6

AF771299

CRIMINAL JUSTICE, LAW ENFORCEMENT AND CORRECTIONS

FEDERAL MANDATORY MINIMUM SENTENCING

ELEMENTS, CONSIDERATIONS, AND STATUTES

CRIMINAL JUSTICE, LAW ENFORCEMENT AND CORRECTIONS

Additional books in this series can be found on Nova's website under the Series tab.

Additional E-books in this series can be found on Nova's website under the E-book tab.

CRIMINAL JUSTICE, LAW ENFORCEMENT AND CORRECTIONS

FEDERAL MANDATORY MINIMUM SENTENCING

ELEMENTS, CONSIDERATIONS, AND STATUTES

CHRISTOPHE SALAUT
EDITOR

nova publishers
New York

Copyright © 2013 by Nova Science Publishers, Inc.

All rights reserved. No part of this book may be reproduced, stored in a retrieval system or transmitted in any form or by any means: electronic, electrostatic, magnetic, tape, mechanical photocopying, recording or otherwise without the written permission of the Publisher.

For permission to use material from this book please contact us:
Telephone 631-231-7269; Fax 631-231-8175
Web Site: http://www.novapublishers.com

NOTICE TO THE READER

The Publisher has taken reasonable care in the preparation of this book, but makes no expressed or implied warranty of any kind and assumes no responsibility for any errors or omissions. No liability is assumed for incidental or consequential damages in connection with or arising out of information contained in this book. The Publisher shall not be liable for any special, consequential, or exemplary damages resulting, in whole or in part, from the readers' use of, or reliance upon, this material. Any parts of this book based on government reports are so indicated and copyright is claimed for those parts to the extent applicable to compilations of such works.

Independent verification should be sought for any data, advice or recommendations contained in this book. In addition, no responsibility is assumed by the publisher for any injury and/or damage to persons or property arising from any methods, products, instructions, ideas or otherwise contained in this publication.

This publication is designed to provide accurate and authoritative information with regard to the subject matter covered herein. It is sold with the clear understanding that the Publisher is not engaged in rendering legal or any other professional services. If legal or any other expert assistance is required, the services of a competent person should be sought. FROM A DECLARATION OF PARTICIPANTS JOINTLY ADOPTED BY A COMMITTEE OF THE AMERICAN BAR ASSOCIATION AND A COMMITTEE OF PUBLISHERS.

Additional color graphics may be available in the e-book version of this book.

Library of Congress Cataloging-in-Publication Data

ISBN: 978-1-62948-557-7

Published by Nova Science Publishers, Inc. † New York

Contents

PREFACE

Federal mandatory minimum sentencing statutes (mandatory minimums) demand that execution or incarceration follow criminal conviction. Among other things, they cover drug dealing, murdering federal officials, and using a gun to commit a federal crime. They have been a feature of federal sentencing since the dawn of the Republic. They circumscribe judicial sentencing discretion, although they impose few limitations upon prosecutorial discretion, or upon the President's power to pardon. They have been criticized as unthinkingly harsh and incompatible with a rational sentencing guideline system; yet they have also been embraced as hallmarks of truth in sentencing and a certain means of incapacitating the criminally dangerous. This book provides an overview of federal statutes and a discussion of some of the constitutional challenges they have faced.

Chapter 1 – Federal mandatory minimum sentencing statutes limit the discretion of a sentencing court to impose a sentence that does not include a term of imprisonment or the death penalty. They have a long history and come in several varieties: the not-less-than, the flat sentence, and piggyback versions. Federal courts may refrain from imposing an otherwise required statutory mandatory minimum sentence when requested by the prosecution on the basis of substantial assistance toward the prosecution of others. First-time, low-level, non-violent offenders may be able to avoid the mandatory minimums under the Controlled Substances Acts, if they are completely forthcoming.

The most common imposed federal mandatory minimum sentences arise under the Controlled Substance and Controlled Substance Import and Export Acts, the provisions punishing the presence of a firearm in connection with a crime of violence or drug trafficking offense, the Armed Career Criminal Act, various sex crimes include child pornography, and aggravated identity theft.

Critics argue that mandatory minimums undermine the rationale and operation of the federal sentencing guidelines which are designed to eliminate unwarranted sentencing disparity. Counter arguments suggest that the guidelines themselves operate to undermine individual sentencing discretion and that the ills attributed to other mandatory minimums are more appropriately assigned to prosecutorial discretion or other sources.

State and federal mandatory minimums have come under constitutional attack on several grounds over the years, and have generally survived. The Eighth Amendment's cruel and unusual punishments clause does bar mandatory capital punishment, and apparently bans any term of imprisonment that is grossly disproportionate to the seriousness of the crime for which it is imposed. The Supreme Court, however, has declined to overturn sentences imposed under the California three strikes law and challenged as cruel and unusual. Double jeopardy, ex post facto, due process, separation of powers, and equal protection challenges have been generally unavailing.

The United States Sentencing Commission's *Mandatory Minimum Penalties in the Federal Criminal Justice System* (2011) recommends consideration of amendments to several of the statutes under which federal mandatory minimum sentences are most often imposed.

Lists of the various federal mandatory minimum sentencing statutes are appended, as is a bibliography of legal materials.

Chapter 2 – Federal law requires a sentencing judge to impose a minimum sentence of imprisonment following conviction for any of a number of federal offenses. Congress has created two exceptions. One is available in all cases when the prosecutor asserts that the defendant has provided substantial assistance in the criminal investigation or prosecution of another, 18 U.S.C. 3553(e). The other, commonly referred to as the safety value, is available, without the government's approval, for a handful of the more commonly prosecuted drug trafficking and unlawful possession offenses that carry minimum sentences, 18 U.S.C. 3553(f).

Qualification for the substantial assistance exception is ordinarily only possible upon the motion of the government. In rare cases, the court may compel the government to file such a motion when the defendant can establish that the refusal to do so was based on constitutionally invalid considerations, or was in derogation of a plea bargain obligation or was the product of bad faith.

Qualification for the safety valve exception requires a defendant to satisfy five criteria. His past criminal record must be minimal; he must not have been a leader, organizer, or supervisor in the commission of the offense; he must not have used violence in the commission or the offense, and the offense must not have resulted in serious injury; and prior to sentencing, he must tell the government all that he knows of the offense and any related misconduct.

Congress has instructed the United States Sentencing Commission to report on the operation of federal mandatory minimum sentencing provisions. A majority of the Federal judges responding to a Commission survey agree that the two exceptions should be expanded. A number of Commission hearing witnesses have also urged that the provisions be amended.

In: Federal Mandatory Minimum Sentencing ISBN: 978-1-62948-557-7
Editor: Christophe Salaut © 2013 Nova Science Publishers, Inc.

Chapter 1

FEDERAL MANDATORY MINIMUM SENTENCING STATUTES*

Charles Doyle

SUMMARY

Federal mandatory minimum sentencing statutes limit the discretion of a sentencing court to impose a sentence that does not include a term of imprisonment or the death penalty. They have a long history and come in several varieties: the not-less-than, the flat sentence, and piggyback versions. Federal courts may refrain from imposing an otherwise required statutory mandatory minimum sentence when requested by the prosecution on the basis of substantial assistance toward the prosecution of others. First-time, low-level, non-violent offenders may be able to avoid the mandatory minimums under the Controlled Substances Acts, if they are completely forthcoming.

The most common imposed federal mandatory minimum sentences arise under the Controlled Substance and Controlled Substance Import and Export Acts, the provisions punishing the presence of a firearm in connection with a crime of violence or drug trafficking offense, the Armed Career Criminal Act, various sex crimes include child pornography, and aggravated identity theft.

---

* This is an edited, reformatted and augmented version of a Congressional Research Service publication, CRS Report for Congress RL32040, dated September 9, 2013.

Critics argue that mandatory minimums undermine the rationale and operation of the federal sentencing guidelines which are designed to eliminate unwarranted sentencing disparity. Counter arguments suggest that the guidelines themselves operate to undermine individual sentencing discretion and that the ills attributed to other mandatory minimums are more appropriately assigned to prosecutorial discretion or other sources.

State and federal mandatory minimums have come under constitutional attack on several grounds over the years, and have generally survived. The Eighth Amendment's cruel and unusual punishments clause does bar mandatory capital punishment, and apparently bans any term of imprisonment that is grossly disproportionate to the seriousness of the crime for which it is imposed. The Supreme Court, however, has declined to overturn sentences imposed under the California three strikes law and challenged as cruel and unusual. Double jeopardy, ex post facto, due process, separation of powers, and equal protection challenges have been generally unavailing.

The United States Sentencing Commission's *Mandatory Minimum Penalties in the Federal Criminal Justice System* (2011) recommends consideration of amendments to several of the statutes under which federal mandatory minimum sentences are most often imposed.

Lists of the various federal mandatory minimum sentencing statutes are appended, as is a bibliography of legal materials.

INTRODUCTION

Federal mandatory minimum sentencing statutes (mandatory minimums) demand that execution or incarceration follow criminal conviction.[1] Among other things, they cover drug dealing, murdering federal officials, and using a gun to commit a federal crime. They have been a feature of federal sentencing since the dawn of the Republic. They circumscribe judicial sentencing discretion,[2] although they impose few limitations upon prosecutorial discretion,[3] or upon the President's power to pardon.[4] They have been criticized as unthinkingly harsh and incompatible with a rational sentencing guideline system; yet they have also been embraced as hallmarks of truth in sentencing and a certain means of incapacitating the criminally dangerous. This is a brief overview of federal statutes in the area and a discussion of some of the constitutional challenges they have faced.[5]

Types of Mandatory Minimums

Mandatory minimums come in many stripes, including some whose status might be disputed. The most widely recognized are those that demand that offenders be sentenced to imprisonment for "not less than" a designated term of imprisonment.[6] Some are triggered by the nature of the offense,[7] others by the criminal record of the offender.[8] A few members of this "not less than" category are less "mandatory" than others, because Congress has provided a partial escape hatch or safety valve. For example, several of the drug-related mandatory minimums are subject to a "safety valve" for small time, first time, non-violent offenders that may render their minimum penalties less than mandatory, or at least less severe.[9] Still others can be avoided at the behest of prosecution for a defendant's substantial assistance against his cohorts.[10] Some of the other "not- less-than" mandatory minimums purport to permit the court to sentence an offender to a fine rather than to a mandatory term of imprisonment.[11]

A second generally recognized category of mandatory minimums consists of the flat or single sentence statutes, the vast majority of which call for life imprisonment.[12] Closely related are the capital punishment statutes that require imposition of either the death penalty or imprisonment for life, or death or imprisonment either for life or for some term of years.[13]

The "piggyback" statutes make up a third class. The piggyback statutes are not themselves mandatory minimums but sentence offenders by reference to underlying statutes including those that impose mandatory minimums.[14]

Until the Supreme Court intervened in *Booker v. United States* to eliminate the binding effect of the Sentencing Guidelines,[15] the final and least obvious group was comprised of statutes whose violation resulted in the imposition of a mandatory minimum term of imprisonment by operation of law, or more precisely by operation of the Sentencing Reform Act and the Sentencing Guidelines issued in its name.[16] After *Booker* and the line of cases that followed, the Guidelines cannot fairly be characterized as a source of mandatory minimum sentences, although they continue to tilt heavily toward incarceration.[17]

History

Mandatory minimums have been with us from the beginning. In fact, the history of our criminal sentencing practices is the story of increased reliance upon judicial or administrative discretion in order to mute the law's severity in individual cases,[18] followed by increased limitations on such discretion in order to curb the resulting arbitrary and discriminatory disparities in punishment.[19] It is a saga in which "competing theories of mandatory and discretionary sentencing have been in varying degrees of ascendancy or decline." [20]

Severity and a want of discretion marked the early criminal law. The sentence which followed a felony conviction was death; except in rare instances no other punishment could be imposed. Over time the courts were given some discretion over sentencing, but the choices were hardly lenient; and corporal punishment and banishment were common.[21]

Yet even early on there were efforts to ease the law's severity. Both the accused and the convicted could be pardoned at the King's will.[22] While Parliament regularly increased the number of crimes, it often replaced common law capital offenses with statutory crimes defined as misdemeanors or subject to the benefit of clergy. The result was the same in either case, a reduced number of capital offenses.[23] In our own country, state legislatures drastically curtailed the number of capital offenses soon after the Revolution.[24]

When the first Congress assembled, it enacted several mandatory minimums, each of them a capital offense.[25] The nineteenth century, however, witnessed the appearance of a host of discretionary schemes designed to ease the harshness of criminal law in individual cases. The courts could suspend sentence and were vested with broad authority in the selection of those sentences they chose to impose.[26] Probation and parole were born and became prominent.[27]

By late in the century at the federal level, the number of mandatory capital offenses had been reduced,[28] and while the number of mandatory minimums had increased,[29] most federal criminal statutes merely established a maximum penalty and left to the discretion of the courts the sentences to be imposed within the maximum. The 1909 federal criminal code revision eliminated most mandatory minimums;[30] soon thereafter federal prisoners were made eligible for parole after service of a third of their sentences (after fifteen years in the case of prisoners with life sentences);[31] and federal courts shortly thereafter received the authority to suspend the imposition or execution of sentence and impose probation.[32] The 1948 federal criminal code revision took much the same tack as its predecessor: it eliminated many, but not all, of the "not-less-than" mandatory minimums and continued in place most of the "flat" sentence mandatory minimums.[33]

By mid-twentieth century, a well-respected commentator could observe that "[t]he individualization of penal dispositions, principally through the institutions of the indeterminate sentence, probation, and parole, is a development whose value few would contest."[34] The contest was joined soon thereafter.[35]

Driven by concerns that broad discretion had led to rootless sentencing, unjustifiable in its leniency in some instances and in its severity in others, legislative bodies moved to curtail discretionary sentencing on several fronts. Determinate sentencing,[36] sentencing commissions and guidelines,[37] and mandatory minimum sentences became more prevalent.[38] Parole and probation were abolished or greatly restricted in several jurisdictions.[39]

The Sentencing Reform Act of 1984 brought this trend to the federal criminal justice system.[40] It repealed the authority of the federal courts to suspend criminal sentences.[41] It abolished federal parole.[42] It created a sentencing guideline system, applicable within the statutory maximum and minimum penalties established by Congress that tightly confined the sentencing discretion of federal judges.[43] The armed career criminal, three strikes, and several of the other prominent drug, child pornography, and gun related mandatory minimums followed in the ensuing years.[44]

Substantial Assistance

> Upon motion of the Government, the court shall have the authority to impose a sentence below a level established by statute as a minimum sentence so as to reflect a defendant's substantial assistance in the investigation or prosecution of another person who has committed an offense. Such sentence shall be imposed in accordance with the guidelines and policy statements issued by the Sentencing Commission pursuant to section 994 of title 28, United States Code.[45]

This substantial assistance provision was enacted with little fanfare in the twilight of the 99th Congress as part of the massive Anti-Drug Abuse Act of 1986, legislation which established or increased a number of mandatory minimum sentencing provisions.[46] The section passed between the date authorizing the Sentencing Guidelines and the date they became effective. Rather than replicate the language of section 3553(e), the Guidelines contain an overlapping section which authorizes a sentencing court to depart from the minimum sentence called for by the Guidelines.[47]

Upon the Motion of the Government

As a general rule, a defendant is entitled to a sentence below an otherwise applicable statutory minimum under the provisions of §3553(e) only if the government agrees.[48] The courts have acknowledged that due process or equal protection or other constitutional guarantees may provide a narrow exception. "Thus, a defendant would be entitled to relief if a prosecutor refused to file a substantial-assistance motion, say, because of the defendant's race or religion."[49] A defendant is entitled to relief if the Government's refusal constitutes a breach of its plea agreement.[50] A defendant is also "entitled to relief if the prosecutor's refusal to move was not rationally related to any legitimate Government end."[51] Some courts have suggested that a defendant is entitled to relief if the prosecution refuses to move under circumstances that "shock the conscience of the court," or that demonstrate bad faith, or for reasons unrelated to substantial assistance.[52]

A majority of the judges who answered the Sentencing Commission's survey agreed that relief under §3553(e) should be available even in the absence of motion from the prosecutor.[53]

A motion under §3553(e) for a sentence beneath the mandatory minimum and a motion under U.S.S.G. §5K1.1 for a sentence beneath the applicable Sentencing Guideline range are not the same. Thus, a motion under §5K1.1 will ordinarily not be construed as a motion under §3553(e).[54]

To Reflect a Defendant's Substantial Assistance

Any sentence imposed below the statutory minimum by virtue of section 3553(e) must be based on the extent of the defendant's assistance; it may not reflect considerations unrelated to such assistance.[55] It has been suggested that a court may use the section 5K1.1 factors for that determination, i.e., "(1) the court's evaluation of the significance and usefulness of the defendant's assistance, taking into consideration the government's evaluation of the assistance rendered; (2) the truthfulness, completeness, and reliability of any information or testimony provided by the defendant; (3) the nature and extent of the defendant's assistance; (4) any injury suffered, or any danger or risk of injury to the defendant or his family resulting from his assistance; [and] (5) the timeliness of the defendant's assistance."[56]

The substantial assistance exception makes possible convictions that might otherwise be unattainable. Yet, it may also lead to "inverted sentencing," i.e., a situation in which "the more serious the defendant's crimes, the lower the sentence – because the greater his wrongs, the more information and assistance he had to offer to a prosecutor;" while in contrast the exception is of no avail to the peripheral offender who can provide no substantial assistance.[57] Perhaps for this reason, most of the judges who responded to the Sentencing Commission survey agreed that a sentencing court should not be limited to assistance-related factors and should be allowed to use the generally permissible sentencing factors when calculating a sentence under §3553(e).[58]

Mandatory Minimums and the Sentencing Guidelines

First Commission Report

Even though guidelines work to reduce judicial sentencing discretion and might once have been characterized as creating a host of new members of the species of mandatory minimums, the not- less-than mandatory minimums have been criticized as incompatible with the federal sentencing guidelines. Early on, perhaps most prominent among its critics was the Sentencing Commission itself. Its 1991 report, after sketching the arguments traditionally offered in support of mandatory minimums,[59] observed that

- only 4 of the 60 mandatory minimums were regularly prosecuted;[60]
- mandatory minimums induce new sentencing disparities;[61]
- due to plea bargaining, 35% of the defendants who might have been charged and sentenced under mandatory minimums were not;[62]
- "disparate application of mandatory minimum sentences ... appears to be related to race;"[63]
- mandatory minimums lack the capacity to consider the range of aggravating and mitigating circumstances that may attend the same offense and as a consequence produce unwarranted sentencing uniformity;[64]
- uneven application deprives mandatory minimums of their potential to deter;[65]
- mandatory minimums breed disparity by transferring judicial discretion to the prosecution;[66]
- in contrast to the calibrated approach of the guidelines, mandatory minimums create cliffs where minuscule factual differences can have enormous sentencing consequences;[67]
- the amendment process of the sentencing guidelines makes them perpetually self-correcting, while mandatory minimums are single-shot efforts at crime control;[68] and

- the most efficient and effective way for Congress to exercise its powers to direct sentencing policy is through the established process of sentencing guidelines, permitting the sophistication of the guidelines structure to work, rather than through mandatory minimums.[69]

The Commission's initial report was quickly followed by a Department of Justice study that concluded that a substantial number of those sentenced under federal mandatory minimums were nonviolent, first-time, lower level drug offenders.[70]

Congress responded with the safety valve provisions of 18 U.S.C. 3553(f) under which the court may disregard various drug mandatory minimums and sentence an offender within the applicable sentencing guideline range as long as the offender was a low level, nonviolent participant with no prior criminal record who has cooperated fully with the government.

Second Commission Report

A number of things changed between the first and second Commission reports. Sentencing under the Guidelines had only been in place for a relatively short period of time when the first report was written. The number of defendants sentenced by federal courts is now almost three times the number sentenced under the Guidelines when the Commission wrote its first report.[71] In the years since, Congress has muted the impact of some mandatory minimums with the safety valve and the Fair Sentencing Act, but it has also added new crimes and increased the penalties for old crimes.[72] Occasionally, that meant new mandatory minimums or increases in old mandatory minimums.[73] The judicial landscape has changed as well. When the Commission issued its first report the Guidelines were largely binding upon sentencing judges.[74] After the Supreme Court's Booker decision and its progeny, they are largely advisory.[75] Finally, in the ensuing years the public policy debate over mandatory minimum sentences has continued before the Commission, before Congress, and in academic circles. The Commission's second report summarizes views of those who favor mandatory minimums and those who oppose them. Proponents contend that mandatory minimum sentences:

- promote sentencing uniformity and prevent sentencing disparity;[76]
- afford greater public protection through certain punishment, deterrence, and incapacitation;[77]

- inflict just desserts;[78]
- induce plea bargains and offender cooperation and thus contribute to law enforcement efficiency;[79] and
- assist state and local law enforcement efforts.[80]

Opponents, on the other hand, contend that mandatory minimum sentences:

- contribute to both excessive uniformity and unwarranted disparity;[81]
- result in disproportionate and excessively severe sentences;[82]
- fail to account for individualized circumstances;[83]
- transfer sentencing discretion from judges to prosecutors;[84]
- constitute neither a deterrent nor an effective law enforcement tool;[85]
- interfere with state law enforcement efforts;[86] and
- adversely impact various demographic groups.[87]

It omits as did the first Commission report at least one argument for mandatory minimums. During the Commission's first decade and a half of operation before *Booker*, the Commission created its own system of mandatory minimum penalties. The Guidelines denied judges sentencing discretion. Imprisonment was mandatory by operation of the Guidelines in the vast majority of cases. True, it occurred by operation of the exercise of a delegation of Congress's legislative authority rather than by direct exercise. Yet the result was same, a mandatory minimum term of imprisonment. The Guideline system was more nuanced, but that is a difference of degree not of kind.

Finally, the most obvious difference between the first and second Commission reports is focus. To an extent the Commission could not provide in its infancy, the second report describes, analyzes, and makes recommendations relating to the four major groups of federal mandatory minimum sentencing statutes: those involving drug crimes, gun crimes, sex crimes, and identity theft crimes.

Constitutional Boundaries

Defendants sentenced to mandatory minimum terms of imprisonment have challenged them on a number of constitutional grounds beginning with Congress's legislative authority and ranging from cruel and unusual punishment through ex post facto and double jeopardy to equal protection and due process. Each constitutional provision defines outer boundaries that a mandatory minimum must be crafted to honor; none confine legislative prerogatives in any substantial way.

Legislative Authority

The federal government is a creature of the Constitution.[88] It enjoys only such powers as can be traced to the Constitution. All other powers are reserved to the states or to the people.[89] Among the powers which the Constitution bestows upon Congress are the powers to define and punish felonies committed upon the high seas, to exercise exclusive legislative authority over certain federal territories and facilities, to make rules governing the armed forces, to regulate interstate and foreign commerce, and to enact legislation necessary and proper for the execution of those and other constitutionally granted powers.[90] It also grants Congress authority to enact legislation "necessary and proper" to the execution of those powers which it vests in Congress or in any officer or department of the federal government.[91]

Many of the federal laws with mandatory minimum sentencing requirements were enacted pursuant to Congress's legislative authority over crimes occurring on the high seas or within federal enclaves,[92] or to its power to regulate commerce.[93] When a statute falls for want of legislative authority, the penalties it would impose fall with it. This has yet to occur in the area of mandatory minimum sentences.

Commerce Clause

"The Congress shall have Power ... To regulate Commerce with Foreign Nations, and among the several States, and with Indian Tribes."[94] This clause vests Congress with authority to regulate three broad categories of interstate commerce. In the words of *United States v. Lopez*, "[f]irst, Congress may regulate the use of the channels of interstate commerce.... Second, Congress is empowered to regulate and protect the instrumentalities of interstate commerce, or persons or things in interstate commerce, even though the threat may come only from intrastate activities.... Finally, Congress' commerce authority includes the power to regulate those activities having a substantial relation to interstate commerce." [95] The Court then proceeded to conclude that the clause did not authorize Congress to enact a particular statute which purported to outlaw possession of a firearm on school property. Since the statute addressed neither the channels nor instrumentalities of interstate commerce, its survival turned upon whether it came within Congress's power to regulate activities that have a substantial impact on interstate commerce.[96] Here, the statute was found wanting. "[B]y its terms" it had "nothing to do with commerce or any sort of economic enterprise."[97] It "contain[ed] no jurisdictional element which would ensure, through case-by-case inquiry, that the firearm possession in question affect[ed] interstate commerce."[98] Its impact on commerce was so remote that to credit it would envision a virtually boundless power and one reserved to the states, the Court felt.[99]

A few years later, the Court reiterated "that Congress may [not] regulate noneconomic, violent criminal conduct based solely on that conduct's aggregate effect on interstate commerce. The Constitution requires a distinction between what is truly national and what is truly local."[100] Yet purely intrastate activities may have a sufficient impact on interstate commerce to bring them within the reach of Congress's Commerce Clause power. So it is in the case of the Controlled Substances Act where several mandatory minimums are found. The Court concluded in *Gonzales v. Raich* that:

> Given the enforcement difficulties that attend distinguishing between marijuana cultivated locally and marijuana grown elsewhere and concerns about diversion into illicit channels, we have no difficulty concluding that Congress had a rational basis for believing that failure to regulate the intrastate manufacture and possession of marijuana would leave a gaping hole in the CSA. Thus ... when it enacted comprehensive legislation to regulate the interstate market in a fungible commodity, Congress was acting well within its authority to 'make all Laws which shall be necessary and proper' to 'regulate Commerce ... among the several States.' That the regulation ensnares some purely intrastate activity is of no moment." [101]

Necessary and Proper

"The Congress shall have Power ... To make all Laws which shall be necessary and proper for carrying into Execution the foregoing Powers, and all other Powers vested by this Constitution in the Government of the United States, or in any Department or Officer thereof." [102] It has never been thought that the Necessary and Proper Clauses empowers only those laws that are absolutely necessary. Instead, "[l]et the end be legitimate, let it be within the scope of the constitution, and all means which are appropriate, which are plainly adapted to that end, which are not prohibited, but consist[ent] with the letter and spirit of the constitution, are constitutional." [103] Thus, the Necessary and Proper Clause makes possible those statutes that are rationally related to the implementation of another constitutional power.[104]

The Court in *Comstock* provided a hint of the scope of Necessary and Proper Clause.[105] The statute there authorized the Attorney General to continue to hold a federal inmate, pending a civil commitment determination, after his scheduled date of release.[106] The Court analyzed the breadth of the power without any explicit reference to any other constitutional power, deciding that:

> [T]he statute is a "necessary and proper" means of exercising the federal authority that permits Congress to create federal criminal laws, to punish their violation, to imprison violators, to provide appropriately for those imprisoned, and to maintain the security of those who are not imprisoned but who may be affected by the imprisonment of others.[107]

Treaty Power

The Constitution grants the President authority to negotiate treaties and the Senate the authority to approve them in the exercise of its advice and consent prerogatives.[108] Almost a century ago, the Court observed that '[i]f the treaty is valid there can be no dispute about the validity of the statute under Article I, §8, as a necessary and proper means to execute the powers of the Government." The Controlled Substances Act, the home of several mandatory minimums, might be considered implementation of various treaties of the United States relating to controlled substances.[109]

Territorial and Maritime

Congress enjoys legislative authority over felonies on the high seas,[110] over matters occurring within the territorial jurisdiction of the United States,[111] and incident to the maritime jurisdiction of the federal courts.[112] It has exercised the authority frequently to enact criminal laws applicable within the territorial and special maritime jurisdiction of the United States. Some of these provisions include mandatory minimums.[113]

Cruel and Unusual Punishment

Mandatory minimums implicate considerations under the Eighth Amendment's cruel and unusual punishments clause.[114] The clause bars mandatory capital punishment statutes,[115] and mandatory imposition on a juvenile of life imprisonment without the possibility of parole.[116] Although the case law is somewhat uncertain, it seems to condemn punishment that is "grossly disproportionate" to the misconduct for which it is imposed;[117] a standard which a sentence imposed under a mandatory minimum statute may breach under extreme circumstances.

Proportionality

During the first century of its existence, there was little recourse to the Amendment's protection,[118] and the early cases involved its proscriptions against particular kinds of punishment rather than of punishments of a particular degree of severity.[119] In *O'Neil v. Vermont*, however, three dissenting justices expressed the view that the cruel and unusual punishments clause's prohibitions extended to "all punishments which by their excessive length or severity are greatly disproportionate to the offences charged."[120]

The views of the *O'Neil* dissenters gained further credence after they were quoted by the Court in *Weems v. United States*, when it invalidated a territorial sentencing scheme which it found both disproportionate in degree and cruel in nature.[121]

Perhaps because of the unusual nature of the penalties involved, the proportionality doctrine suggested in *Weems* lay dormant for over sixty years.[122] It reappeared in the capital punishment cases following *Furman v. Georgia*.[123]

When the capital punishment statutes enacted in response to *Furman* came before the Court, one of the threshold questions was whether capital punishment was a per se violation of the cruel and unusual punishments clause. For a plurality of the Court, that question could only be answered by determining whether capital punishment was necessarily "grossly out of proportion to the severity of [any] crime."[124] In the case of murder, "when a life has been taken deliberately by the offender, [the Court could not] say that the punishment is invariably disproportionate to the crime."[125]

In *Coker v. Georgia*, a plurality of the Court found "that death is indeed a disproportionate penalty for the crime of raping an adult woman."[126] It did so after considering the general repudiation of the death penalty in such cases by the legislatures of other jurisdictions; the infrequency with which juries in Georgia had been willing to impose the death penalty for rape of adult woman; and the comparative severity Georgia used to punish other equally or more serious crimes. The Court employed much the same method of analysis in later capital punishment cases which raised the proportionality doctrine.[127]

Initial efforts to carry the proportionality doctrine to noncapital cases proved unsuccessful. Shortly after *Coker*, a petitioner, convicted under a recidivist statute which called for an automatic life sentence upon a third felony conviction, sought to persuade the Court that the Eighth Amendment precluded such a sentence based upon a comparative analysis of the severity of the treatment of recidivism in other jurisdictions, *Rummel v. Estelle.*[128] The majority of the Court was not persuaded. The proportionality doctrine had only been employed in capital punishment cases and *Weems*, it noted. Both involved punishments, different in nature, from those in *Rummel.*[129]

Moreover, the petitioner had failed to convincingly establish any objective criteria to evidence gross disproportionality. Without some objectively identifiable "bright light" marking disproportionality, the Court feared application of the proportionality doctrine would constitute subjective policy making, a task more appropriately left to the legislative bodies.[130]

Any thoughts that the proportionality doctrine might have been abandoned were dashed almost immediately by *Solem v. Helm.*[131] *Solem* declared that imposition of a mandatory term of life imprisonment under a state recidivist statute constituted cruel and unusual punishment. The "objective criteria" which guided a proportionality analysis included, "(i) the gravity of the offense and the harshness of the penalty; (ii) the sentences imposed on the other criminals in the same jurisdiction; and (iii) the sentences imposed for commission of the same crime in other jurisdictions."[132]

Individualized consideration. Consideration of the defendant's unique circumstances is one of the foundations of the Court's Eighth Amendment jurisprudence in capital punishment cases. *Furman* found that the Eighth Amendment's cruel and unusual punishments clause, made binding upon the states by the due process clause of the Fourteenth Amendment, precluded imposition of the death penalty at the unguided discretion of the judge or jury.

The states initially travelled one of two paths to avoid the problems of unguided discretion identified in *Furman*. Some eliminated discretion; others provided guidance. The second approach passed constitutional muster, *Gregg v. Georgia.*[133] The first did not, *Woodson v. North Carolina.*[134] Mandatory capital punishment offended the Eighth Amendment on three grounds, it was said in *Woodson*. It was contrary to the evolving standards of decency which mark the threshold of the Amendment's protection.[135] It failed to address the objections of *Furman* to imposition of the death penalty at the *unguided* discretion of the judge or jury.[136] And it failed to permit consideration of individual characteristics of the crime and offender:

> A process that accords no significance to relevant facets of the character and record of the individual offender or the circumstances of the particular offense excludes from consideration in fixing the ultimate punishment of death the possibility of compassionate or mitigating factors stemming from the diverse frailties of humankind. It treats all persons convicted of a designated offense not as uniquely individual human beings, but as members of a faceless, undifferentiated mass to be subjected to the blind infliction of the penalty of death....
>
> Consideration of both the offender and the offense in order to arrive at a just and appropriate sentence has been viewed as a progressive and humanizing development. While the prevailing practice of individualizing sentencing determinations generally reflects simply enlightened policy rather than a constitutional imperative, we believe that in capital cases the fundamental respect for humanity underlying the Eighth Amendment, requires consideration of the character and record of the individual offender and the circumstances of the particular offense as a constitutionally indispensable part of the process of inflicting the penalty of death. 428 U.S. at 304 (citations omitted).[137]

The Court regularly and consistently recognized the individual considerations requirement in subsequent capital punishment cases.[138] Although the language cited above and other dicta[139] would seem to apply with similar force in noncapital cases, the Court emphasized that the doctrine was limited to capital cases.[140] The gravity of the offense appears to the most critical factor in non-capital cases, but the seriousness of the offense may be judged at least in part by the record and other circumstances of the individual who committed it.

Gravity of the Offense

The defendant in *Harmelin v. Michigan*[141] was a first time offender convicted of possession of 672 grams of cocaine, enough for possibly as many as 65,000 individual doses. Under the laws of the State of Michigan, the conviction carried with it a mandatory sentence of life imprisonment without the possibility of parole.

Harmelin contended that the sentence violated both the individual consideration and proportionality doctrines of the Eighth Amendment. A majority of the Court rejected the individual considerations argument and a plurality refused to accept the proportionality assertion.

The Court noted that in its opinions "[t]he penalty of death differs from all other forms of criminal punishment.... in its total irrevocability."[142] In view of the differences, the majority saw no reason "to extend this so-called individualized capital-sentencing doctrine to an individualized mandatory life in prison without parole sentencing doctrine." [143]

The proportionality question proved somewhat more difficult. Justice Scalia and Chief Justice Rehnquist simply refused to recognize an Eighth Amendment proportionality requirement, at least in noncapital cases.[144] For three other justices, Kennedy, O'Connor and Souter, a sentence which satisfies the first of the *Solem* tests, seriousness of the offense, need not survive or even face comparisons with sentences for other crimes in the same jurisdiction and for the same crime in other jurisdictions.[145] More precisely, the plurality emphasized that "the Eighth Amendment does not require strict proportionality between crime and sentence. Rather, it forbids only extreme sentences that are grossly disproportionate to the crime."[146] In the case of Harmelin, the sentence was not grossly disproportionate because of the severity of his crime, that is, "the pernicious effects of the drug epidemic in this country ... demonstrate that the ... legislature could with reason conclude that the threat posed to the individual and society by possession of this large an amount of cocaine – in terms of violence, crime, and social displacement – is momentous enough to warrant the deterrence and retribution of a life sentence without parole."[147]

The plurality opinion also contains several useful observations about the constitutionality of mandatory sentences per se.[148]

Deference to legislative judgment notwithstanding, when the Court later applied the same gross disproportionality standard in an excessive fines context, it seemed to imply that even misconduct legislatively classified as a fairly serious crime (a felony) might lack the gravity to support boundless sanctions. *United States v. Bajakajian*[149] involved the confiscation of $357,144 as a consequence of trying to carry it out of the United States without reporting it, a willful act punishable by imprisonment for not more than 5 years, 31 U.S.C. 5322. In the eyes of the Court, the crime involved a "minimal level of culpability." Moreover, "[t]he harm ... caused was also minimal. Failure to report this currency affected only one party, the Government, and in a relatively minor way.... Had his crime gone undetected, the Government would have been deprived only of the information that $357,144 had left the country.... Comparing the gravity of respondent's crime with the $357,144 forfeiture the Government seeks, we conclude that such a forfeiture would be grossly disproportional to the gravity of his offense."[150]

Did this mean that long mandatory minimum terms of imprisonment triggered by misconduct that a court might treat as a misdemeanor under California's three strikes law might fall because it could result in grossly disproportionate sentences? Four justices said yes, but three said no, and they were joined by two others who said the law survived constitutional scrutiny regardless of proportionality.

The question arose from the sentencing of an oft-convicted defendant to imprisonment for not less than 25 years pursuant to the California recidivist statute as a result of his attempt to steal three golf clubs valued at just under $400 a piece, *Ewing v. California*.[151] Under California law, the trial court might have chosen to avoid the three strikes statute either by sentencing the attempted theft as a misdemeanor or by ignoring the nature of the earlier convictions.[152] It chose not to. The California appellate courts rejected Ewing's Eighth Amendment challenges.[153] As did a majority of the Members of the Supreme Court.

Justices Scalia and Thomas "concluded that the Eighth Amendment's prohibition of 'cruel and unusual punishments' [is] not a 'guarantee' against disproportionate sentences" and that Ewing's sentence did not constitute cruel and unusual punishment in violation of the Eight Amendment.[154] Justice O'Connor, joined by Justice Kennedy and Chief Justice Rehnquist, believe that the cruel and unusual punishments clause includes a "narrow proportionality principle that applies to noncapital sentences."[155] They note that standing alone the theft of property valued at nearly $1,200 "should not be taken lightly."[156] Moreover, "[i]n weighing the gravity of Ewing's offense, we must place in the scales not only his current felony, but also his long history of felony recidivism."[157] Thus, "Ewing's sentence of 25 years to life in prison, for the offense of felony grand theft under the three strikes law, is not grossly disproportionate and therefore does not violate the Eighth Amendment's prohibition on cruel and unusual punishments."[158]

Class of Offenders

Proportionality is balance: the severity of the punishment weighted against gravity of the offense. Justice O'Connor's *Ewing* opinion indicates that certain of a defendant's individual circumstances, his criminal record for instance, enhance gravity of the offense. Other cases hold out the possibility that other individualistic circumstances, such as the defendant's mental capacity or maturity, may enhance the severity of the punishment. These cases also have their origin in the death penalty cases.

The first of these, *Atkins v. Virginia*, held that the Eighth Amendment barred execution of a mentally retarded defendant.[159] In the years leading up to *Atkins*, a substantial number of state legislatures in capital punishment states, had banned execution of the mentally retarded.[160] Elsewhere, though permitted in law, the practice has been abandoned in fact.[161] This, coupled with the fact that a want of defendant capacity undermines the normal expectations and justifications of the criminal justice system, marked execution of the mentally retarded as an Eighth Amendment impermissible excessive punishment.[162]

For much the same reason, the Court shortly thereafter in *Roper v. Simmons*, declared that the Eighth Amendment prohibited imposing the death penalty for a crime committed as a juvenile.[163] Next, the Court carried the *Atkins-Roper* line of cases beyond the capital punishment realm. In *Graham v. Florida*, Justice Kennedy explained that "[t]he Court's cases addressing the proportionality of sentences fall within two general classifications. The first involves challenges to the length of term-of-years sentences given all the circumstances of a particular case. The second comprises cases in which the Court implements the proportionality standard by certain categorical restrictions on the death penalty." [164] In the first line of cases, the *Solem-Harmelin- Ewing* line, the Court employs a proportionality standard and "it has been difficult for the challenger to establish a lack of proportionality." [165]

In the second line of cases, the *Atkins-Roper* line, *Graham* recognized a two-step approach used when the challenge is based on a characteristic of the defendant, such as his mental capacity as in *Atkins* or his age as in *Roper*.[166] First, the Court "considers 'objective indicia of society's standards, as expressed in legislative enactments and state practice' to determine whether there is a national consensus against the sentencing practice at issue."[167] Second, "guided by 'the standards elaborated by controlling precedents and by the Court's own understanding and interpretation of the Eighth Amendment's text, history, meaning, and purpose,' the Court must determine in the exercise of its own independent judgment whether the punishment in question violates the Constitution."[168]

Graham challenged his sentence of life imprisonment without the possibility of parole imposed the commission of a nonhomicide, armed robbery, committed while a child. Using this *Atkins- Roper* approach the Court concluded that the Eighth Amendment precluded Graham's sentence. It carried that logic forward in *Miller v. Alabama*.[169] The *Miller* defendants had been convicted of capital murder committed while juveniles and had been sentenced to life imprisonment without the possibility of parole.[170] That the Eighth Amendment does not permit, the Court held.[171] The *Miller* sentencing procedures suffered from two previously identified constitutional defects. First, they barred consideration of the mitigating impact of the defendant's age:

> By removing youth from the balance – by subjecting a juvenile to the same life-without- parole sentence applicable to an adult – these laws prohibit a sentencing authority from assessing whether the law's harshest term of imprisonment proportionately punishes a juvenile offender. That contravenes *Graham's* (also *Roper's*) foundational principle: that imposition of a State's most severe penalties on juvenile offenders cannot proceed as though they were not children.[172]

Second, the procedure not only failed to account a paramount culpability-reducing factor, but it also failed to account for the severity of the sentence when imposed upon a child:

> *Graham* makes plain these mandatory scheme's defects in another way: by likening life- without-parole sentences imposed on juveniles to the death penalty itself. Life-without- parole terms, the Court wrote, share some characteristics with death sentences that are shared by no other sentences. Imprisoning an offender until he dies alters the remainder of his life by a forfeiture that is irrevocable. And this lengthiest possible incarceration is an especially harsh punishment for a juvenile because he will almost inevitably serve more years and a greater percentage of his life in prison than an adult offender. The penalty when imposed on a teenage, as compared with an older person, is therefore the same in name only. All of that suggested a distinctive set of legal rules: In part because we viewed this ultimate penalty for juveniles as akin to the death penalty, we treated it similarly to that most severe punishment.[173]

Thus, under the current state of the law, the Eighth Amendment bars imposition of a mandatory life term of imprisonment upon juveniles and most likely a particular term of imprisonment in those exceptionally rare cases when the punishment is grossly disproportionate to the offense.

Juries, Grand Juries, and Due Process

The Constitution demands that no person "be held to answer for a capital or otherwise infamous crime, unless on a presentment or indictment of a grand jury" and that "[i]n all criminal prosecutions, the accused shall enjoy the right to a speedy and public trial, by an impartial jury."[174] Moreover, due process requires that the prosecution prove beyond a reasonable doubt "every fact necessary to constitute the crime" with which an accused is charged, *In re Winship*.[175] After *Winship*, the question arose whether a statute might authorize or require a more severe penalty for a particular crime based on a fact – not included in the indictment, not found by the jury, and not proven beyond a reasonable doubt. Pennsylvania passed a law under which various serious crimes (rape, robbery, kidnapping and the like) were subject to a mandatory minimum penalty of imprisonment for five years, if the judge after conviction found by a preponderance of the evidence that the defendant had been in visible possession of a firearm during the commission of the offense.[176] Had the Pennsylvania statute created a new series of crimes? For example, had it supplemented its crime of rape with a new crime of rape while in visible possession of a firearm? And if so, did the fact of visible possession have to be proven to the jury beyond a reasonable doubt? [177]

The Supreme Court concluded that visible possession of a firearm under the statute was not an element of a new series of crimes, but was instead a sentencing consideration that had been given a legislatively prescribed weight.[178] As such, the Pennsylvania statutory scheme neither offended due process nor triggered any right to a separate jury finding.[179]

There followed a number of state and federal statutes under which facts that might earlier have been treated as elements of a new crime were simply classified as sentencing factors. In some instances, the new sentencing factor permitted imposition of a penalty far in excess of that otherwise available for the underlying offense. For instance, the Supreme Court found no constitutional defect in a statute which punished a deported alien for returning to the United States by imprisonment for not more than 2 years, but which permitted the alien to be sentenced to imprisonment for not more than 20 years upon a post-trial, judicial determination that the alien had been convicted of a serious crime following deportation.[180]

Perhaps uneasy with the implications, the Court soon made it clear that, "under the Due Process Clause of the Fifth Amendment and the notice and jury trial guarantees of the Sixth Amendment, any fact (other than prior conviction) that increases the *maximum* penalty for a crime must be charged in an indictment, submitted to a jury, and proven beyond a reasonable doubt," *Apprendi v. New Jersey.*[181] Side opinions questioned the continued vitality of *McMillan*'s mandatory minimum determination in light of the *Apprendi.*[182]

Initially unwilling to extend *Apprendi* to mandatory minimums in *Harris,*[183] the Court did so in *Alleyne v. United States.*[184] Alleyne was convicted under the statute that imposes a series of mandatory minimum penalties upon defendants who carry a firearm during and in furtherance of a crime of violence (5 years for carrying; 7 years for brandishing; 10 years for discharging).[185] The jury found him guilty of carrying; the court concluded the gun had been brandished.[186] The Sixth Amendment requires that the question of brandishing had to be found by the jury, the Court declared:

> Harris drew a distinction between facts that increase the statutory maximum and facts that increase only the mandatory minimum. We conclude that this distinction is inconsistent with our decision in Apprendi and with the original meaning of the Sixth Amendment. Any fact that, by law, increases the penalty for a crime is an element that must be submitted to the jury and found beyond a reasonable doubt. Mandatory minimum sentences increase the penalty for a crime. It follows, then, that any fact that increases the mandatory minimum is an element that must be submitted to the jury.[187]

Neither the Sixth Amendment, *Apprendi*, nor *Alleyne* limits Congress's authority to establish mandatory minimum sentences nor limits the authority of the courts to impose them. They simply dictate the procedural safeguards that must accompany the exercise of that authority.

Separation of Powers

While "it remains a basic principle of our constitutional scheme that one branch of the Government may not intrude upon the central prerogatives of another," [188] the Supreme Court has observed that "Congress has the power to define criminal punishments without giving the courts any sentencing discretion." [189] Thus, the lower federal courts have regularly upheld mandatory minimum statutes when challenged on separation of powers grounds,[190] and the Supreme Court has denied any separation of powers infirmity in the federal sentencing guideline system which at the time might have been thought to produce its own form of mandatory minimums.[191]

Drug Crimes

Federal law regulates the cultivation, manufacture, distribution, export, import, and possession of certain plants, drugs, and chemicals, which it designates as controlled substances and classifies according to medicinal value and potential for abuse under the Controlled Substances Act and the Controlled Substances Import and Export Act.[192] The Acts contain a number of mandatory minimum penalty provisions. Most involve possession with the intent to distribute (traffic) substantial amounts of eight controlled substances which are considered highly susceptible to abuse.[193] The mandatory minimums are structured so that more severe sentences attend cases involving very substantial quantities,[194] death or serious bodily injury,[195] or repeat offenders.[196]

The penalties of the underlying offense apply to anyone who attempts or conspires to commit any controlled substance offense that carries a mandatory minimum.[197]

The eight trigger substances are heroin, powder cocaine, cocaine base (crack), PCP, LSD, propanamide, methamphetamine, and marijuana. Each comes with one set of mandatory minimums for trafficking a substantial amount and a second, high set of mandatory minimums for ten times that amount. The first set (841(b)(1)(B) levels) has the following thresholds:

heroin - 100 grams;[198]
powder cocaine - 500 grams;[199]
crack - 28 grams;[200]
PCP - 100 grams;[201]
LSD - 1 gram;[202]
propanamide - 40 grams;[203]
methamphetamine - 5 grams;[204]
marijuana - 100 kilograms.[205]

The second set (841(b)(1)(A) levels):

heroin - 1 kilogram;[206]
powder cocaine – 5 kilograms;[207]
crack - 280 grams;[208]
PCP - 100 grams;[209]
LSD - 10 grams;[210]
propanamide - 400 grams;[211]
methamphetamine - 50 grams;[212]
marijuana – 1,000 kilograms.[213]

In addition to the volume mandatory minimums for these eight, trafficking in lesser amounts of those substances, or in other schedule I or schedule II controlled substances, or in various "date rape" drugs carries mandatory minimums if the business results in death or serious bodily injury.[214]

Table 1. Federal Drug Offenses: Mandatory Minimum Terms of Imprisonment

Substance	Minimum	Maximum
Trafficking 841(b)(1)(A) substance (e.g., 1 kilo or more of heroin)	10 years	life
if death or serious injury results	20 years	life
repeat offender	20 years	life
repeat offender if death or serious injury results	life	life
Trafficking 841(b)(1)(B) substance (e.g., 100 grams or more of heroin)	5 years	40 years
if death or serious injury results	20 years	life
repeat offender	10 years	life
repeat offender if death or serious injury results	life	life
Trafficking lesser amounts of 841(b)(1) substances; other schedule I or II substances; or date rape drugs: if death or serious injury results	20 years	life
repeat offender if death or serious injury results	life	life
Simple possession of a controlled substance with 1 prior conviction	15 days	2 years
Simple possession of a controlled substance with 2 or more priors	90 days	3 years
Drug kingpin	20 years	life
repeat offender	30 years	life
large operation (e.g., gross $10 million + per year)	life	life
killing in furtherance	20 years	life/death
Unless a higher minimum applies, distribution of a controlled substance to a pregnant woman, to or using a child.	1 year	2x usual penalty; 3x for repeat offenders
Unless a higher minimum applies, distribution of a controlled substance proximate to a school or other prohibited location	1 year	2x usual penalty
repeat offender	3 years	3x usual penalty
Narco-terrorism involving 841(b)(1) substances	2x usual minimum	life

Severe mandatory minimum penalties also follow conviction under the continuing criminal enterprise ("drug kingpin") section. Section 848(c) defines a continuing criminal enterprise as one in which an individual derives substantial income from directing five or more others in the commission of various controlled substance felonies.[215] The offense itself carries a term of imprisonment of not less than 20 years and may be increased to not more than 30 years for repeat offenders.[216] Furthermore, anyone who kills in furtherance of the enterprise is punishable by imprisonment for not less than 20 years and may be put to death.[217] Large scale drug kingpins who traffic in vast amounts of any of the eight 841(b)(1) substances or who realize vast fortunes from such trafficking receive a mandatory life term of imprisonment upon conviction.[218]

Narco-terrorists who traffic in the threshold amounts of the eight 841(b)(1) substances are punishable by imprisonment for not less than twice the mandatory minimum that would otherwise apply.[219]

As reflected in the chart below, less stringent mandatory minimum sentences await repeat offenders convicted of simple possession[220] and those who traffic controlled substances, not otherwise accompanied by mandatory minimums, to pregnant women,[221] children,[222] or in proximity of a school, playground or other prohibited location.[223]

Possession with Intent

Conviction of possession with intent to distribute various controlled substances forms the basis for imposition of a mandatory minimum sentence under §841(b). To support a conviction, "the government must show that the defendant had (1) knowing (2) possession of the drugs and (3) an intent to distribute them."[224] The government need not prove that the defendant knew the particular type or quantity of the controlled substance he intended to distribute.[225] Culpable possession may be either actual or constructive.[226] "Constructive possession exists where the defendant has the power to exercise control or dominion over the item. In drug cases, constructive possession is an appreciable ability to guide the destiny of the contraband." [227] As for the intent to distribute, it "can be proven circumstantially from, among other things, the quantity of cocaine and the existence of implements such as scales commonly used in connection with the distribution of cocaine." [228] Moreover, although proof of sale or gift will suffice, intent to distribute demands no more than an intent to transfer.[229]

The escalating mandatory minimums that apply to offenders with "a prior conviction for a felony drug offense" extend to those classified as misdemeanors under state law but punishable by imprisonment for more than a year.[230] They also apply even though the underlying state felony conviction has been expunged.[231] On the other hand, there is apparently at least a division among the circuits over whether the government's failure to comply with the procedure for establishing a prior conviction,[232] and therefore to alert the defendant of the prospect of an enhanced mandatory minimum, is jurisdictional.[233]

The second Sentencing Commission report made several recommendations relating to repeat offender mandatory minimums. It suggested that the escalator approach in some instances might be unduly severe.[234] It also expressed the view that exclusion of simple possession offenses and greater compatibility with state sentence provisions might be advisable.[235]

The mandatory minimums apply with equal force to those who attempt to possess with intent to distribute,[236] or who conspire to do so,[237] or who aids and abets another to do so.[238] "To prove the crime of attempted knowing or intentional possession, with intent to distribute, of a controlled substance, the government must show: (1) the defendant acted with the intent to possess a controlled substance with the intent to distribute; and (2) the defendant engaged in conduct which constitutes a substantial step toward commission of the offense."[239]

"To establish a conspiracy, the government must prove: (1) the existence of an agreement among two or more people to achieve an illegal purpose; (2) the defendant's knowledge of the agreement; and (3) that the defendant knowingly joined and participated in the agreement."[240] The agreement may be inferred circumstantially.[241] Conspirators need to know the scheme's general outline, but every conspirator need not be informed of the plot's every detail.[242]

"To convict under a theory of aiding and abetting, the Government must prove: (1) the substantive offense was committed; (2) the defendant contributed to and furthered the offense; and (3) the defendant intended to aid in its commission."[243]

Drug Kingpin

Conviction of a Continuing Criminal Enterprise (CCE or Drug Kingpin) offense is punishable by imposition of a mandatory minimum. To secure a conviction, the government must establish "1) a felony violation of the federal narcotics laws; 2) as part of a continuing series of three or more related felony violations of federal narcotics laws; 3) in concert with five or more other persons; 4) for whom [the defendant] is an organizer, manager or supervision; [and] 5) from which [the defendant] derives substantial income or resources."[244]

The homicide mandatory minimum found in the drug kingpin statute sets a 20-year minimum term of imprisonment for killings associated with a kingpin offense or for killings of law enforcement officers associated with certain other controlled substance offenses.[245]

Safety Valve

Low level drug offenders can escape some of the mandatory minimum sentences if they qualify for the safety valve found in 18 U.S.C. 3553(f). Congress created the safety valve after it became concerned that the mandatory minimum sentencing provisions could have resulted in equally severe penalties for both the more and the less culpable offenders.[246] It is available to qualified offenders convicted of violations of the possession with intent, the simple possession, attempt, or conspiracy provisions of the Controlled Substances or Controlled Substances Import and Export Acts.[247]

It is not available to avoid the mandatory minimum sentences that attend other offenses, even those closely related to the covered offenses. For instance, §860 (21 U.S.C. 860) which outlaws violations of section 841 near schools, playgrounds or public housing facilities and sets the penalties for violation at twice what they would be under section 841, is not covered. Those charged with a violation of section 860 are not eligible for relief under the safety valve provisions.[248] In addition, safety valve relief is not available to those convicted under the Maritime Drug Law Enforcement Act, even though the act proscribes conduct closely related to the smuggling and trafficking activities punished under sections 960 and 963.249.

For the convictions to which the safety valve does apply, the defendant must convince the sentencing court by a preponderance of the evidence that he satisfies each of safety valve's five requirements.[250] He may not have more than one criminal history point.[251] He may not have used violence or a dangerous weapon in connection with the offense.[252] He may not have been an organizer or leader of the drug enterprise.[253] He must have provided the government with all the information and evidence at his disposal.[254] Finally, the offense may not have resulted in serious injury or death.[255]

One Criminal History Point

The criminal history point qualification refers to the defendant's criminal record. The Sentencing Guidelines assign criminal history points based on a defendant's past criminal record. Two or more points are assigned for every prior sentence of imprisonment or juvenile confinement of sixty days or more or for offenses committed while the defendant was in prison, was an escaped prisoner, or was on probation, parole, or supervised release.[256] A single point is assigned for every other federal or state prior sentence of conviction, subject to certain exceptions.[257]

Foreign sentences of imprisonment are not counted;[258] nor are sentences imposed by tribal courts;[259] nor summary court martial sentences;[260] nor sentences imposed for expunged, reversed, vacated, or invalidated convictions;[261] nor sentences for certain petty offenses or minor misdemeanors.[262] The Sentencing Guidelines list two classes of these minor misdemeanor or petty offenses that are not counted for criminal history purposes and thus for safety valve purposes. One class consists of eight types of minor offenses, like hunting and fishing violations or juvenile truancy, that are not counted regardless of the sentence imposed.[263] The other class consists of arguable more serious offenses, such as gambling or prostitution, that are only excused if the offender was sentenced no more severely than to imprisonment for thirty days or less or to probation for less than a year.[264] Both classes also include similar offenses to those listed "by whatever name they are known."[265]

Two-thirds of the judges who responded to the Commission's survey favored expanding the safety valve criminal history criterion to encompass those with 2 or 3 criminal history points,[266] although fewer than one quarter favored expansion of the criterion further.[267] Some of the Commission's hearing witnesses concurred.[268] The Commission's second report, in fact, recommends that Congress "consider expanding the safety valve ... to include certain offenders who receive two, or perhaps three, criminal history points under the guidelines."[269]

Only the Non-violent

The safety valve has two disqualifications designed to reserve its benefits to the non-violent. The weapon or threat of violence disqualification turns upon the defendant's conduct or the conduct of those he "aided or abetted, counseled, commanded, induced, procured, or willfully caused."[270] It is not triggered by the conduct of a co-conspirator, unless the defendant aided, abetted, counsel ... the co-conspirator's violence or possession.[271]

Disqualifying firearm possession may be either actual or constructive.[272] Constructive possession is the dominion or control over a firearm or the place where one is located.[273] Disqualification requires the threat of violence or possession of a firearm "in connection with the offense."[274] In many instances, possession of a firearm in a location where drugs are stored or transported, or where transactions occur, will be enough to support an inference of possession in connection with the drug offense of conviction.[275]

The Sentencing Guidelines define 'serious bodily injury" for purposes of section 3553(f)(3) as an "injury involving extreme physical pain or the protracted impairment of a function of a bodily member, organ, or mental faculty; or requiring medical intervention such as surgery, hospitalization, or physical rehabilitation."[276] On its face, the definition would include serious bodily injuries, such as hospitalization, suffered by the defendant as a result of the offense.[277]

Unlike the gun and violence disqualification in section 3553(f)(2), the serious injury disqualification in section 3553(f)(3) may be triggered by the conduct of a co-conspirator.[278]

Only Single or Low Level Offenders

The Sentence Guidelines disqualify anyone who receives a guideline level increase for their aggravated role in the offense.[279] Thus, by implication, it does not require a defendant to have received a guideline increase based on his minimal or minor participation in a group offense nor does it disqualify a defendant who acted alone.[280]

Tell All

The most heavily litigated safety valve criterion requires full disclosure on the part of the defendant. The requirement extends not only to information concerning the crimes of conviction, but also to information concerning other crimes that "were part of the same course of conduct or of a common scheme or plan," including uncharged related conduct.[281]

Neither section 3553(f) nor the Sentencing Guidelines explain what form the defendants' full disclosure must take. At least one court has held that under rare circumstances disclosure through the defendant's testimony at trial may suffice.[282] Most often the defendant provides the information during an interview with prosecutors or by a proffer. The defendant must disclose the information to the prosecutor, however. Disclosure to the probation officer during preparation of the presentence report is not sufficient.[283] Moreover, a defendant does not necessarily qualify for relief merely because he has proffered a statement and invited the prosecution to identify any addition information it seeks; for "the government is under no obligation to solicit information from a defendant."[284] On the other hand, past lies do not render a defendant ineligible for relief under the truthful disclosure criterion of the safety value, although they may undermine his creditability.[285]

FIREARMS OFFENSES

Section 924(c)

Mandatory minimums are found in two federal firearms statutes. One, the Armed Career Criminal Act, deals exclusively with recidivists.[286] The other, §924(c), attaches one of several mandatory minimum terms of imprisonment whenever a firearm is used or possessed during and in relation to a federal crime of violence or drug trafficking.[287] Section 924(c) has been the subject of repeated Supreme Court litigation[288] and regular congressional amendment since its inception in 1968.[289]

Section 924(c), in its current form, imposes one of several different minimum sentences when a firearm is used or possessed in furtherance of another federal crime of violence or of drug trafficking. The mandatory minimums, imposed in addition to the sentence imposed for the underlying crime of violence or drug trafficking, vary depending upon the circumstances:

- imprisonment for not less than five years, unless one of higher mandatory minimums below applies;
- imprisonment for not less than seven years, if a firearm is brandished;
- imprisonment for not less than 10 years, if a firearm is discharged;
- imprisonment for not less than 10 years, if a firearm is a short-barreled rifle or shotgun or is a semi-automatic weapon;
- imprisonment for not less than 15 years, if the offense involves the armor piercing ammunition;
- imprisonment for not less than 25 years, if the offender has a prior conviction for violation of §924(c);
- imprisonment for not less than 30 years, if the firearm is a machine gun or destructive device or is equipped with a silencer; and

- imprisonment for life, if the offender has a prior conviction for violation of §924(c) and if the firearm is a machine gun or destructive device or is equipped with a silencer.290

A "firearm" for purposes of section 924(c) includes not only guns ("weapons ... which will or [are]designed to or may readily be converted to expel a projectile by the action of an explosive"), but silencers and explosives as well.[291] It includes firearms that are not loaded or are broken;[292] it does not, however, include toys or imitations.[293]

The mandatory minimums apply to "any person, who, during and in relation to any [federal] crime of violence or drug trafficking crime ... uses or carries a firearm, or who, in furtherance of any such crime, possesses a firearm." [294] Originally, section 924(c) condemned only "use" of a firearm in connection with certain federal offenses.[295] Then, the Supreme Court pointed out in *Bailey* that the word "use" demands more than simple possession.[296] Congress amended the section thereafter to outlaw not only use during and in relation to a predicate offense, but possession "in furtherance" of a predicate drug trafficking or violent offense as well.[297]

Predicate Offenses

The drug trafficking predicates include any felony violation of the Controlled Substances Act, the Controlled Substances Import and Export Act, or the Maritime Drug Law Enforcement Act.[298] The crime of violence predicates are statutorily defined as any federal felony that satisfies either of two tests, i.e. (1) if it "has as an element the use, attempted use, or threatened use of physical force against the person or property of another," or (2) if it "by its nature, involves a substantial risk that physical force against the person or property of another may be used in the course of committing the offense."[299]

The Supreme Court has addressed several other aspects of section 924(c), but it has yet to decide what constitutes a crime of violence for purposes of the section. In *Leocal v. Ashcroft*, however, it had occasion to examine the question under 18 U.S.C. 16 which defines crimes of violence in virtually the same terms.[300]

There, it reasoned that the wording of the definition precluded its application to the crime of driving under the influence and causing injury. When the statute speaks of the element involving the "*use* ... of physical force against the person or property another" – as both sections 16 and 924(c)(3) do – it means "a higher degree of intent than negligent or merely accidental conduct."[301] When, like sections 16 and 924(c)(3), it speaks of a "risk that physical force against the person or property of another may be used in the course of committing the offense," it means the "risk that the use of physical force against another might be *required* in committing the offense," not the risk that physical force might inadvertently or negligently visited upon another.[302] "The ordinary meaning of this term [(the use physical force)] ... 'calls to mind a tradition of crimes that involve the possibility of more closely related, *active* violence'").[303]

The circuit courts have found a wide range of federal crimes fit the definition.[304] One has used the *Leocal* tests to reconcile the conflicting views in other circuits and decide that firearm possession offenses are not crimes of violence for purposes of section 924(c).[305]

Possession in Furtherance

The possession prong of the offense requires that the defendant "(1) knowingly, (2) possessed a firearm, (3) in furtherance of any [federal] drug trafficking crime."[306] The "in furtherance" element compels the government to show some nexus between possession of a firearm and a predicate offense, that is, to show that the firearm furthered, advanced, moved forward, promoted, or in some way facilitated the predicate offense.[307] This requires more than proof of the presence of a firearm in the same location as the predicate offense.[308] Most circuits have identified specific factors that commonly allow a court to distinguish guilty possession from innocent "possession at the scene," particularly in a drug case, i.e., "(1) type of drug activity [or violent crime] that is being conducted, (2) accessibility of the firearm, (3) the type of the weapon, (4) whether the possession is illegal, (5) whether the gun is loaded, (6) the proximity to the drugs or drug profits, and (7) the time and circumstances under which the gun is found."[309]

Although the Supreme Court has made it clear that acquiring a firearm in an illegal drug transaction does not constitute "use" in violation of the section 924(c),[310] several of the circuits have found that such acquisition may constitute "possession in furtherance."[311]

Use or Carry

The "use" outlawed in the use or carriage branch of section 924(c) requires that a firearm be actively employed during and in relation to a predicate offense, i.e., either a crime of violence or a drug trafficking offense.[312] A defendant "uses" a firearm during or in relation to a drug trafficking offense when he uses it to acquire drugs in a drug deal,[313] or when he uses it as collateral in a drug deal,[314] but not when he accepts a firearm in exchange for drugs in a drug deal.[315] The "carry[ing]" that the section outlaws encompasses instances when a firearm is carried on the defendant's person as well as when it is simply readily accessible in vehicle during and in relation to a predicate offense.[316]

A firearm is used or carried "during or in relation" to a predicate offense when it has "some purpose or effect with respect" to the predicate offense; "its presence or involvement cannot be the result of accident or coincidence."[317] The government must show that the availability of the firearm played an integral role in the predicate offense.[318]

Discharge and Brandish

The basic five-year mandatory minimum penalty for using, carrying, or possessing a firearm in the course of a predicate offense becomes a seven-year mandatory minimum if a firearm was brandished during the course of the offense and becomes a 10-year mandatory minimum if a firearm was discharged during the course of the offense.[319] The discharge provision applies even if the firearm is discharged inadvertently.[320] Whether a firearm is discharged or brandished is a question that after *Alleyne* must be presented to the jury and proven beyond a reasonable doubt.[321] A firearm is brandished for these purposes when (1) it is displayed or its presence made known (2) in order to intimidate another.[322] Intimidation is a necessary feature of brandishing, but it is no less present when the fear is induced by using the gun as a club rather than merely displaying it.[323]

Short Barrels, Semiautomatics, Machine Guns, and Bombs

For some time, section 924(c) consisted of a single long paragraph. When Congress added the "possession in furtherance" language, it parsed the section. Now, the general, brandish, and discharge mandatory penalties provisions appear in one part.[324] The provisions for offenses involving a short-barreled rifle or shotgun, a semiautomatic assault weapon, a silencer, a machinegun, or explosives appear in a second part.[325] The provisions for second and consequent convictions appear in a third part.[326]

The circuits are apparently divided over the question of whether the government must show that the defendant knew that the firearm at issue was of a particular type (i.e., short-barreled rifle or shotgun, machine gun, or bomb).[327]

Prior to the division, the Supreme Court had identified as an element of a separate offense (rather than a sentencing factor) the question of whether a machinegun was the firearm used during and in relation to a predicate offense.[328] Thereafter, it concluded that the division was a matter of style rather than substance. Thus, the answer remains the same – use of a short-barreled rifle, semiautomatic assault weapon, silencer, machine gun, or bomb is not a sentencing factor, but an element of a separate offense to be charged and proved to the jury beyond a reasonable doubt.[329] The question of whether a second or subsequent conviction has occurred, however, remains a sentencing factor.[330]

Other Sentencing Considerations

The penalties under section 924(c) were once flat sentences, e.g., the penalty for use of a firearm during the course of a predicate offense was a five-year term of imprisonment.[331] Now, they are simply mandatory minimums, each carrying an unspecified maximum term of life imprisonment.[332]

A court may not avoid the mandatory minimums called for in section 924(c)(1) by imposing a probationary sentence,[333] or by ordering that a 924(c)(1) minimum mandatory sentence be served concurrently with some other sentence.[334] Nor may a court mute the impact of a mandatory minimum sentence by artificially reducing the sentence for the predicate offense.[335]

If a criminal episode involves more than one predicate offense, more than one violation of section 924(c) may be punished.[336] Moreover, the second or subsequent convictions which trigger enhanced mandatory minimum penalties need not be the product of separate trials, but may be part of the same verdict. Thus, a defendant charged and convicted in a single trial on several counts may be subject to multiple, consecutive, mandatory minimum terms of imprisonment.[337]

A number of defendants have sought refuge in the clause of section 924(c) which introduces the section's mandatory minimum penalties with an exception: "[e]xcept to the extent that a greater minimum sentence is otherwise provided by this subsection or by any other provision of law." Defendants at one time argued that the mandatory minimums of section 924(c) become inapplicable, if they are subject to a higher mandatory minimum under the predicate drug trafficking offense under the Armed Career Criminal Act (18 U.S.C. 924(e)), or some other provision of law.[338] The Supreme Court rejected the argument in *Abbott*.[339] The clause means that the standard five-year minimum applies except in cases where the facts trigger one of section 924(c)'s higher minimums.[340]

Armor Piercing Ammunition

Section 924(c) has a separate provision which outlaws predicate crime-related use, carriage, or possession of armor piercing ammunition.[341] The provision, added in 2005, greatly resembles a pre-existing provision in 18 U.S.C. 929.[342] There are two significant differences. Section 924(c)(5) carries a 15-year mandatory minimum with special provisions if a death results from the commission of the offense. Section 929 carries a five-year mandatory minimum with no mention of death-resulting offenses. Yet, section 929 specifically excludes the possibility of probation or concurrent sentencing; while section 924(c)(5) makes no mention of either. Neither provision appears to have been prosecuted with any regularity.

Aiding, Abetting, and Conspiracy

As a general rule, conspirators are liable for any foreseeable crimes committed by any of their co- conspirators in furtherance of the conspiracy.[343] The rule applies when a defendant's co- conspirator has committed a violation of section 924(c).[344]

Under federal law, moreover, anyone who commands, counsels, aids, or abets the commission of a federal offense by another is punishable as though he had committed the crime himself, 18 U.S.C. 2.[345] Here too, the general proposition applies to section 924(c). "[A] defendant is liable of aiding and abetting the use of a firearm during a crime of violence if he (1) knows his cohort used a firearm in the underlying crime, and (2) knowingly and actively participates in that underlying crime."[346]

Second Amendment

> A well regulated Militia, being necessary to the security of a free State, the right of the people to keep and bear Arms, shall not be infringed.[347]

The Supreme Court has explained that the Second Amendment confers an individual right to possess and carry weapons for the defense of his or her person, family, and home.[348] The Court has been quick to point out, however, that the right is not absolute. Without providing a full panoply of exceptions, it observed that the Amendment permits such things as "longstanding prohibitions on the possession of firearms by felons and the mentally ill, [and] laws forbidding the carrying of firearms in sensitive places such as schools and government buildings, [and] laws imposing conditions and qualifications on the commercial sale of arms."[349] Consistent with this theme, the circuit courts have held that the Second Amendment cast no constitutional doubt upon §924(c).[350]

Double Jeopardy

The Fifth Amendment declares that "No person shall be ... subject for the same offence to be twice put in jeopardy of life or limb...."[351] The double jeopardy clause protects against both successive prosecutions and successive punishments for the same offense.[352] The initial test for whether a defendant has been twice tried or punished for the same offense or two different offenses is whether each of the two purported offenses requires proof that the other does not.[353] Thus, without violating the double jeopardy clause, an individual may be convicted and sentenced for two violations of section 924(c), if each has a different predicate offense.[354] On the other hand, there is no consensus over whether a single predicate offense may support conviction and sentencing for two or more violations of section 924(c).[355] Moreover, the conviction for a serious offense will ordinarily preclude prosecution or punishment for a lesser included offense, since the lesser offense consists of only elements found in the more serious offense.[356] For example, a defendant may not be convicted and punished for both a violation of section 924(c)(use of a firearm in furtherance of a robbery) and of section 924(j)(use of the same firearm in the same robbery resulting in death).[357]

Sentencing Commission

More than 60% of the judges who responded to the Commission's survey felt that the mandatory minimum sentencing provisions of section 924(c) were appropriate.[358] Nevertheless, the Commission recommended that Congress consider several modifications:

i. Amend the length of section 924(c) penalties

Congress should consider amending the mandatory minimum penalties established at section 924(c), particularly the penalties for "second or subsequent" violations of the statute, to lesser terms. Section 924(c), for example, requires a 25-year mandatory minimum penalty for offenders convicted of a "second or subsequent" violation of the statute. Reducing the length of the mandatory minimum penalty would reduce the risk of excessive severity, permit the guidelines to better account for the variety of mitigating and aggravating factors that may be present in the particular case, and mitigate the inconsistencies in application produced by the severity of the existing mandatory minimum penalties.

ii. Make section 924(c) a "true" recidivist statute

Congress should consider amending section 924(c) so that the increased mandatory minimum penalties for a "second or subsequent" offense apply only to *prior* convictions. In those circumstances, the mandatory minimum penalties for multiple violations of section 924(c) charged in the same indictment would continue to apply consecutively, but would require significantly shorter sentences for offenders who do not have a prior conviction under section 924(c). This would reduce the potential for overly severe sentences for offenders who have not previously been convicted of an offense under section 924(c), and ameliorate some of the demographic impacts resulting from stacking.

iii. Give discretion to impose concurrent sentences for multiple section 924(c) violations

Congress should consider amending section 924(c) to give the sentencing court limited discretion to impose sentences for multiple violations of section 924(c) concurrently. Congress has recently used this approach in enacting the offense of aggravated identity theft and the accompanying mandatory penalty at 18 U.S.C. § 1028A. This limited discretion would provide the flexibility to impose sentences that appropriately reflect the gravity of the offense and reduce the risk that an offender will receive an excessively severe punishment.

iv. Amend statutory definitions

Congress should consider clarifying the statutory definitions of the underlying and predicate offenses that trigger mandatory minimum penalties under section 924(c) and the Armed Career Criminal Act to reduce the risk of inconsistent application and the litigation that those definitions have fostered. To further reduce the risk of inconsistent application, Congress also should consider more finely tailoring the definitions of the predicate offenses that trigger the Armed Career Criminal Act's mandatory minimum penalty.[359]

Armed Career Criminal Act (18 U.S.C. 924(e))

The Armed Career Criminal Act (ACCA) establishes a 15-year mandatory minimum term of imprisonment for defendants convicted of unlawful possession of a firearm under section 18 U.S.C. 922(g) who have three prior convictions for violent felonies or serious drug offenses.[360] Although §922(g) bans firearm possession for nine categories of individuals, it applies most often to defendants with prior felony convictions for obvious reasons.[361] More often than not, the prior convictions are for violations of state law.

Predicate Offenses

The elements of a §924(e) violation consist of an unlawful possession offense coupled with three qualifying prior convictions. The prior convictions must be for either violent felonies or serious drug offenses and must have been committed on different occasions.[362] "[T]o trigger a sentence enhancement under the ACCA, a defendant's prior felony convictions must involve separate criminal episodes. However, offenses are considered distinct criminal episodes if they occurred on occasions different from one another. Two offenses are committed on occasions different from one another if it is possible to discern the point at which the first offense is completed and the second offense beings."[363] Thus, separate drug deals on separate days will constitute offenses committed on different occasions though they involve the same parties and location.[364] The fact that two crimes occurred on a different occasion, however, must be clear on the judicial record; recourse to police records will not do.[365]

Application of section 924(e) provides no opportunity to challenge the validity of the underlying predicate offenses.[366]

Serious Drug Offenses

The section defines serious drug offenses as those violations of state or federal drug law punishable by imprisonment for 10 years or more.[367] Conviction under a statute which carries a 10-year maximum for repeat offenders qualifies, even though the maximum term for first-time offenders is five years.[368] It is the maximum permissible term which determines qualification, even when discretionary sentencing guidelines called for a term of less than 10 years,[369] or when the defendant was in fact sentenced to a lesser term of imprisonment.[370] The drug offense must be at least a 10-year felony at the time of prior conviction to qualify as a predicate offense under §924(e).[371]

As long as the attempt is punishable by imprisonment for 10 years or more, the term "serious drug offense" includes attempts to commit a serious drug offense.[372]

Violent Felonies

The assessment of whether a past crime constitutes a violent felony for purposes of section 924(e) is more complicated than whether a drug offense is a serious drug offense for such purposes. The task involves an examination of "how the law defines the offense and not ... how an individual offender might have committed on a particular occasion."[373] Violent felony predicates come in two varieties: offenses involving the use of physical force and offenses of the burglary/arson/ extortion class.[374]

Physical force. The physical force category consists of those offenses that have "as an element the use, attempted use, or threatened use of physical force against the person of another."[375] "Physical force" here means "violent force – that is, force capable of causing physical pain or injury to another person."[376] Thus, it does not include state convictions for intentional touching of another, such as the Florida statute in *Johnson*.[377]

Burglary et al. The second variety of violent felony predicates consists of the crimes of burglary, arson, extortion, use of explosives, and any other offense that "otherwise involves conduct that presents a serious potential risk of physical injury to another." [378] The crimes found in the residual clause (crimes that "otherwise involve ... ") are only those similar to the enumerated crimes of burglary, arson, extortion and the use of explosives, those marked by "purposeful, violent and aggressive conduct."[379] Thus, the class includes "def[ying] a law enforcement command by fleeing in a car,"[380] but does not include convictions for driving under the influence of alcohol or failing to report to begin serving a term of imprisonment.[381] The statutory elements of the crime of prior conviction determine whether the conviction qualifies for purposes of the residual clause.[382] While a court may inquiry minimally into the facts of a given case when a statute provides alternative elements (one qualifying and the other not) for the offense of conviction, it may not do so when the statute condemns broadly both qualified and unqualified misconduct.[383]

Legislative Authority

Congress's constitutional authority to regulate interstate and foreign commerce is among its most sweeping prerogatives, but the power is not boundless. It permits regulation of the use of the channels of commerce, of the instrumentalities of commerce, of the things that move there, and of those activities which substantially impact commerce.[384] Absent such a nexus, it does not permit Congress to enact legislation proscribing possession of a firearm on school grounds, as the Supreme Court observed in *Lopez*.[385] Section 922(g)[386] outlaws receipt by a felon of a firearm "which has been shipped or transported in interstate or foreign commerce." This, in the view of the circuit courts to address the issue, is sufficient to bring within Congress's commerce clause power the prohibitions of section 922(g), that section 924(e) makes punishable.[387]

Second Amendment

In §924(e) cases, the courts ordinarily proceed no further in their Second Amendment analysis than to the threshold possession offense, for example, 18 U.S.C. 922(g)(1)(prohibiting firearm possession by convicted felons). Pointing to the statement in *Heller*, they conclude that the possession offense does not offend the Second Amendment.[388] From which it seems to follow that §924(e), at least when it imposes a mandatory minimum sanction upon felons who violate section 922(g)(1), is similarly inoffensive.[389]

Apprendi and Recidivism

The Supreme Court in *Almendarez-Torres* identified the fact of a prior conviction as a sentencing factor. It rejected the argument that the Fifth and Sixth Amendments required that the fact of a defendant's prior conviction be charged in the indictment and found by the jury beyond a reasonable doubt.[390] Yet almost immediately thereafter, it seemed to repudiate the broad implications of *Almendarez-Torres*, while clinging to its narrow holding, "under the Due Process Clause of the Fifth Amendment and the notice and jury trial guarantees of the Sixth Amendment, any fact (*other than prior conviction*) that increases the maximum penalty for a crime must be charged in an indictment, submitted to a jury, and proven beyond a reasonable doubt."[391]

And so the Court continued in *Blakely* and *Booker* – unless the defendant waived, a jury must decide any sentence enhancing fact, other than the fact of a prior conviction.[392] The Court waivered slightly in *Shepard* where a plurality held that a sentencing court may look no further than the judicial record of a prior conviction when faced with a dispute over whether a section 924(e) defendant was convicted earlier of a qualifying predicate offense.[393] Justice Thomas, upon whose concurrence the result rested, however, opined that "*Almendarez-Torres* ... has been eroded by this Court's subsequent Sixth Amendment jurisprudence, and a majority of the Court now recognizes that *Almendarez-Torres* was wrongly decided."[394]

Nevertheless, the Court has yet to revisit *Almendarez-Torres*,[395] and the lower federal courts continue to adhere to it in section 924(e) cases: the fact of a prior qualifying conviction need not be charged in the indictment nor proved to the jury beyond a reasonable doubt.[396]

Table 2. Federal Sex Offenses: Mandatory Minimum Terms of Imprisonment

Citation	Offense	Mandatory Minimum Term Imprisonment
18 U.S.C. 2241(a)	aggravated sexual assault (by threat or force)(including attempt)	any term of years
18 .S.C.2241(b)	aggravated sexual assault (upon an incapacitated victim)(including attempt)	any term of years
18 U.S.C. 2241(c)	a. sexual act (victim under 12 or victim under 16 and at least 4 years the offender's junior)(including attempt)	a. 30 years
	b. with a prior conviction	b. life
18 U.S.C. 1591	a. sex trafficking by force or fraud or of a child under 14	a. 15 years
	b. sex trafficking of a child (14 to 18)(w/o force or fraud)	b. 10 years
18 U.S.C. 2422(b)	enticing or coercing a child under 18 to engage in prostitution (including attempt)(Mann Act)	10 years
18 U.S.C. 2423(a)	transporting a child under 18 for illicit sexual purposes (including attempt) (Mann Act)	10 years
18 U.S.C. 2245	murder in the course of a Mann Act, sex trafficking, or production of child pornography offense	any term of years
18 U.S.C. 2251	child pornography: inducing a child under 18 to produce, custodial involvement in production, or advertising (including attempt)	
	a. death results	a. 30 years
	b. 2 or more prior convictions	b. 35 years
	c. 1 prior conviction	c. 25 years
	d. otherwise	d. 15 years
18 U.S.C. 2251A	child pornography: custodial involvement in production	30 years
18 U.S.C. 2252	a. child pornography (real): transportation, receipt, or sale (including attempt)	a. 5 years
	b. prior conviction	b. 15 years
	c. child pornography (real): recidivist possession	c. 10 years
18 U.S.C. 2252A	a. child pornography (real or virtual): transportation, receipt, promotion, sale, or distribution to a child (including attempt)	a. 5 years
	b. prior conviction	b. 15 years
	c. child pornography (real or virtual): recidivist possession	c. 10 years
18 U.S.C. 2252A(g)	child exploitation enterprise; 3 or more instances involve 3 or more others and multiple victims of child pornography, child sex trafficking, or Mann Act violations involving a child	20 years
18 U.S.C. 3559(e)	federal sex offense (sex trafficking, sexual assault, Mann Act, or production of child pornography violation), involving a victim under 17, by an offender with a prior federal or state equivalent conviction and sentence	life

Eighth Amendment

Defendants sentenced under section 924(e) have suggested two Eighth Amendment issues. First, they argue that their sentences are disproportionate to their offenses. Second, they contend that crimes committed when they were juveniles may not be used as predicates.

The Eighth Amendment prohibits the infliction of cruel and unusual punishments.[397] It has been said to prohibit sentences that are "grossly disproportionate" to the crime.[398] Under varying theories, the Supreme Court has held that it permits the imposition of life imprisonment without the possibility of parole of a first-time offender convicted of large scale drug trafficking;[399] and permits the imposition of a sentence of imprisonment for 25 years to life following a "three strikes" conviction resting on three nonviolent grand theft convictions.[400] On the other hand, the Court held in *Ewing* that the Eighth Amendment precludes execution for a capital offense committed by a juvenile,[401] and most recently in *Graham* that it precludes imprisonment for life without parole for a non-homicide offense committed by a juvenile.[402]

The lower federal courts have consistently rejected general claims that sentences under 924(e) were grossly disproportionate to the crimes involved.[403] In cases decided before *Graham*, the lower federal courts had also rejected claims that the Eighth Amendment precluded use of a juvenile predicate offense to trigger sentencing of an adult under section 924(e).[404] To date, there have been no subsequent federal appellate court decisions directly on point. Two circuits, however, have found no Eighth Amendment impediment to mandatory life imprisonment sentences imposed under provisions other than section 924(e) upon adults convicted of drug trafficking and based in part on predicate juvenile offenses.[405]

Double Jeopardy

The Fifth Amendment ensures that no "person be subject for the same offence to be twice put in jeopardy of life or limb."[406] The double jeopardy clause protects against both successive prosecutions and successive punishments for the same offense.[407] The test for whether a defendant has been twice tried or punished for the same offense or tried or punished for two different offenses is whether each of the two purported offenses requires proof that the other does not.[408] Defendants have argued to no avail that the double jeopardy clause bars reliance on the predicate offenses or on section 922(g) to trigger section 924(e).[409]

Almost 60% of those responding to the Sentencing Commission survey indicated that they considered the section 924(e) mandatory minimum sentences appropriate.[410]

SEX OFFENSES

Congress increased the number of federal sex offenses and their attendant mandatory minimum sentences beginning in 1978 with the enactment of the first federal child pornography statutes.[411] It filled out the complement of federal sex offenses with mandatory minimum sentences of imprisonment at fairly regular intervals thereafter.[412] The current array includes:

Federal Enclaves and Prisons

Federal sex offenses, and consequently the mandatory minimums that accompany them, involve either federal enclaves, interstate travel, or commerce, and are roughly arranged within title 18 of the *United States Code* accordingly. Chapter 109A outlaws rape and other forms of sexual abuse and sexual contact when committed in federal enclaves or federal prisons. Chapter 110 outlaws child pornography. Chapter 117 outlaws sexual activities that have travel or commercial attributes.

Chapter 109A reaches a relatively wide range of sexual misconduct under relatively narrow jurisdiction circumstances. It applies in the special maritime and territorial jurisdiction of the United States. It applies as well in federal prisons and other institutions where individuals are held in federal custody by contract or agreement with federal authorities, regardless of whether they are located within the territorial jurisdiction of the United States.[413]

Within the United States, the "territorial jurisdiction of the United States" refers to those areas over which Congress enjoys state-like legislative jurisdiction.[414] It includes some, or parts of some, military installations, Indian reservations, national parks, and national forests.[415] Outside of the United States, it includes overseas federal facilities and residences with respect to offenses committed by or against U.S. nationals.[416] Felonies proscribed when committed within the territorial jurisdiction of the United States are also proscribed when committed outside the United States by members of the Armed Forces, or employees of the Armed Forces, or those accompanying the Armed Forces.[417]

The "maritime jurisdiction of the United States" includes vessels of U.S. registry, vessels owned by Americans, and vessels scheduled to arrive in, or depart from, the United States with respect to crimes committed by or against a U.S. national.[418]

Prosecution of the mandatory minimum offenses of chapter 109A and each of the other mandatory minimum federal sex offenses may begin at any time.[419] There is no applicable statute of limitations, although in rare instances due process may preclude prosecution of a stale complaint.[420]

Offenses

Chapter 109A violations trigger mandatory minimum sentencing provisions when:

- the offender commits or attempts to commit a sexual act by force or threat or by rendering the victim unconscious or intoxicated (aggravated sexual abuse);[421]
- a sexual act is committed against a minor under the age of 12, or under the age of 16, if is there is disparity of 4 years or more between the age of the victim and the age of the offender (aggravated sexual abuse of a child);[422]
- the offender commits or attempts to commit a sexual act by threat or when the victim is incapacitated (sexual abuse);[423]
- had the sexual contact been a sexual act, it would have been punishable as sexual abuse or aggravated sexual abuse (abusive sexual contact);[424] or
- the offense is a federal sex offense, including an offense subject to a mandatory minimum sentence, committed against a minor by an offender with a prior state or federal conviction for a sex offense committed against a minor (repeated sexual offense).[425]

Definitions

Chapter 109A offenses each involve some form of "sexual act" or "sexual contact." The term "sexual act" includes oral sexual activity as well as sexual penetration by sex organ, foreign object, or digitally.[426] It also covers touching the genitalia of a child under the age of 16 for purposes of humiliation or sexual gratification.[427] The term "sexual contact" includes touching any of the sexually sensitive areas of the body of another for purposes of humiliation or sexual gratification.[428]

Aggravated Sexual Abuse

Section 2241 of chapter 109A proscribes two types of aggravated sexual abuse, each punishable by a mandatory minimum term of imprisonment. First, under the prison and territorial conditions noted above, subsections 2241(a) and (b) outlaw causing, or attempting to cause, another person to engage in a sexual act, when it is accomplished by force, threat, rendering the victim unconscious, or by substantially incapacitating the victim using drugs or intoxicants.[429] Such misconduct is punishable by fine, or by imprisonment for any term of years or for life, or by both a fine and imprisonment, regardless of the age of the victim.[430]

Second, under prison and territorial conditions or when the offender crosses a state border with intent to commit the offense, subsection 2241(c) criminalizes engaging or attempting to engage in a sexual act with a child under 12 years of age (or under 16 years of age, if the offender is 4 years or more the victim's senior).[431] The offense is punishable by imprisonment for not less than 30 years or for life.[432] The mandatory minimum sentencing requirement cannot be overcome by the general sentencing instruction in 18 U.S.C. 3553(a) that a sentence imposed should be no greater than necessary to serve the sentencing purposes identified in that section.[433] The offense is punishable by life imprisonment, if the offender has a prior comparable federal or state conviction.[434]

A defendant may be guilty of an attempted violation of subsection 2241(a), (b), or (c), when he intends to commit the offense and takes a substantial step toward its completion.[435] The prosecution under subsection 2241(c) need not show that the defendant knew that the victim was under 12 years of age,[436] and the greater protection afforded victims under the age of 12 offends neither the equal protection nor due process clauses of the Constitution.[437] The courts have held that a 30-year mandatory minimum sentence for violation of subsection 2241(c) is not so disproportionate as to constitute unconstitutional cruel and unusual punishment,[438] nor does its imposition upon Native Americans violate the equal protection clause.[439] Although abusive sexual contact is a lesser included offense of aggravated sexual abuse, both may be prosecuted without offending the double jeopardy clause, when they involve distinct criminal acts, even if occurring in the same criminal episode.[440]

Sexual Abuse

Section 2242 makes sexual abuse a federal crime when comparable jurisdiction conditions exist, that is, when it is committed within the special maritime and territorial jurisdiction of the United States or equivalent overseas locations or in a federal prison or other federal custodial institution.[441] Sexual abuse is punishable by a fine and a mandatory minimum term of imprisonment for any term of years or for life, regardless of the age of the victim.[442] The offense may be committed by using or attempting to use threats to cause another to engage in a sexual act or by engaging or attempting to engage in a sexual act with an incapacitated victim.[443] A victim who is asleep or incapacitated by intoxication is considered incapacitated for purposes of sexual abuse.[444] A victim with reduced mental capacity may also be considered more susceptible to threats.[445]

Abusive Sexual Contact

Section 2244 proscribes abusive sexual contact, that is, engaging in sexual contact (touching) under circumstances (threats, force, etc.) that would constitute abuse under section 2241 or 2242 had the contact been a sexual act (penetration).[446] Abusive sexual contact is punishable by a fine and a mandatory term of imprisonment for any term of years or for life when engaging in a sexual act under similar circumstances would have violated subsection 2241(c)(victim under 12 or under 16 if the offender is more than 4 years the victim's senior).[447] Abusive sexual contact is not otherwise punishable by a mandatory minimum term of imprisonment.[448]

Repeated Sex Offenses against Children

A defendant, guilty of a "federal sex offense" against a child and previously convicted of a federal or state felonious sex offense committed against a child, must be sentenced to life imprisonment under 18 U.S.C. 3559(e).[449] A child for purposes of subsection 3559(e) is a minor under the age of 17.[450] The federal predicate offenses for purposes of the subsection include both violations of chapter 109A and similar federal and state offenses, that is, violations of "section 1591 (relating to sex trafficking of children), 2241 (relating to aggravated sexual abuse), 2242 (relating to sexual abuse), 2244(a)(1) (relating to abusive sexual contact), 2245 (relating to sexual abuse resulting in death), 2251 (relating to sexual exploitation of children), 2251A (relating to selling or buying of children), 2422(b) (relating to coercion and enticement of a minor into prostitution), 2423(a) (relating to transportation of minors);" or any state equivalent felony.[451]

The defendant must also have been convicted and sentenced prior to the commission of the second offense.[452] An equivalent state offense qualifies as a subsection 3559(e) predicate when it consists of conduct that would be a federal offense should it occur under one of two jurisdictional circumstances—(1) the offense involves use of the mails or interstate commerce, or (2) the offense occurs on a federal enclave, prison, or facility, or in Indian country.[453] Although the predicate state offense must be committed against a child, the victim's status as a child need not be an element of the state offense.[454] Moreover, the state predicate offense need have no federal nexus at the time of commission; it is enough that it would have been a federal offense under the designated jurisdictional circumstances.[455]

A qualified defendant must be sentenced under subsection 3559(e), notwithstanding the fact that he might otherwise have been sentenced under the less severe recidivist provisions of 18 U.S.C. 2551(e).[456]

Subsection 3559(e) provides defendants with a narrow affirmative defense when either the offense of conviction or the predicate offense arises under subsection 2422(b)(relating to inducing another to engage in prostitution) or under subsection 2423(a)(relating to transportation of a child for illicit sexual purposes). To claim the benefits of the defense, an accused must show by clear and convincing evidence that "(A) the sexual act or activity was consensual and not for the purpose of commercial or pecuniary gain; (B) the sexual act or activity would not be punishable by more than one year in prison under the law of the State in which it occurred; or (C) no sexual act or activity occurred."[457]

Travel and Commerce

Several mandatory minimum sentencing statutes punish sexual misconduct based on Congress's legislative authority to regulate interstate and foreign commerce. Most are found in chapter 117 (relating to transportation for illegal sexual activity), but a few others appear in either chapter 109A (relating to sexual abuse) or chapter 77 (relating to peonage, slavery, and human trafficking).

Generally known as the Mann Act or the White Slave Act or the White Slave Traffic Act,[458] chapter 117 has five sections that proscribe travel or the use of the facilities of interstate or foreign commerce when they relate to sexual misconduct: (1) 18 U.S.C. 2421 that outlaws transporting or attempting to transport another in interstate or foreign commerce for purpose of prostitution or other illicit sexual activity; (2) 18 U.S.C. 2422 that outlaws either (a) enticing or attempting to entice another to engage such travel for such a purpose or (b) using or attempting to use the facilities of interstate commerce for such enticement of a minor for such purpose; (3) 18 U.S.C. 2423 that outlaws travel under various circumstances for illegal purposes; (4) 18 U.S.C. 2424 that outlaws false or incomplete filings relating to foreign nationals maintained in a house of prostitution; and (5) 18 U.S.C. 2425 that outlaws the use of the facilities of interstate commerce to communicate information relating to a juvenile for illicit sexual purposes. Sections 2422 and 2423 contain mandatory minimum sentencing provisions; the others do not.

Coercion and Enticement

Subsection 2422(b) requires imposition of a fine and a mandatory minimum term of imprisonment of 10 years for using the facilities of interstate commerce to coerce or entice a child under 18 years of age to engage in prostitution or other illicit sexual activity.[459] Subsection 2422(a) punishes such misconduct involving an adult victim with imprisonment for not more than 20 years with no minimum sentence required.

Coercion or enticement in violation of subsection 2422(b) consists of "(1) use of a facility of interstate commerce (2) to knowingly persuade, induce, entire, or coerce (3) an individual under the age of 18 (4) to engage in illegal sexual activity."[460] The subsection also proscribes any attempt to engage in such conduct.[461] Conviction for attempt requires proof of an intent to violate the subsection and of a substantial step beyond mere preparation toward accomplishment of that intent.[462] The intent required is the intent to entice or coerce—not the intent to engage in the illicit sexual act.[463] The effort to entice need not be addressed to a child directly; culpability may result from efforts to entice through an adult intermediary.[464] An offender who is misled as to the existence of an actual child victim is no less culpable.[465]

Convictions under subsection 2422(b) have withstood a number of constitutional challenges. Defendants have generally been unable establish that they have been exposed to grossly disproportionate sentences in violation of the Eighth Amendment;[466] or suffered a Fifth Amendment deprivation of due process in the form of entrapment,[467] the loss of judicial sentencing discretion,[468] or the denial of equal protection;[469] or lost First Amendment freedom by exposure to vague and overbroad laws;[470] or fallen victim to an unconstitutional violation of separation of powers.[471]

Transportation of a Minor

Section 2423 establishes four sex-related travel offenses and condemns attempts or conspiracies to commit them as well. Subsection 2423(a), which bans interstate or foreign transportation of a child under 18 years of age for criminal sexual purposes, carries a mandatory minimum sentence of imprisonment of 10 years;[472] the same mandatory minimum applies to attempts or conspiracies to violate the subsection.[473] The other three subsections—travel for illicit sexual purposes; travel and illicit sexual conduct overseas; and facilitation of travel for illicit sexual purposes—punish violations by imprisonment for not more than 30 years, with no minimum term of imprisonment required.[474]

"To obtain a conviction under §2423(a), the government must prove beyond a reasonable doubt that the defendant: (1) knowingly transported a minor across state lines, (2) with the intent to engage in sexual activity with the minor, and (3) that the minor was under eighteen at the time of the offense."[475] The government need not show that the defendant knew the minor was underage.[476] Nor must it show that illicit sexual activity was the sole purpose or even the dominant purpose for the travel, as long as it constituted a significant consideration.[477]

Travel to Sexually Abuse a Child

The Mann Act's prohibitions on an offender's travel for illicit sexual purposes carry no mandatory minimum penalties. However, chapter 109A, which ordinarily deals with prison and territorial offenses, provides for such a penalty. As noted earlier, subsection 2241(c) establishes a mandatory minimum sentence of imprisonment of not less than 30 years for "[w]hoever crosses a State line with intent to engage in a sexual act with a person who has not attained the age of 12 years ... or attempts to do so."[478] Recidivists face a mandatory term of life imprisonment.[479] Subsection 2241(d) provides that the government need not establish that the defendant knew that the victim was underage.[480]

Commercial Sex Trafficking of a Child or by Force

Section 1591 of chapter 77 establishes a pair of mandatory minimum sentencing provisions when commercial sex trafficking occurs in or affecting interstate or foreign commerce or within the special maritime or territorial jurisdiction of the United States. One outlaws sex trafficking; the other profiting from it.[481] In either case, violations are punishable by a fine and imprisonment for not less than 10 years, if the child is between the ages of 14 and 18 and no force or coercion is involved.[482] Otherwise, violations are punishable by a fine and imprisonment for not less than 15 years.[483]

Parsed to their elements the two offenses provide:

I.

- (1) Whoever
- (2)
  - (A) in or affecting interstate or foreign commerce, or
  - (B) within the special maritime and territorial jurisdiction of the United States,
- (3) knowingly (4)(A) recruits,
  - (B) ntices,
  - (C) arbors,
  - (D) transports,
  - (E) provides,
  - (F) obtains, or
  - (G) maintains by any means
- (5) a person;
- (6)
  - (A) knowing, or
  - (B)in reckless disregard of the fact,
- (7) that
  - (A) means of force,
  - (B) threats of force,
  - (C) fraud,
  - (D) coercion, or
  - (E) any combination of such means
- (8)
  - (A) will be used to cause the person to engage in a commercial sex act, or (B)
    - (i) that the person has not attained the age of 18 years and
    - (ii) will be caused to engage in a commercial sex act…[484]

II.

- (1) Whoever
- (2) knowingly
- (3) benefits
  - (A) financially or
  - (B) by receiving anything of value,
- (4) from participation in a venture in which
  - (A) person was
  - (B)
    - (i) recruited,
    - (ii) enticed,

(iii) arbored,
(iv) transported,
(v) rovided,
(vi) btained, or
(vii)maintained by any means

(C)
(i) in or affecting interstate or foreign commerce, or
(ii) within the special maritime and territorial jurisdiction of the United States,

(5)
(A) knowing, or
(B) reckless disregard of the fact,

(6) that (A) means of force,
(B) threats of force,
(C) fraud,
(D) coercion, or
(E) any combination of such means

(7)
(A) will be used to cause the person to engage in a commercial sex act, or
(B)
(i) that the person has not attained the age of 18 years and
(ii) will be caused to engage in a commercial sex act…[485]

The courts have held that the interstate commerce prong of the two offenses comes within the reach of Congress's authority to regulate interstate and foreign commerce.[486] To pass muster, the defendant's misconduct must have at least some minimal effect on interstate or foreign commerce.[487] The prosecution, however, need not prove that the defendant knew that his activities were occurring in or affecting commerce.[488] Moreover, while as a general rule, the defendant must be shown to have known that his juvenile victim was underage,[489] the statute relieves the government of the obligation, if the defendant has had sufficient opportunity to observe the victim and thus presumably to discern the victim's age.[490]

Murder in the Course of Certain Sexual Offenses

Section 2245 establishes a mandatory minimum sentence of imprisonment for any term of years for murder committed during the course of a violation of sex trafficking (18 U.S.C. 1591), child pornography (18 U.S.C. 2251, 2251A, 2260), or Mann Act violations (18 U.S.C. 18 U.S.C. 2421, 2422, 2423, 2425), regardless of the age of the victim.[491] Other sections of the Code establish a mandatory minimum term of life imprisonment for murder in the course of the other federal sex offenses, that is, those committed while in federal custody or within the special maritime or territorial jurisdiction of the United States.[492] Section 2251 establishes a 30-year mandatory minimum term of imprisonment when the production of, attempted production of, or conspiracy to produce, child pornography results in a death.[493]

Child Pornography

Four federal child pornography sections establish mandatory minimum terms of imprisonment for violations: 18 U.S.C. 2251 (relating to sexual exploitation of children), 18 U.S.C. 2251A (relating to selling or buying children), 18 U.S.C. 2252 (relating to certain activities relating to material involving sexual exploitation of children), and 18 U.S.C. 2252A (relating to certain activities relating to material constituting or containing child pornography).

Production of Child Pornography

Section 2251 creates a series of mandatory minimum terms of imprisonment for the production of, attempted production of, and conspiracy to produce, child pornography or related misconduct under various jurisdictional circumstances. First time offenders are punishable by a fine and imprisonment for not less than 15 years; offenders with a prior conviction face a fine and imprisonment for not less than 25 years; and offenders with 2 or more prior convictions must be fined and sentenced to imprisonment for at least 35 years.[494] Should a death result from the commission of such offense, the offender must be imprisoned for at least 30 years.[495]

Section 2251 outlaws four substantive offenses: the use of a child to produce child pornography, subsection 2251(a); the participation of a parent or other custodian of a child in such production, subsection 2251(b); the overseas production of such material, subsection 2251(c); and the advertising of such material, subsection 2251(d). Subsection 2251(e) applies the same penalties to attempts or conspiracies to commit any of the four substantive offenses.

The elements common to all four are a child under 18 years of age[496] and at least the goal of creating a visual depiction of sexually explicit conduct of the child.[497] A majority of courts have held that neither the statute nor the Constitution requires the prosecution to show that the defendant knew the child was underage and that mistake of age constitutes no defense.[498]

"Visual depiction" includes photographs, video, and computer disks.[499] "Sexually explicit conduct" is defined to encompass various sexual acts as well as "lascivious exhibition[s]" of an individual's pubic area.[500] The lower federal appellate courts have endorsed the so-call *Dost* factors as a guide to determine when the otherwise lawful depiction of nudity has become a lascivious exhibition.[501]

Subsection 2251(a): Use of a Child to Produce

Subsection 2251(a) outlaws employment, use, or inducement of a child to produce a visual depiction of sexually explicit conduct under a range of jurisdictional circumstances, or by virtue of subsection (e) attempting or conspiring to do so.[502] The jurisdictional circumstances include interstate or territorial transportation of the child, anticipated or actual transmission or transportation of the depiction in or affecting interstate commerce, and use of materials transported in interstate commerce.[503] The courts have held that subsection 2251(a) constitutes a valid exercise of Congress's legislative power under the commerce clause.[504] Moreover, they have concluded that its mandatory minimum term of imprisonment does not offend the Eighth Amendment's prohibition against cruel and unusual punishments.[505]

Subsection 2251(b): Permitting the Use of a Child to Produce

Subsection 2251(b) applies the mandatory minimums of subsection 2251(e) to a parent, or other custodian of a child under 18 years of age, who permits, attempts to permit, or conspires to permit a child to be used for the visual depiction of sexually explicit conduct under jurisdictional circumstances comparable to those that apply to subsection 2251(a).[506] A related provision with a more substantial mandatory minimum sentence of imprison appears in 18 U.S.C. 2251A and differs primarily in its requirement of a transfer of custody or control.[507]

Subsection 2251(c): Overseas Production

Subsection 2251(c) applies the mandatory minimums of subsection 2251(e) to the overseas use, attempted use, or conspiracy to use, a child in the visual depiction of sexually explicit conduct with the intent to transport, or the transportation of, the depiction into the United States.[508]

Subsection 2251(d): Advertising

Subsection 2251(d) applies the mandatory minimums of subsection 2251(e) to anyone who "knowingly makes, prints, or publishes, or causes to be made, printed, published any notice or advertisement seeking or offering child pornography"[509] or to anyone seeking or offering to participate in the production of child pornography under various jurisdictional circumstances.[510] Federal jurisdiction exists if the notice or advertisement is transported or transmitted using the facilities of interstate commerce or the defendant anticipates that it will be.[511] The notice or advertisement need not "specifically state that it offers or seeks a visual depiction to violate §2251(c)(1)(A);" all that is required is that its implications are clear.[512]

Selling or Buying Children for Pornographic Purposes

Section 2251A demands a mandatory minimum sentence of imprisonment of 30 years for those convicted of relinquishing or acquiring custody or control of a child under 18 years of age knowing or intending that the child will be used to produce visual depictions of sexually explicit conduct, under certain jurisdictional circumstances.[513]

"Custody or control" is statutorily defined to "include[] temporary supervision over or responsibility for a minor whether legally or illegally obtained."[514] "The statute does not require transfer of full parental authority; something less than the control a parent exercises—including ...limitations on time and scope—suffices to violate the law."[515] Moreover, "the terms contained in the title of §2251A(b)—buying and selling—do not exclusively define the statute's reach."[516] The statute's reach extends as well to instances where the defendant acquires custody or control of the child by paying the victim herself.[517]

Federal jurisdiction over the offense exists if it occurred within the territorial jurisdiction of the United States, if it involved travel in or affecting interstate commerce, or if the offer was transported or transmitted through the facilities in or affecting interstate commerce.[518]

Certain Activities Involving Child Pornography (Real Child)

Three of the four offenses created in 18 U.S.C. 2252 require imposition of a sentence of imprisonment for not less than 5 years: transportation, receipt, or possession with intent to sell, of visual depictions of sexually explicit conduct involving a child under 18 years of age—under various jurisdictional circumstances.[519] Attempts or conspiracies to commit those offenses carry the same mandatory minimum penalties.[520] Simple possession by a first time offender is not punishable by a mandatory minimum term of imprisonment.[521] Defendants charged with any of the four offenses, who have a prior similar conviction, face increased mandatory minimum sentences of imprisonment.[522]

Transporting

The mandatory minimum sentences of subsection 2252(b)(1) apply to those convicted of violating subsection 2252(a)(1) which outlaws the transportation or transmission of child pornography in or affecting interstate commerce or by using the facilities of interstate commerce.[523] The mandatory minimum sentences apply as well to those convicted of attempting or conspiring to violate the subsection.[524]

"Under Section 2252(a)(1), the government must prove that: (1) the defendant knowingly transported or shipped, (2) in interstate or foreign commerce, (3) any visual depiction involving the use of a minor engaging in sexually explicit conduct."[525] The government must also prove that the visual depiction was of an actual child not a mere computer simulation,[526] and that the defendant knew the child was underage.[527]

Moreover, simply because the statute indicates that transportation may take the form of computer transmission "does not mean that use of a computer is a required element of the crime."[528]

For purposes of subsection 2252(a)(1), "interstate commerce" includes commerce to and from the possessions and the territories of the United States, and "foreign commerce" includes travel between foreign nations by way of the United States.[529] The government, however, need not prove that the defendants know of the interstate or foreign commercial nature of the transportation or shipment.[530]

When the government seeks the 15-year recidivist mandatory minimum sentence and the "state law [upon which the prior conviction was based] covers conduct some of which is within, and the rest of which is outside, the scope of a recidivist statute, the federal court may examine the [state] charging papers (and any guilty-plea colloquy) to classify the conviction."[531]

Receipt or Distribution

The same mandatory minimum terms of imprisonment apply when the defendant is convicted of receipt or distribution of, attempted receipt or distribution of, or conspiracy to receive or distribute, child pornography, under the same jurisdictional circumstances—not less than 15 years with a prior conviction; not less than 5 years otherwise.[532]

"The elements of receipt under 18 U.S.C. 2252(a)(2) require the defendant to knowingly receive an item of child pornography, and the item to be transported in interstate or foreign commerce" or otherwise satisfy the subsection's jurisdictional requirements.[533]

> To be sure, the exact contours of the crime of "knowingly receiving" electronic child pornography in a constantly shifting technological background are murky. Part of the problem is that computers connected to the internet store vast quantities of data about which many users know nothing. As a user browses the internet, the computer stores images and text and other kinds of data in its temporary memory the way a ship passing through the ocean collects barnacles that cling to its hull. Thus, there is some risk that the computer of an internet user not intending to access child pornography may be infected with child pornography. Understandably, our sister circuits have struggled with whether to impute knowledge from the presence of illicit files found in such temporary storage.[534]

Ultimately, the facts of a given case will determine whether the defendant is the unwitting victim of technology or knowingly received child pornography.[535] The government's burden includes proving that the defendant knew that child depicted was real and underage.[536]

For purposes of the jurisdictional element, "the government prove[s] images traveled interstate when it introduce[s] evidence that the defendant received images that were transmitted over the Internet."[537]

To be guilty of attempted violation of subsection 2252(b)(2), the defendant must have intended to receive or distribute child pornography and taken a substantial step toward the achievement of that goal.[538]

When a court faces the question of whether a defendant must be sentenced to the mandatory minimum 15-year term of imprisonment reserved for recidivists in a case where the prior conviction occurred under a statute proscribing both qualifying and non-qualifying offenses, the court "may refer to the charging document, the terms of a plea agreement, the transcript of the colloquy, jury instructions, and other comparable judicial records."[539]

Sale or Possession with Intent to Sell

Subsection 2252(a)(3), which prohibits the sale of, or possession with intent to sell, child pornography under various jurisdiction circumstances, requires imposition of a 5-year mandatory minimum term of imprisonment as well (a minimum of 15 years for recidivists).[540] The same penalties must be assessed upon conviction of an attempt or conspiracy to violate the subsection.[541] Jurisdiction exists if the offense occurs within the special maritime and territorial jurisdiction of the United States, on a federal facility or Indian reservation.[542] It also exists if interstate commerce is implicated in the offense.[543]

Recidivist Possession

Recidivists in possession of child pornography must be sentenced to 10-year minimum term of imprisonment under subsection 2252(a)(4), as must a recidivist convicted of attempting or conspiring to violate the subsection.[544] The necessary jurisdictional circumstances are the same as those which apply in the case of the sale offense under subsection 2252(a)(3).[545]

Qualifying prior convictions may include convictions under either state or federal law.[546] The offender's prior state conviction must be "related to" one of the statutorily described offenses and involve a minor, but the statute of conviction need not list a minor victim as an element of the offense.[547] "[T]he sentencing court looks to the fact of conviction and the statutory definition of the prior offense and determines whether the full range of conduct encompassed by the statute qualifies to enhance the sentence."[548] In this exercise, "[i]f the statute [of prior conviction] criminalizes both conduct that would qualify a defendant for an enhancement, as well as conduct that would not do so, the court may refer to the charging document, the terms of a plea agreement, the transcript of the colloquy, jury instructions, and the comparable judicial records to determine the basis for the guilty plea or verdict [in the prior case]."[549]

Subsection 2252(a)(4) has two distinctive features. First, offenders are not subject to a mandatory minimum term of imprisonment, unless the recidivist provisions are tripped.[550] Second, subsection 2252(c) provides a narrow explicit statutory defense, available when possession is minimal and the individual destroys the material or reveals it to authorities.[551]

Certain Activities Involving Child Pornography (Real and Virtual)

Sections 2252 and 2252A were almost identical at one point.[552] Section 2252 covered only visual depictions of sexual activity involving an actual child. Section 2252A covered visual depictions of sexual activity involving a digitally created child as well.[553] Other changes have occurred over the years, but that essential distinction remains. So too do the mandatory minimum terms of imprisonment that attend comparable violations of either section.

At least a 5-year term of imprisonment must be imposed for a violation, attempt to violate, or conspiracy to violate any of five child pornography-related offenses found in subsection 2252A: transportation; receiving or distributing; reproducing or promoting; selling or possession with intent to sell; or providing to a child.[554] Recidivists must be sentenced to imprisonment for not less than 15 years (not less than 10 years for a recidivist guilty of simple possession).[555] As discussed below, a 20-year mandatory term of imprisonment attends conviction for a child exploitation enterprise offense involving multiple violations of subsection 2252A(a) and related child abuse offenses that involve several children and several collaborators.[556]

Transporting

A 5-year mandatory term of imprisonment must be imposed on "[a]ny person who - (1) knowingly mails, or transports or ships using any means or facility of interstate or foreign commerce or in or affecting interstate or foreign commerce by any means, including by computer, any child pornography."[557] A mandatory 15-year term of imprisonment awaits recidivists.[558]

The subsection's recently expanded jurisdictional statement ("using any means ... affecting ... commerce") eliminates the split among the lower federal appellate courts over whether the earlier version of the statute covered any Internet use, or use where actual interstate transportation can be shown.[559] On the other hand, the use of a computer is not an element of the offense; the offense may be committed with or without the use of computer.[560]

Defendants accused of violating the transportation prohibition of subsection 2252A(a)(1) enjoy a relatively narrow affirmative defense.[561] The defense is available, if, after giving the required pre- trial notice, the defendant establishes that the alleged child pornography did not involve the use of a real child or the image of a real child.[562]

Receipt or Distribution

Section 2252A punishes the knowing receipt or distribution of child pornography, committed under certain jurisdictional circumstances, with imprisonment for not less than 5 years.[563] It punishes attempt and conspiracy in the same manner.[564] It imposes a minimum 15-year term of imprisonment upon recidivists.[565] The offense must be committed knowingly; inadvertent receipt is not a violation.[566] Knowing violation occurs, for instance, when the defendant "intentionally views, acquires, or accepts child pornography on a computer from an outside source."[567]

Attempted violation requires evidence of an intent to commit the offense and a substantial step beyond mere preparation toward that goal.[568] Factual impossibility, such as the absence of a real child in a sting situation, poses no obstacle to conviction for attempt.[569]

Possession of child pornography under subsection 2252A(a)(5) is a lesser included offense to the crime of receipt of child pornography under subsection 2252A(a)(2).[570] The Constitution's double jeopardy clause thus precludes punishment under both subsections for the same misconduct.[571] Punishment under both subsections is permissible, however, when each addresses a different violation.[572] The double jeopardy clause may also bar punishment for receipt of child pornography under both subsection 2252(a)(2) and 2252A(a)(2), unless the offenses involve different violations; for example, the 2252A(a)(2) offense involves a digital image and the other involves a real child.[573]

Reproduction or Promotion

Knowingly reproducing or promoting child pornography carries the same 5-year mandatory minimum term of imprisonment (15 years for recidivists).[574] Reproduction and the promotion offenses are distinct. Both offenses, however, rest on a broad claim of federal jurisdiction: utilization of a means or facility "affecting interstate or foreign commerce" by any manner "including by computer."[575]

The Supreme Court in *Williams* held that neither the reproduction nor promotion proscription violates either First Amendment over breadth restrictions or Fifth Amendment due process vagueness limitations.[576] The Court dissected several of subsection 2252A(a)(3)'s features in the course of its analysis.

First, it observed that the knowledge requirement applies to both the reproduction and promotion offenses.[577] Second, it said that the action elements of the promotion offense—"advertises, promotes, presents, distributes, or solicits"—bespeaks a transaction, although not necessarily a commercial transaction.[578] "That is to say, the statute penalizes speech that accompanies or seeks to induce a transfer of child pornography—via production or physical delivery—from one person to another."[579]

For the promotion offense, the advertisement, promotion, or presentation must be advanced with one of two intents: either "in a manner that reflects belief" that child pornography is being offered, or in a manner that is calculated to induce another to believe child pornography is being offered. As for the first, the manner of advertisement, promotion, or presentation "must objectively manifest a belief that the material is child pornography; a mere belief, without an accompanying statement or action that would lead a reasonable person to understand that the defendant holds that belief, is insufficient."[580] As for the second, "the defendant must 'intend' that the listener believe the material to be child pornography, and must select a manner of 'advertising, promoting, presenting, distributing, or soliciting' the material that he thinks will engender the belief—whether or not a reasonable person would think the same."[581]

Defendants charged with the reproduction offense may invoke the narrow affirmative defense covering pornography that involves only adults; defendants charged with the promotion offense may not.[582]

Sale or Intent to Sell

The same 5- and 15-year mandatory minimum terms of imprisonment follow conviction for selling or possession with intent to sell child pornography if committed under a wide range of jurisdictional circumstances, or for attempting or conspiring to do so.[583] Jurisdiction exists if the offense occurs on federal enclaves or facilities or in Indian country.[584] It also exists if the offense involves transportation using a means or facility in or affecting interstate or foreign commerce.[585]

The affirmative defense available when children have not been used in the pornography may be claimed by defendants charged with selling or intent to sell child pornography.[586]

Offering Child Pornography to a Child

Section 2252A requires a fine and a minimum term of imprisonment of 5 years for offering child pornography to a child with the intent to induce the child to engage in illegal activity, or attempting or conspiring to do so.[587] It requires a fine and a minimum term of 15 years for recidivists.[588] The offense is punishable if the offer, the pornography, or the material used to produce the pornography, was transported using a means or facility in or affecting interstate or foreign commerce.[589] The defendants charged under the offering offense of subsection 2252A(a)(6) may not claim the affirmative defense available elsewhere for when the pornography involves only adults.[590]

Recidivist Possession

There is no mandatory minimum term of imprisonment for conviction of simple possession of child pornography.[591] However, there is a 10-year mandatory minimum term of imprisonment for conviction of possession by a recidivist.[592] The possession which triggers the minimum sentence may occur in Indian country or on federal enclaves or facilities.[593] Interstate commerce may also provide a basis for jurisdiction.[594] Defendants charged with possession may assert the affirmative, adults-only pornography defense, if they do so in a timely fashion.[595]

Child Molesting Enterprises

Subsection 2252A(g) outlaws "child exploitation enterprises," a crime punishable by a fine and imprisonment "for any term of years not less than 20 or for life."[596] The crime's federal predicate felony offenses include not only pornography, but sex trafficking, kidnaping a child, sex abuse of a child, and Mann Act violations involving a child. More precisely, the penalty applies to:

(1) Whoever
(2) in concert with three or more other persons
(3) commits a series of predicate offenses
(4) constituting three or more separate incidents
(5) involving more than one victim
(6) when the predicate offenses involve felony violations of:
18 U.S.C. 1591 (relating to sex trafficking of a child or by force)
18 U.S.C. 1201 (relating to kidnaping of a child)
18 U.S.C. ch. 109A (relating to sexual abuse of a child)
18 U.S.C. ch. 110 (relating to pornography but not including record-keeping violations), or
18 U.S.C. ch. 117 (relating to sex offenses involving travel).[597]

Each predicate offense need not involve more than one victim nor be committed in concert with three other offenders; it is enough that the series of predicate offenses, taken in total involve more than one victim and three or more other offenders.[598] The Constitution's double jeopardy clause bars punishment for both a violation of subsection 2252A(g) and for conspiracy to violate the underlying predicate offenses.[599]

Sentencing Commission

A majority of the judges responding to the Sentencing Commission survey thought that the mandatory minimum sentences for production and distribution of child pornography and other child exploitation offenses were generally appropriate. Well over two-thirds, however, considered those for receipt of child pornography too high.[600]

The Commission's report on mandatory minimum sentencing statutes noted that its "review of available sentencing data [relating to sex offenses] indicates that further study of these penalties is needed before it can offer specific recommendations in this area." [601] It concluded preliminarily, however, that "the mandatory minimum penalties for certain non-contact child pornography offenses may be excessively severe and as a result are being applied inconsistently." [602]

IDENTITY THEFT

Aggravated identity theft is punishable by imprisonment for two years, and by imprisonment for five years if the offense involves a federal crime of terrorism.[603] Aggravated identity theft only occurs when the identity theft happens "during and in relation" to one of several other federal crimes. It has the effect of establishing a mandatory minimum for each of those predicate offenses that would not otherwise exist.

More than half of the judges who responded to a United States Sentencing Commission survey felt that the two-year mandatory minimum was a generally appropriate sentence.[604] The Sentencing Commission's report on mandatory minimum penalties makes little if any mention of the five-year terrorism penalty and instead directs its attention to the two-year identity theft mandatory minimum.[605] The Commission further confines itself to comparatively complimentary observations rather than recommendations, due to the provision's relatively recent emergence and its somewhat unique characteristics.[606]

Section 1028A, parsed to its elements, declares:

- Whoever
- during and in relation to
- any felony enumerated in
  - subsection (c) [predicate offense], [or]

  - section 2332b(g)(5)(B) [predicate terrorist offense]
- knowingly
- transfers, possesses, or uses
- without lawful authority
- a means of identification
- of another person

shall, in addition to the punishment provided for such [predicate offense or predicate terrorist offense], be sentenced to a term of imprisonment of 2 years [or a term of imprisonment of 5 years in the case of terrorist predicate offense].[607]

Whoever

Section 1028A only punishes aggravated identity theft by individuals. Most federal crimes outlaw misconduct by both individuals and organizations, such as corporations, firms, and other legal entities. The Dictionary Act explains that "[i]n determining the meaning of any Act of Congress, unless the context indicates otherwise ... the words 'person' and 'whoever' include corporations, companies, associations, firms, partnerships, societies, and joint stock companies, as well as individuals."[608] Section 1028A is one of those situations when "the context indicates otherwise."

Entities other than individuals can be fined, but they cannot be imprisoned. Section 1028A punishes violations with a flat term of imprisonment, but no fine. Thus, only individuals may be punished for violating the section. For the same reason, persons other than individuals may not incur criminal liability indirectly as principals under 18 U.S.C. 2.[609] Principals are subject to the same penalties, in this case only imprisonment.[610]

Persons other than individuals may, however, incur criminal liability as conspirators. The federal conspiracy statute outlaws conspiracy to commit any federal crime, including aggravated identity theft.[611] It makes conspiracy punishable by both a fine and a term imprisonment.[612] Thus, it seems possible for a person other than an individual to incur criminal liability for conspiracy to commit aggravated identity theft.

During and in Relation to

The phrase "during and in relation to" describes the connection, necessary for a violation under the section, between the predicate offense and the other identity theft elements. The phrase also appears in the mandatory minimums of 18 U.S.C. 924(c) that apply when a firearm is used "during and in relation to" certain crimes of violence or drug trafficking.[613]

There, the Supreme Court has said the "in relation to" portion of the phrase requires that the firearm "must facilitate or have the potential of facilitating" the predicate offense.[614] This suggests that the "phrase 'in relation to' in §1028A ... means that the 'in relation to' element is met if the identity theft 'facilitates or has the potential of facilitating' that predicate felony."[615] Whether the identity theft occurs "during" the predicate offense depends on the duration of the predicate offense.[616]

Subsection (c) Felony Predicates

Section 1028A recognizes two classes of predicate offenses – one of which involves terrorist offenses and carries a five-year term of imprisonment; the other of which does not and carries a two-year term. Proof of the commission of one of the qualifying predicate offenses is an element of aggravated identity theft.[617] The defendant, however, need not otherwise be charged or convicted of the predicate offense.[618] Moreover, the Constitution's double jeopardy clause, which prohibits multiple punishments for the same offense, bars prosecution for both aggravated identity theft and the parallel identity theft provision.[619] Attached is the list of more than 60 federal theft, fraud, immigration, and related felonies for which the two-year mandatory minimum sentencing provision provides a sentencing floor when identity theft is involved.

Federal Crimes of Terrorism Predicates

The terrorist predicate offenses are the federal crimes of terrorism, listed in 18 U.S.C. 2332b(g)(5)(B), regardless of whether the predicate offense was committed for a terrorist purpose.[620] A list of the close to 50 terrorist predicate offenses also appears below as an attachment. The five-year aggravated identity theft offense seems to have been infrequently prosecuted thus far.[621]

Knowingly

The Supreme Court in *Flores-Figueroa* made clear that the knowledge element colors each of the other elements.[622] The government must prove that the defendant was aware that he transferred, possessed, or used something.[623] It must prove that the defendant was aware that he was doing so without lawful authority.[624] Finally, it must prove that the defendant was aware that the something he unlawfully possessed, transferred, or used was that of another person.[625]

Transfers, Possesses, or Uses

What constitutes a proscribed transfer, possession, or use appears to have been a matter of dispute only rarely, perhaps because of the limitations posed by the other elements. For example, the requirement that possession be knowing and in relation to a predicate offense cabins the otherwise natural scope of the term "possession."

Without Lawful Authority

The "lawful authority" element addresses whether the law permits the defendant to use the identification of another, not whether the defendant has the permission of another to borrow the means of identification. Thus, "the use of another person's social security number to commit a qualifying felony, even with that person's permission, serve[s] as use 'without lawful authority' in violation of §1028A." [626] Moreover, a defendant may be guilty of using the means of identity of another without lawful authority for certain purposes, even though he has lawful authority to use the identification for other purposes.[627]

A Means of Identification

The term "means of identification" in the aggravated identify theft provision draws its meaning from the definition of that term in the generic identity theft provision, 18 U.S.C. 1028.[628] "The 'overriding requirement' of [that] definition is that the means of identification 'must be sufficient to identify a specific individual.'"[629] One court has suggested that use of no more than the name of another would be insufficient,[630] but others have indicated that forging the signature of another constitutes use of the means of identification of another without lawful authority.[631]

Of Another Person

The statute does not extend to the use of a "fake id" that does not identified with a real person.[632] On the other hand, the "other person" element reaches both the living and dead.[633] Moreover, although only an individual may engage in aggravated identity theft, the victim of such a theft might well include persons who are legal entities rather than individuals.

Sentencing

Aggravated identity theft sentencing is distinctive in a number of ways. First, violations carry a flat mandatory two-year sentence of imprisonment or a flat mandatory five years for terrorism related offenses.[634] Most federal criminal statutes provide a maximum term of imprisonment ("shall be imprisoned for not more than … ").[635] If they require a mandatory minimum sentence, it is usually well below the maximum ("shall be imprisoned not less than … ") or the maximum is unstated.[636]

Second, it explicitly states that the sentence imposed for the predicate offenses may not be reduced to account for the mandatory minimum.[637] Third, it explicitly states that as a general rule the two- or five-year sentence may not be served concurrently with any sentence imposed for the predicate offense or another.[638] Finally, it establishes an exception to the general rule under which multiple mandatory minimum sentences under the section may be served concurrently at the discretion of the court when consistent with the Sentencing Guidelines.[639]

The Sentencing Guidelines suggest that in exercising its discretion as to whether to impose consecutive or concurrent sentences for multiple aggravated identity theft violations, a court should consider the statutory sentencing factors mentioned in 18 U.S.C. 3553(a)(2), as well as the nature and seriousness of the offense and the extent to which predicate offenses are related.[640] If the purposes of subsection 3553(a)(2) are better served by imposing consecutive sentences, the court may do so even if the predicate offenses are "grouped" (i.e., are closely related).[641]

As in the case of other mandatory minimum sentencing statutes, a court may sentence a defendant convicted of aggravated identity theft to a term of less than two years pursuant to subsection 3553(e).[642] The prosecution must seek the exception, which is only available on the basis of the defendant's substantial assistance in the investigation or prosecution of a federal crime.[643]

Sentencing Commission Report

The Sentencing Commission's assessment of sentencing under the provision is guardedly laudatory: "The problems associated with certain mandatory minimum penalties are not observed, or are not as pronounced, in identity theft offenses. The Commission believes this is due, in part, to 18 U.S.C. §1028A requiring a relatively short mandatory penalty and not requiring stacking of penalties for multiple counts. The statute is relatively new and is used in only a handful of districts, however, so specific findings are difficult to make at this time."[644]

Attachments

Two-Year Predicate Offenses

18 U.S.C. 641 (relating to theft of public money, property, or rewards),

18 U.S.C. 656 (relating to theft, embezzlement, or misapplication by bank officer or employee), 18 U.S.C. 664 (relating to theft from employee benefit plans),

18 U.S.C. 911 (relating to false personation of citizenship),

18 U.S.C. 922(a)(6) (relating to false statements in connection with the acquisition of a firearm),

18 U.S.C. ch. 47 (any provision contained in this chapter (relating to fraud and false statements), other than this section (section 1028A) or section 1028(a)(7):

18 U.S.C. 1001 (relating to false statements or entries generally),

18 U.S.C. 1002 (relating to possession of false papers to defraud United States),

18 U.S.C. 1003 (relating to demands against the United States involving $1,000 or more), 18 U.S.C. 1004 (relating to certification of checks),

18 U.S.C. 1005 (relating to bank entries, reports and transactions),

18 U.S.C. 1006 (relating to Federal credit institution entries, reports and transactions),

18 U.S.C. 1007 (relating to Federal Deposit Insurance Corporation transactions),

18 U.S.C. 1010 (relating to Department of Housing and Urban Development and Federal Housing Administration transactions),

18 U.S.C. 1011 (relating to Federal land bank mortgage transactions),

18 U.S.C. 1014 (relating to loan and credit applications generally; renewals and discounts; crop insurance),

18 U.S.C. 1015 (relating to naturalization, citizenship or alien registry),

18 U.S.C. 1016 (relating to acknowledgment of appearance or oath),

18 U.S.C. 1017 (relating to government seals wrongfully used and instruments wrongfully sealed),

18 U.S.C. 1019 (relating to certificates by consular officers),

18 U.S.C. 1020 (relating to highway projects),

18 U.S.C. 1021 (relating to title records),

18 U.S.C. 1022 (relating to delivery of certificate, voucher, receipt for military or naval property),

18 U.S.C. 1023 (relating to insufficient delivery of money or property for military or naval service),

18 U.S.C. 1024 (relating to purchase or receipt of military, naval, or veteran's facilities property),

18 U.S.C. 1025 (relating to false pretenses on high seas and other waters involving $1,000 or more),

18 U.S.C. 1027 (relating to false statements and concealment of facts in relation to documents required by the Employee Retirement Income Security Act of 1974),

18 U.S.C. 1028 (relating to felony violations involving fraud and related activity in connection with identification documents and information),

18 U.S.C. 1029 (relating to fraud and related activity in connection with access devices),

18 U.S.C. 1030 (relating to felony violations involving fraud and related activity in connection with computers,

18 U.S.C. 1031 (relating to major fraud against the United States),

18 U.S.C. 1032 (relating to concealment of assets from conservator, receiver, or liquidating agent of financial institution),

18 U.S.C. 1033 (relating to crimes by or affecting persons engaged in the business of insurance whose activities affect interstate commerce),

18 U.S.C. 1035 (relating to false statements relating to health care matters),

18 U.S.C. 1036 (relating to entry by false pretenses to any real property, vessel, or aircraft of the United States or secure area of any airport or seaport),

18 U.S.C. 1036 (relating to fraud and related activity in connection with electronic mail),

18 U.S.C. 1038 (relating to false information and hoaxes),

18 U.S.C. 1039 (relating to fraud and related activity in connection with obtaining confidential phone records information of a covered entity),

18 U.S.C. 1040 (relating to fraud in connection with major disaster or emergency benefits),

18 U.S.C. ch. 63 (any provision contained in chapter 63 (relating to mail, bank, and wire fraud); 18 U.S.C. 1341 (relating to mail fraud),

18 U.S.C. 1342 (relating to fraudulent use of false name or address for postal purposes), 18 U.S.C. 1343 (relating to wire fraud),

18 U.S.C. 1344 (relating to bank fraud),

18 U.S.C. 1347 (relating to health care fraud), 18 U.S.C. 1348 (relating to securities fraud),

18 U.S.C. 1349 (relating to attempts or conspiracies to violate the provisions of chapter 63),

18 U.S.C. 1350 (relating to certification of corporate financial reports),

18 U.S.C. 1351 (relating to fraud in foreign labor contracting),

18 U.S.C. ch. 69 (any provision contained in chapter 69 (relating to nationality and citizenship);

18 U.S.C. 1421 (relating to accounts of court officers),

18 U.S.C. 1422 (relating to fees in naturalization proceedings),

18 U.S.C. 1423 (relating to misuse of evidence of citizenship or naturalization),

18 U.S.C. 1424 (relating to misuse of papers in naturalization proceedings),

18 U.S.C. 1425 (relating to procurement of citizenship or naturalization unlawfully),

18 U.S.C. 1426 (relating to reproduction of naturalization or citizenship papers),

18 U.S.C. 1427 (relating to sale of naturalization or citizenship papers),

18 U.S.C. 1428 (relating to surrender of canceled naturalization certificate),

18 U.S.C. 1429 (relating to neglect or refusal to answer naturalization-related subpoena)

18 U.S.C. ch. 75 (any provision contained in chapter 75 (relating to passports and visas); 18 U.S.C. 1541 (relating to issuance without authority),

18 U.S.C. 1542 (relating to false statement in application and use of passport),

18 U.S.C. 1543 (relating to forgery or false use of passport),

18 U.S.C. 1544 (relating to misuse of passport),

18 U.S.C. 1545 (relating to safe conduct violation),

18 U.S.C. 1546 (relating to fraud and misuse of visas, permits, and other documents),

15 U.S.C. 6823 (section 523 of the Gramm-Leach-Bliley Act (relating to obtaining customer information by false pretenses)),

8 U.S.C. 1253 (section 243 of the Immigration and Nationality Act (relating to willfully failing to leave the United States after deportation)),

8 U.S.C. 1306 (section 266 of the Immigration and Nationality Act (relating to creating a counterfeit alien registration card)),

8 U.S.C. ch.12 (any provision contained in chapter 8 of title II of the Immigration and Nationality Act

(8 U.S.C. 1321 et seq.) (relating to various immigration offenses);

8 U.S.C. 1321 (relating to prevention of unauthorized landing of aliens),

8 U.S.C. 1324c(e) (relating to document fraud),

8 U.S.C. 1325 (relating to marriage fraud),

8 U.S.C. 1326 (relating to reentry of removed aliens),

8 U.S.C. 1327 (relating to aid or assisting certain aliens to enter),
8 U.S.C. 1328 (relating to importation of alien for immoral purpose)

42 U.S.C. 408 (section 208 of the Social Security Act (relating to penalties for miscellaneous misconduct)),
42 U.S.C. 1011 (section 811 of the Social Security Act (relating to fraud)),
42 U.S.C. 1307(b) (section 1107(b) of the Social Security Act (relating to false statements)),
42 U.S.C. 1320a-7b(a) (section 1128B(a) of the Social Security Act (relating to fraud),
42 U.S.C. 1383a (section 1632 of the Social Security Act (relating to fraud)).

Terrorist Predicate Offenses
18 U.S.C. 32 (relating to destruction of aircraft or aircraft facilities),
18 U.S.C. 37 (relating to violence at international airports),
18 U.S.C. 81 (relating to arson within special maritime and territorial jurisdiction),
18 U.S.C. 175 or 175b (relating to biological weapons),
18 U.S.C. 175c (relating to variola virus),

18 U.S.C. 229 (relating to chemical weapons),
18 U.S.C. 351 (a), (b), (c), (d) (relating to congressional, cabinet, and Supreme Court killing, kidnaping, or attempts or conspiracies to kill or kidnap),
18 U.S.C. 831 (relating to nuclear materials),
18 U.S.C. 832 (relating to participation in nuclear and weapons of mass destruction threats to the U.S.)
18 U.S.C. 842(m) or (n) (relating to plastic explosives),

18 U.S.C. 844(f)(2) or (3) (relating to arson and bombing of Federal property risking or causing death),
18 U.S.C. 844(i) (relating to arson and bombing of property used in interstate commerce),
18 U.S.C. 930(c) (relating to killing or attempted killing during an attack on a Federal facility with a dangerous weapon),
18 U.S.C. 956(a)(1) (relating to conspiracy to murder, kidnap, or maim persons abroad),

18 U.S.C. 1030(a)(1) (relating to protection of computers),

18 U.S.C. 1030(a)(5)(A) resulting in damage as defined in 1030(c)(4)(A)(i)(II) through (VI) (relating to protection of computers),

18 U.S.C. 1114 (relating to killing or attempted killing of officers and employees of the United States),

18 U.S.C. 1116 (relating to murder or manslaughter of foreign officials, official guests, or internationally protected persons),

18 U.S.C. 1203 (relating to hostage taking),

18 U.S.C. 1361 (relating to government property or contracts),

18 U.S.C. 1362 (relating to destruction of communication lines, stations, or systems),

18 U.S.C. 1363 (relating to injury to buildings or property within special maritime and territorial jurisdiction of the United States),

18 U.S.C. 1366(a) (relating to destruction of an energy facility),

18 U.S.C. 1751(a), (b), (c), or (d) (relating to Presidential and Presidential staff killing, kidnaping, or attempts or conspiracies to kill or kidnap),

18 U.S.C. 1992 (relating to terrorist attacks and other acts of violence against mass transit)

18 U.S.C. 2155 (relating to destruction of national defense materials, premises, or utilities),

18 U.S.C. 2156 (relating to national defense material, premises, or utilities),

18 U.S.C. 2280 (relating to violence against maritime navigation),

18 U.S.C. 2281 (relating to violence against maritime fixed platforms),

18 U.S.C. 2332 (relating to certain homicides and other violence against U.S. nationals occurring outside of the U.S.),

18 U.S.C. 2332a (relating to use of weapons of mass destruction),

18 U.S.C. 2332b (relating to acts of terrorism transcending national boundaries),

18 U.S.C. 2332f (relating to bombing of public places and facilities),

18 U.S.C. 2332g (relating to missile systems designed to destroy aircraft),

18 U.S.C. 2332h (relating to radiological dispersal devices),

18 U.S.C. 2339 (relating to harboring terrorists),

18 U.S.C. 2339A (relating to providing material support to terrorists),

18 U.S.C.

2339B (relating to providing material support to terrorist organizations),

18 U.S.C. 2339C (relating to financing of terrorism),

18 U.S.C. 2339D (relating to military-type training from a foreign terrorist organization),

18 U.S.C. 2340A (relating to torture),

21 U.S.C. 960a (section 1010A of the Controlled Substances Import and Export Act) (relating to narco- terrorism),

42 U.S.C. 2122 (section 92 of the Atomic Energy Act of 1954)(relating to prohibitions governing atomic weapons)

42 U.S.C. 2284 (section 236 of the Atomic Energy Act of 1954 (relating to sabotage of nuclear facilities or fuel)

49 U.S.C. 46502 (relating to aircraft piracy),

49 U.S.C. 46504 (second sentence)(relating to assault on a flight crew with a dangerous weapon),

49 U.S.C. 46505(b)(3) or (c) (relating to explosive or incendiary devices, or endangerment of human life by means of weapons, on aircraft),

49 U.S.C. 46506 (if homicide or attempted homicide is involved)(relating to application of certain criminal laws to acts on aircraft),

49 U.S.C. 60123(b) (relating to destruction of interstate gas or hazardous liquid pipeline facility).

THREE STRIKES (18 U.S.C. 3559(C))

A defendant convicted of a federal "serious violent felony" must be sentenced to life imprisonment under the so-called three strikes law, 18 U.S.C. 3559(c), if he has two prior state or federal violent felony convictions or one such conviction and a serious drug offense conviction.[645]

Over 60% of the federal district court judges responding to the Sentencing Commission survey indicated they considered federal mandatory minimum sentences too high.[646] Although the survey asked specifically about sentences under other mandatory minimum statutes, it provided no opportunity for a response focused on section 3559(c).[647]

Notice and Objections

Section 3559(c) requires prosecutors to follow the notice provisions of 21 U.S.C. 851(a), if they elect to ask the court to sentence a defendant under the three strikes provision.[648] Section 851(a), in turn, requires prosecutors to notify the court and the defendant of the government's intention to seek the application of section 3559(c) and the description of the prior convictions upon which the government will rely.[649] Without such notice, the court may not impose an enhanced sentence.[650] The purpose of the requirement "is to ensure the defendant is aware before trial that he faces possible sentence enhancement as he assesses his legal options and to afford him a chance to contest allegations of prior convictions."[651] As long as that dual purpose is served, however, a want of meticulous compliance or complete accuracy will not preclude enhanced sentencing.[652] The objections most often raised are constitutional challenges and those that question the qualifications of prior convictions as predicate offenses.

Predicate Offenses

Serious Drug Offenses

Serious drug offenses for purposes of section 3559(c) consist of (a) federal drug kingpin offenses;[653] (b) the most severely punished of the federal drug trafficking offenses;[654] (c) the smuggling counterpart of the such trafficking offenses;[655] and (d) state equivalents of any of these three.[656] When the prosecution relies upon a state drug trafficking conviction, for example, it must show that the amount of drugs involved warranted treating it as an equivalent.[657]

Serious Violent Felonies

The federal three strikes provision recognizes convictions for two categories of serious violent felonies – one enumerated, the other general. The inventory of enumerated serious violent felonies consists of the federal or state crimes of:

- murder (as described in section 1111);
- manslaughter other than involuntary manslaughter (as described in section 1112);
- assault with intent to commit murder (as described in section 113(a));

- assault with intent to commit rape; aggravated sexual abuse and sexual abuse (as described in sections 2241 and 2242);
- abusive sexual contact (as described in sections 2244(a)(1) and (a)(2);
- kidnapping;[658]
- aircraft piracy (as described in section 46502 of Title 49);
- robbery (as described in section 2111, 2113, or 2118);
- carjacking (as described in 2119);
- extortion;[659]
- arson;[660]
- firearms use;[661]
- firearms possession (as described in section 924(c)); or
- attempt, conspiracy, or solicitation to commit any of the above offenses.[662]

The more general, unenumerated category consists of "any other [state or federal] offense punishable by a maximum term of imprisonment of 10 years or more that has as an element the use, attempted use, or threatened use of physical force against the person of another or that, by its nature, involves a substantial risk that physical force against the person of another may be used in the course of committing the offense."[663]

There are statutory exceptions for both categories. Among the enumerated offenses, arson offenses do not qualify as predicate offenses, if the defendant can establish by clear and convincing evidence that he reasonably believed the offense posed no threat to human life and that it in fact did not.[664] Moreover, neither robbery, attempted robbery, conspiracy to commit robbery, nor solicitation to commit robbery qualify, if the defendant can establish by clear and convincing evidence that the offense involved neither the use nor threatened use of a dangerous weapon and that no one suffered serious bodily injury as a consequence of the crime.[665]

Among the unenumerated offenses, this same no-weapon, no-injury standard applies – those otherwise qualifying 10-year felonies, marked by the use or threatened use of physical force against another, do not qualify as predicate offenses, if the defendant can establish by clear and convincing evidence that no weapon was used, and no injury sustained, in the course of the offense.[666]

The question of what constitutes a conviction for an unenumerated "serious violent felony" under §3559(c) seems to have proven as perplexing as what constitutes a "violent felony" conviction under the Armed Career Criminal Act (ACCA).[667] Recent Supreme Court construction of the term "violent felony" in the ACCA may provide clarification for future cases arising under section 3559(c).[668]

Constitutional Considerations

Defendants sentenced under §3559(c) have raised many of the same constitutional arguments asserted by defendants subject to other mandatory minimum sentences. Here too, their arguments have been largely unavailing. *Almendarez-Torres* blocks the contention that prior convictions must be noted in the indictment and proven to the jury beyond a reasonable doubt.[669] Defendants who claimed that §3559(c) has a disparate racial impact and therefore offends equal protection have been unable to show, as they must, that it was crafted for that purpose.[670] The Eighth Amendment's grossly disproportionate standard has proven too formidable for defendants sentenced under the section to overcome.[671] The courts remain to be convinced that the mandatory minimum features of the section pose any separation of powers impediments.[672] Defendants who invoke double jeopardy have been reminded that "the Supreme Court has long since determined that recidivist statutes do not violate double jeopardy because 'the enhanced punishment imposed for the later offense is not to be viewed as either a new jeopardy or additional penalty for the earlier crimes, but instead as a stiffened penalty for the latest crime, which is considered to be an aggravated offense because a repetitive one.'"[673] Much the same response has awaited those in §3559(c) cases who seek refuge in ex post facto, "the use of predicate felonies to enhance a defendant's sentence does not violate the Ex Post Facto Clause because such enhancements do not represent additional penalties for earlier crimes, but rather stiffen the penalty for the latest crime committed by the defendant." [674]

LIST OF FEDERAL MANDATORY MINIMUM SENTENCING STATUTES

(* Mandatory Minimum Term of Imprisonment *or* a Fine)[675]
(+ Safety Valve Offenses)

Imprisonment for Not Less Than a Specified Term of Years or Life

2 U.S.C. 192 (contempt of Congress: imprisonment for not less than 1 nor more than 12 months)

*2 U.S.C. 390** (contempt of Congress in a contested election case: imprisonment for not less than 1 nor more than 12 months *or* a fine of not less than $100 nor more than $1,000)

*7 U.S.C. 13a** (failure to comply with certain Commodities Futures Exchange Commission cease and desist orders: a fine of not more than $500,000 *or* imprisonment for not less than 6 months nor more than 1 year or both) (+ imprisonment at the discretion of the court)

*7 U.S.C. 15b** (violation of regulations relating to cotton futures contracts: a fine of not less than $100 nor more than $500 and at the discretion of the court imprisonment for not less than 30 nor more than 90 days)

*7 U.S.C. 195** (failure to comply with certain orders of the Secretary under the Packers and Stockyards Act: a fine of not less than $500 nor more than $10,000, *or* imprisonment for not less than 6 months nor more than 5 years or both) (+ imprisonment at the discretion of the court)

7U.S.C. 2024 (2d conviction for fraudulent use of a food stamp access device worth between $100 and $5,000: imprisonment for not less than 6 months nor more than 5 years)

8 U.S.C. 1324 (unlawfully bringing in aliens for profit or knowing the alien will commit a felony within the U.S.: a fine and imprisonment for not less than 3 nor more than 10 years (1st and 2d violations) and imprisonment for not less than 5 nor more than 15 years (3d and subsequent violations))

8 U.S.C. 1326(b)(3)(reentry of certain aliens after exclusion or removal: imprisonment for 10 years)

*8 U.S.C. 1534** (disclosure of classified information by a special attorney in immigration removal cases: imprisonment for not less than 10 nor more than 25 years)

*12 U.S.C. 617** (price fixing by officers of corporations organized to do foreign banking: a fine of not less than $1,000 nor more than $5,000 *or* imprisonment for not less than 1 nor more than 5 years, or both in the discretion of the court)

12 U.S.C. 630 (embezzlement by officers of corporations organized to do foreign banking: imprisonment for not less than 2 nor more than 10 years)

*15 U.S.C. 8** (trusts in restraint of import trade: a fine of not less than $100 nor more than $5,000 and imprisonment, in the discretion of the court, for a term not less than three months nor exceeding twelve months)

*15 U.S.C. 1245** (possession of a ballistic knife during the commission of a federal crime of violence: imprisoned not less than five years and not more than ten years, or both)

*16 U.S.C. 413** (damaging structures or vegetation on a national military park: a fine of not more than $1,000 *or* imprisonment for not less than 5 nor more than 30 days or both)

*16 U.S.C. 414** (trespassing for hunting purposes on a national military park: a fine of not more than $1,000 *or* imprisonment for not less than 5 nor more than 30 days or both)

18 U.S.C. 33 (destruction of commercial motor vehicles or their facilities involving high-level radioactive waste: any term of years but not less than 30 years)

18 U.S.C. 175c(c)(1)(unlawful possession of variola virus: imprisonment for not less than 25 years or for life)

18 U.S.C. 175c(c)(2)(unlawful use, attempted use, or possession and threat to use variola virus: imprisonment for not less than 30 years or for life)

18 U.S.C. 225 (continuing financial crimes enterprise: imprisonment for not less than 10 years and "may be life")

*18 U.S.C. 844(f)** (burning or bombing federal property: imprisonment for not less than 5 years nor more than 20 years; not less than 7 nor more than 40 years' imprisonment if the offense involves personal injury or a substantial risk of personal injury; if death results, death or imprisonment for not less than 20 years or life)

18 U.S.C. 844(h) (use of fire or explosives to commit a federal felony or possession of explosives during the commission of a federal felony: imprisonment for 10 years' for 1st offense, 20 for the second and any subsequent offense)

*18 U.S.C. 844(i)** (burning or bombing property affecting interstate commerce: imprisonment for not less than 5 years nor more than 20 years; not less than 7 nor more than 40 years' imprisonment if the offense involves personal injury or a substantial risk of personal injury; if death results, death or imprisonment for not less than 20 years or life)

18 U.S.C. 844(o) (transfer of explosives knowing they will be used to commit a crime of violence or drug trafficking offense: imprisonment for 10 years for 1st offense, 20 for the second and any subsequent offense)

18 U.S.C. 924(c)(1) (use of or possession of a firearm during the commission of a crime of violence or drug trafficking: imprisonment for not less 5 years generally; imprisonment for not less than 7 years if the firearm is brandished; imprisonment for not less than 10 years if the firearm is discharged or involves a short-barreled rifle or shotgun; imprisonment for not less than 25 years for second or subsequent offenses; imprisonment for not less than 30 years for a machinegun or silencer; life imprisonment for second or subsequent machinegun or silencer offense)

18 U.S.C. 924(c)(5) (possession or use of armor piercing ammunition during the commission of a crime of violence or drug trafficking: not less than 15 years' imprisonment)

18 U.S.C. 924(e)(1) (possession of firearm by a three time violent felony or serious drug dealer: not less than 15 years' imprisonment)

18 U.S.C. 929 (use of armor piercing ammunition during the commission of a crime of violence or drug trafficking: not less than 5 years)

18 U.S.C. 1028A (aggravated identity theft in furtherance of designated predicate offenses: imprisonment for 5 years if the predicate offense is a federal crime of terrorism; imprisonment for 2 years if the predicate offense is not a federal crime of terrorism)

18 U.S.C. 1121(b) (killing a state law enforcement officer by a federal prisoner or while transferring a prisoner interstate: not less than 20 years and may be punishable by death or life imprisonment)

*18 U.S.C. 1122** (selling HIV infected blood: not less than 1 nor more than 10 years)

18 U.S.C. 1591 (sex trafficking using force or children, imprisonment for any term of years not less than 10 years or for life; not less than 15 years or for life if the child is under 14 years of age at the time)

*18 U.S.C. 1658(b)** (causing a shipwreck for plunder or preventing escape from a shipwreck: imprisonment for not less than 10 years)

*18 U.S.C. 1917** (interfering with civil service examinations: imprisonment for not less than 10 days nor more than 1 year *or* a fine of not less than $100 or both)(+ imprisonment at the discretion of the court)

18 U.S.C. 1992 (wrecking a train carrying high level radioactive waste or spent nuclear fuel: imprisonment for any term of years not less than 30 or for life)

18 U.S.C. 2113(e) (killing or hostage taking during the course of robbing a federally insured bank: not less than 10 years; death or life imprisonment if death results)

18 U.S.C. 2250 (unregistered sex offender who commits a federal crime of violence: imprisonment for not less than 5 years nor more than 30 years)

18 U.S.C. 2251 (sexual exploitation of children: imprisonment for not less than 15 nor more than 30 years; upon a 2d conviction, imprisonment for not less than 25 nor more than 50 years; upon a 3d conviction, imprisonment for not less than 35 years nor more than life; where death results, death or imprisonment for any term of years not less than 30 years or life)

18 U.S.C. 2251A (selling or buying a child for purposes sexual exploitation: imprisonment for not less than 30 years or for life)

18 U.S.C. 2252(b)(1) (trafficking in material related to sexual exploitation of children: imprisonment for not less than 5 nor more than 20 years; 2d and subsequent offenses, not less than 15 years nor more than 40 years)

18 U.S.C. 2252(b)(2) (possession of pornography depicting a child under 12 years of age by an offender with a prior similar conviction: imprisonment for not less than 10 nor more than 20 years)

18 U.S.C. 2252A(b)(1) (trafficking in material related to sexual exploitation of children including by computer: imprisonment for not less than 5 nor more than 20 years; 2d and subsequent offenses, not less than 15 years nor more than 40 years)

18 U.S.C. 2252A(b)(2) (2d or subsequent conviction for possession of child pornography: imprisonment for not less than10 nor more than 20 years)

*18 U.S.C. 2257** (2d and subsequent violation of the recordkeeping requirements concerning sexual exploitation of children: imprisonment for not less than 2 nor more than 10 years)

*18 U.S.C. 2257A** (2d and subsequent violation of the recordkeeping requirements concerning simulated sexual activity: imprisonment for not less than 2 nor more than 10 years)

18 U.S.C. 2260(c)(1) (production material involving sexual exploitation of children for importation into the U.S.: imprisonment for not less than 15 nor more than 30 years; upon a 2d conviction, imprisonment for not less than 25 nor more than 50 years; upon a 3d conviction, imprisonment for not less than 35 years nor more than life; where death results, death or imprisonment for any term of years not less than 30 years or life)

18 U.S.C. 2260(c)(2) (trafficking in material related to sexual exploitation of children for importation into the U.S: imprisonment for not less than 5 nor more than 20 years; 2d and subsequent offenses, not less than 15 years nor more than 40 years)

18 U.S.C. 2260A (federal sex offenses by registered sex offenders: imprisonment for a consecutive 10 years)

18 U.S.C. 2261(b)(6) (stalking in violation of court order: imprisonment for not less than 1 year)

18 U.S.C. 2332g(c)(1) (unlawful possession of an anti-aircraft missile: imprisonment for not less than 25 years or for life)

18 U.S.C. 2332g(c)(2)(use, attempted used, or possession and threat to use an anti-aircraft missile: imprisonment for not less than 30 years or for life)

18 U.S.C. 2332h(c)(1)(unlawful possession of a radiological dispersal device: imprisonment for not less than 25 years or for life)

18 U.S.C. 2332h(c)(2)(unlawful use, attempted used, or possession and threat to use an radiological dispersal device: imprisonment for not less than 30 years or for life)

18 U.S.C. 2381 (treason: death or imprisonment for not less than 5 years)

18 U.S.C. 2422 (coercing or entice a child to engage in sexual activity: imprisonment for not less than 10 years or for life)

18 U.S.C. 2423 (transportation of a child for immoral purpose: imprisonment for not less than 10 years or for life)

18 U.S.C. 3559(c) (3 strikes: an offender convicted of a serious violent felony after having been convicted for 2 or more serious violent felonies or serious drug offenses must be sentenced to life imprisonment)

18 U.S.C. 3559(e) (2 strikes: an offender convicted of a serious sex offense against a child after having been convicted of an earlier serious sex offense must be sentenced to life imprisonment)

19 U.S.C. 283 (failure to pay duty on saloon stores: not less than 3 months nor more than 2 years imprisonment)

*21 U.S.C. 212** (offenses involving the practice of pharmacy in the consular districts of China: a fine of not less than $50 nor more than $100 *or* imprisonment for not less than 1 month nor more than 60 days, or both) (+ imprisonment at the discretion of the court)

21 U.S.C. 622 (bribery of a meat inspector: not less than 1 nor more than 3 years' imprisonment)

21 U.S.C. 841(b)(1)(A)+ (drug trafficker where the offender has 2 or more prior convictions for violation of 21 U.S.C. 849(drug dealing at a truck stop), 859 (dealing to minors), 860 (dealing near a school), 861 (using minors to deal): mandatory life imprisonment)

21 U.S.C. 841(b)(1)(A)+* (drug trafficking in very substantial amounts of controlled substances (e.g., a kilogram or more of heroin: imprisonment for not less than 10 years nor more than life; imprisonment for not less than 20 years nor more than life if the offender has a prior felony drug conviction or if death or serious bodily injury results)

21 U.S.C. 841(b)(1)(B)+* (drug trafficking in substantial amounts of controlled substances (e.g., 100 grams of heroin: imprisonment for not less than 5 nor more than 40 years; imprisonment for not less than 20 years nor more than life if death or serious bodily injury results; imprisonment for not less than 10 years nor more than life if the offender has a prior drug felony conviction)

21 U.S.C. 841(b)(1)(C)+* (drug trafficking in schedule I or II controlled substances or 1 gram of flunitrazepam: imprisonment for not less than 20 years nor more than life if death or serious bodily injury results; imprisonment for life if the offender has a prior drug felony conviction and death or serious bodily injury results)

21 U.S.C. 844+* (simple possession of a controlled substance: imprisonment for not less than 90 days nor more than 3 years if the offender has 2 or more prior drug convictions; imprisonment for not less than 15 days nor more than 2 years if the offender has a prior drug conviction)

21 U.S.C. 846 *+(attempts and conspiracies to violate any of the offenses in the Controlled Substances Act carry the same sentences as the underlying offenses)

21 U.S.C. 848(a) (drug kingpin - continuing criminal enterprise violations: imprisonment for not less than 30 years nor more than life for previous offenders, not less than 20 years nor more than life otherwise)

21 U.S.C. 848(b) (drug kingpin violations involving large enterprises: life imprisonment)

21 U.S.C. 848(e)(1) (killing in furtherance of a serious drug trafficking violations or killing a law enforcement official in furtherance of a controlled substance violation: death, life imprisonment, or imprisonment for a term of years not less than 20 years)

21 U.S.C. 859 (distribution of controlled substances to those under 21 years of age): imprisonment for not more than twice the otherwise applicable maximum term, but not less than the greater of the otherwise applicable minimum term or 1 year imprisonment; three times the otherwise applicable maximum term for 2d offenders)

21 U.S.C. 860 (distribution of controlled substances near schools and colleges: imprisonment for not more than twice the otherwise applicable maximum term, but not less than the greater of the otherwise applicable minimum term or 1 year imprisonment; three times the otherwise applicable maximum term but not less than the greater of the otherwise applicable minimum term or 3 years' imprisonment for 2d offenders)

21 U.S.C. 861 (use of those under 21 years of age to distribute controlled substances: imprisonment for not more than twice the otherwise applicable maximum term, but not less than the greater of the otherwise applicable minimum term or 1 year imprisonment; three times the otherwise applicable maximum term for subsequent offenses)

21 U.S.C. 960(b)(1)+* (illicit drug importing/exporting of very substantial amounts of controlled substances (e.g., a kilogram or more of heroin):

imprisonment for not less than 10 years nor more than life; imprisonment for not less than 20 years nor more than life if the offender has a prior felony drug conviction or if death or serious bodily injury results)

21 U.S.C. 960(b)(2)+ (illicit drug importing/exporting of substantial amounts of controlled substances (e.g., 100 grams of heroin): imprisonment for not less than 5 nor more than 40 years; imprisonment for not less than 20 years nor more than life if death or serious bodily injury results; imprisonment for not less than 10 years nor more than life if the offender has a prior drug felony conviction)

21 U.S.C. 960(b)(3)+ (illicit drug importing/exporting of schedule I or II controlled substances or 1 gram of flunitrazepam: imprisonment for not more than 20 years, but not less than 20 years nor more than life if death or serious bodily injury results; imprisonment for not more than 30 years if the offender has a prior drug felony conviction; imprisonment for life if the offender has a prior drug felony conviction and death or serious bodily injury results)

21 U.S.C. 963+ (attempt or conspiracy to commit any of the drug import/export offenses are subject to the same penalties as the underlying offense)

*22 U.S.C. 422*1 (perjury before consular officers: imprisonment for not less than 1 nor more than 3 years)

*33 U.S.C. 410** (violation of floating timber regulations: a fine of not less than $500 nor more than $2,500 or imprisonment for not less than 30 days nor more than 1 year, or both in the discretion of the court)

*33 U.S.C. 411** (certain navigable waters offenses: a fine of not more than $2,500 *or* imprisonment for not less than 30 days nor more than 1 year, or both in the discretion of the court)

*33 U.S.C. 441** (deposit of refuse in various harbors: a fine of not less than $250 nor more than $2,500 or imprisonment for not less than 30 days nor more than 1 year, or both "as the judge before whom conviction is obtained shall decide") (+ imprisonment at the discretion of the court)

33 U.S.C. 447 (bribery of harbor employees: not less than 6 months' nor more than 1 year imprisonment)

*46 U.S.C. 58109** (violations of the Merchant Marine Act: a fine or "imprisonment for not less than one year or more than five years, or by both fine and imprisonment")

47 U.S.C. 13 (refuse to afford telegraph service: a fine of not more than $1,000 and may be imprisonment for not less than 6 months)

*47 U.S.C. 220** (false entries in communication common carrier records: a fine of not less than $1,000 nor more than $5,000 *or* imprisonment for not less than 1 nor more than 3 years)

Death or Imprisonment for Any Term of Years or for Life

8 U.S.C. 1324(1) (bringing in or harboring aliens where death results)

*18 U.S.C. 36** (drive-by shooting constituting 1st degree murder)

18 U.S.C. 37 (violence at international airports where death results)

18 U.S.C. 175 (development or possession of biological weapons)

*18 U.S.C. 241** (conspiracy against civil rights where death results)

*18 U.S.C. 242** (deprivation civil rights under color of law where death results)

*18 U.S.C. 245** (discriminatory obstruction of enjoyment federal protected activities where death results)

*18 U.S.C. 247** (obstruction of the exercise of religious beliefs where death results) *18 U.S.C. 351* (conspiracy to kill or kidnap a Member of Congress if death results) *18 U.S.C. 351* (kidnapping a Member of Congress if death results)

18 U.S.C. 794 (espionage)

18 U.S.C. 844(d) (use of fire or explosives unlawfully where death results)

18 U.S.C. 924(j)(1) (murder while in possession of a firearm during the commission of a crime of violence or drug trafficking)

18 U.S.C. 1512 (tampering with a federal witness or informant involving murder) *18 U.S.C. 1513* (retaliating against a federal witness or informant involving murder) *18 U.S.C. 1751* (kidnapping the President where death results)

18 U.S.C. 1751 (conspiracy to kill or kidnap the President where death results)

18 U.S.C. 1992 (terrorist attack on mass transit where death results)

18 U.S.C. 2119 (car jacking where death results)

18 U.S.C. 2241 (aggravated sexual assault of a child under 12 years of age in the special maritime and territorial jurisdiction of the U.S.: death, imprisonment for any term of years not less than 30, or for life)

18 U.S.C. 2245 (sexual abuse where death results)

18 U.S.C. 2251 (sexual exploitation of children where death results)

*18 U.S.C. 2280** (violence against maritime navigation where death results)

*18 U.S.C. 2281** (violence against maritime fixed platform where death results)

*18 U.S.C. 2282A** (interference with maritime commerce where death results)

*18 U.S.C. 2283** (unlawful maritime transportation of explosive, biological, chemical, radioactive or nuclear material where death results)

*18 U.S.C. 2284** (maritime transportation of terrorists)

18 U.S.C. 2291 (destruction of vessels or maritime facilities where death results)

*18 U.S.C. 2320** (trafficking in counterfeit goods or services where death results)

*18 U.S.C. 2332** (terrorist murder of an American outside the U.S.)

18 U.S.C. 2332a (use of weapons of mass destruction where death results)

18 U.S.C. 2332b (acts of terrorism transcending national boundaries where death results)

18 U.S.C. 2332f (bombing public places where death results)

18 U.S.C. 2340A (torture where death results)

*18 U.S.C. 2441** (war crimes where death results)

18 U.S.C. 2442 (recruiting or using child soldiers where death results)

18 U.S.C. 3559(f)(1) (murder of a child in violation of federal law: death, life imprisonment or imprisonment for not more than 30 years)

Death or Imprisonment for Life

15 U.S.C. 1825(a)(2)(C) (1st degree murder of those enforcing the Horse Protection Act)

18 U.S.C. 34 (destruction of aircraft, commercial motor vehicles or their facilities where death results)

18 U.S.C. 115 (kidnapping with death resulting of the member of the family of a federal official or employee to obstruct or retaliate)

18 U.S.C. 115 (1st degree murder of the member of the family of a federal official or employee to obstruct or retaliate)

18 U.S.C. 229A (unlawful possession of chemical weapons where death results)

18 U.S.C. 351 (1st degree murder of a Member of Congress)

18 U.S.C. 924(c)(5) (1st degree murder using armor piercing ammunition during the commission of a crime of violence or drug trafficking)

18 U.S.C. 930(c) (1st degree murder while in possession of a firearm in a federal building)

*18 U.S.C. 1091** (genocide where death results)

18 U.S.C. 1111 (1st degree murder within the special maritime and territorial jurisdiction of the U.S.)

18 U.S.C. 1114 (1st degree murder of a federal officer or employee)

18 U.S.C. 1116 (1st degree murder of a foreign dignitary)

18 U.S.C. 1118 (murder by a federal prisoner)

18 U.S.C. 1119 (1st degree murder of an American by an American overseas)

18 U.S.C. 1120 (1st degree murder by an escaped federal prisoner)

18 U.S.C. 1121 (1st degree murder of one assisting in a federal criminal investigation)

18 U.S.C. 1201 (kidnapping where death results)

18 U.S.C. 1203 (hostage taking where death results)

18 U.S.C. 1503 (1st degree murder committed to obstruction of federal judicial proceedings)

18 U.S.C. 1512 (1st degree murder involving witness tampering)

18 U.S.C. 1513 (1st degree murder involving witness retaliation)

18 U.S.C. 1716 (mailing injurious articles with intent to injury or damage property where death results)

18 U.S.C. 1751 (1st degree murder of the President)

18 U.S.C. 1841 (1st degree murder of an unborn child)

18 U.S.C. 1958 (use of interstate facilities in furtherance of a murder-for-hire where death results)

18 U.S.C. 1959 (murder in aid of racketeering activity)

18 U.S.C. 1992 (attack in mass transit where death results)

18 U.S.C. 2113(e) (killing or hostage taking during the course of robbing a federally insured bank: not less than 10 years; death or life imprisonment if death results)

18 U.S.C. 3559 (federal violent felony or violation of 18 U.S.C. 2422 (coercing or enticing interstate travel for sexual purposes), 2423(transporting minors for sexual purposes), or 2251(sexual exploitation of children) resulting in the death of a child under 14 years of age)

21 U.S.C. 461 (1st degree murder of a poultry inspector)

21 U.S.C. 675 (1st degree murder of a meat inspector)

49 U.S.C. 46502 (air piracy where death results)

Imprisonment for Any Term of Years or Life

15 U.S.C. 1825(a)(2)(C) (2d degree murder of those enforcing the Horse Protection Act)

*18 U.S.C. 36** (drive-by shooting constituting murder other than 1st degree murder)

*18 U.S.C. 38** (fraud involving aircraft or space vehicle part whose failure results in death)

18 U.S.C. 43 (animal enterprise terrorism where death results)

*18 U.S.C. 81** (arson within the special maritime and territorial jurisdiction of the United States)

18 U.S.C. 115 (kidnapping or conspiring to kidnap the member of the family of a federal official or employee to obstruct or retaliate)

18 U.S.C. 115 (2d degree murder of the member of the family of a federal official or employee to obstruct or retaliate)

18 U.S.C. 115 (conspiracy to murder the member of the family of a federal official or employee to obstruct or retaliate)

*18 U.S.C. 175** (unlawful possession of biological weapons)

*18 U.S.C. 229A** (unlawful possession of chemical weapons: imprisonment for any term of years)

*18 U.S.C. 241** (conspiracy against civil rights involving attempts to kill, or kidnap, attempted kidnapping, sexual assault or attempted sexual assault)

*18 U.S.C. 242** (deprivation of rights under color of law involving attempts to kill, or kidnap, attempted kidnaping, sexual assault or attempted sexual assault)

*18 U.S.C. 245** (discriminatory obstruction of enjoyment federal protected activities involving attempts to kill, or kidnap, attempted kidnapping, sexual assault or attempted sexual assault)

*18 U.S.C. 248** (interference with access to clinic entrances where death results)

*18 U.S.C. 249** (hate crime where death results or involving attempts to kill, or kidnap, attempted kidnapping, sexual assault or attempted sexual assault)

18 U.S.C. 351(c),(d) (attempt or conspiracy to kill or kidnap a Member of Congress)

18 U.S.C. 351(b) (kidnapping a Member of Congress)

18 U.S.C. 351(a) (2d degree murder of a Member of Congress)

18 U.S.C. 831 (prohibited transactions in nuclear material where death or serious bodily injury results)

18 U.S.C. 832 (attempt to use, conspiracy to use, threaten to use, or use of radiological weapon)

18 U.S.C. 924(c)(5) (2d degree murder using armor piercing ammunition during the commission of a crime of violence or drug trafficking)

18 U.S.C. 924(o) (conspiracy to violate 18 U.S.C. 924(c)(use of or possession of a machinegun or firearm equipped with a silencer during the commission of a crime of violence or drug trafficking))

18 U.S.C. 930(c) (2d degree murder while in possession of a firearm in a federal building)

18 U.S.C. 956 (conspiracy to murder or kidnap in a foreign country)

*18 U.S.C. 1030** (intentionally causing computer damage that results in death)

*18 U.S.C. 1038** (terrorism hoax where death results)

18 U.S.C. 1111 (2d degree murder within the special maritime and territorial jurisdiction of the U.S.)

18 U.S.C. 1114 (2d degree murder of a federal officer or employee)

18 U.S.C. 1116 (2d degree murder of a foreign dignitary)

18 U.S.C. 1117 (conspiracy to commit murder in violation of 18 U.S.C. 1111 (within the special maritime and territorial jurisdiction of the U.S.), 1114 (of a federal officer or employee), 1116 (of a foreign dignitary), or 1119 (of an American by an American overseas)

18 U.S.C. 1119 (2d degree murder of an American by an American overseas)

18 U.S.C. 1120 (2d degree murder by an escaped federal prisoner)

18 U.S.C. 1121 (2d degree murder of one assisting in a federal criminal investigation)

18 U.S.C. 1201 (kidnapping or conspiracy to kidnap)

18 U.S.C. 1203 (hostage taking)

*18 U.S.C. 1347** (health care fraud resulting in death)

*18 U.S.C. 1365** (tampering with consumer products where death results)

18 U.S.C. 1366 (destruction of energy facilities where death results)

18 U.S.C. 1503 (2d degree murder committed to obstruction of federal judicial proceedings)

18 U.S.C. 1512 (2d degree murder involving witness tampering)

18 U.S.C. 1513 (2d degree murder involving witness retaliation)

*18 U.S.C. 1581** (peonage involving kidnapping or rape or where death results)

*18 U.S.C. 1583** (enticement into slavery involving kidnapping or rape or where death results)

*18 U.S.C. 1584** (sale into involuntary servitude involving kidnapping or rape or where death results)

*18 U.S.C. 1589** (forced labor involving kidnapping or rape or where death results)

*18 U.S.C. 1590** (slave trafficking involving kidnapping or rape or where death results)

*18 U.S.C. 1594** (conspiracy sex trafficking by force or of children)

18 U.S.C. 1751 (2d degree murder of the President)

18 U.S.C. 1751 (kidnapping the President)

18 U.S.C. 1751 (attempting to kill or kidnap the President) *18 U.S.C. 1751* (conspiracy to kill or kidnap the President) *18 U.S.C. 1751* (aggravated assault of the President)

18 U.S.C. 1841 (2d degree murder of an unborn child)

*18 U.S.C. 1864** (booby traps on federal lands where death results)

18 U.S.C. 1952 (Travel Act violations (interstate travel in aid of racketeering enterprises) where death results)

18 U.S.C. 1959 (kidnapping in aid of racketeering activity)

*18 U.S.C. 1992** (attack on mass transit shipper carrying high level radioactive waste or spent nuclear fuel unless the offense results in death (may be punished by death if death results))

*18 U.S.C. 2118** (robbery or burglary involving controlled substances where death results)

18 U.S.C. 2155 (destruction of national defense material where death results)

*18 U.S.C. 2199** (stowaways on vessels or aircraft where death results)

*18 U.S.C. 2237** (failure to heave to or to resist law enforcement boarding where death results or involving attempts to kill, or kidnap, attempted kidnapping, sexual assault or attempted sexual assault)

18 U.S.C. 2242 (sexual abuse committed in special maritime or territorial jurisdiction of the United States)

18 U.S.C. 2244 (sexual contact with a child under the age of 12 (or under the age of 16 when at least 4 years younger than the offender) committed in special maritime or territorial jurisdiction of the United States)

18 U.S.C. 2261 (interstate domestic violence if death results)

18 U.S.C. 2261A (interstate stalking if death results)

18 U.S.C. 2262 (interstate violation of protection order if death results)

18 U.S.C. 2272 (destruction of vessel by owner)

18 U.S.C. 2280 (maritime transportation of terrorists)

18 U.S.C. 2332 (terrorist conspiracy to murder an American outside the U.S.)

18 U.S.C. 2332a (use of weapons of mass destruction)

18 U.S.C. 2332b (acts of terrorism transcending national boundaries involving a kidnapping)

18 U.S.C. 2339A (providing material support to terrorists where death results)

18 U.S.C. 2339B (providing material support to terrorist organizations where death results)

*18 U.S.C. 2441** (war crimes)

18 U.S.C. 3559(f)(2)(kidnapping or maiming of a child in violation of federal law: imprisonment for any term of years or for life but not less than 25 years)

18 U.S.C. 3559(f)(3)(a crime of violence involving serious injury or use of a dangerous weapon committed against a child in violation of federal law: imprisonment for any term of years or fore life but not less than 10 years)

21 U.S.C. 461 (2d degree murder of a poultry inspector)

21 U.S.C. 675 (2d degree murder of a meat inspector)

42 U.S.C. 2000e-13 (killing EEOC personnel)

*42 U.S.C. 2272** (atomic energy violations to injure the U.S. or aid a foreign nation)

*42 U.S.C. 2274** (communication of restricted data)

*42 U.S.C. 2275** (receipt of restricted data)

*42 U.S.C. 2276** (tampering with restricted data)

42 U.S.C. 2284 (sabotaging nuclear facilities where death results)

*42 U.S.C. 3631** (housing discrimination where death results)

49 U.S.C. 46503 (interfering with airport security screening personnel while armed with a dangerous weapon)

49 U.S.C. 46504 (interference with flight crew involving a dangerous weapon)

49 U.S.C. 46505 (carrying a weapon or explosive on an aircraft where death results)

49 U.S.C. 60123 (damaging pipelines where death results)

Imprisonment for Life

18 U.S.C. 175c(c)(3)(unlawful possession of variola virus where death results)

18 U.S.C. 924(c) (2d conviction for commission of a crime of violence or drug trafficking while armed with a machinegun or firearm with a silencer)

18 U.S.C. 1651 (piracy)

18 U.S.C. 1652 (piracy)

18 U.S.C. 1653 (piracy)

18 U.S.C. 1655 (seaman laying violent hands upon a commander)

18 U.S.C. 1661 (robbery ashore by pirates: imprisonment for life)

18 U.S.C. 1963 (racketeer and corrupt influenced organization (RICO) offenses where the predicate offense)

18 U.S.C. 2332g(c)(3) (unlawful possession of an anti-aircraft missile where death results)

18 U.S.C. 2332h(c)(3)(unlawful possession of a radiological dispersal device where death results)

Imprisonment for Any Term of Years

21U.S.C.860a (manufacturing or trafficking methamphetamine where children are present)

Imprisonment for the Same, or Some Multiple of, the Sentence for a Predicate Offense When the Predicate Requires Imposition of a Mandatory Minimum Sentence

18 U.S.C. 2 (aiding and abetting any of the offenses listed – offenders are treated as principals in the predicate offense)

18 U.S.C. 1841 (commission of various predicate offenses upon an unborn child)

18 U.S.C. 2247 (doubles the otherwise applicable penalties for sexual abuse violations if the offender has a prior sex offense conviction)

18 U.S.C. 2426 (doubles the otherwise applicable penalties for Mann Act (transportation for illegal sexual activity) violations if the offender has a prior sex offense conviction)

21 U.S.C. 846 (attempts or conspiracies to violate any provision of the Controlled Substance Act is subject to the same penalties as the completed offense)

21 U.S.C. 860(c) (use of one under 21 years of age to distribution of controlled substances near schools and colleges: imprisonment for not more than three times the otherwise applicable sentence)

*21 U.S.C. 860a** (narco-terrorism: imprisonment for less than twice the minimum punishment under 21 U.S.C. 841(b)(1)(trafficking in controlled substances))

21 U.S.C. 962 (violation of the drug import/export law by an offender with a prior conviction for violation of those provisions is punishable by imprisonment for twice the term otherwise authorized)

21 U.S.C. 963 (attempts or conspiracies to violate any provision of the Controlled Substance Import and Export Act are subject to the same penalties as the completed offense)

BIBLIOGRAPHY

Books and Articles

Albonetti, The Effects of the "Safety Valve" Amendment on Length of Imprisonment for Cocaine Trafficking/Manufacturing Offenders: Mitigating the Effects of Mandatory Minimum Penalties and Offender's Ethnicity, 87, IOWA LAW REVIEW, 401 (2002)

Blackstone, COMMENTARIES ON THE LAWS OF ENGLAND (1765)

Blumstein, Cohen, Martin & Tonry, RESEARCH ON SENTENCING: THE SEARCH FOR REFORM (1983)

Bottomed, Parole in Transition: A Comparative Study of Origins, Developments, and Prospects for the 1990s, 12 CRIME & JUSTICE: A REVIEW OF RESEARCH 319 (1990)

Bowman, The Quality of Mercy Must be Restrained and Other Lessons in Learning to Love the Federal Sentencing Guidelines, 1996 WISCONSIN LAW REVIEW 679 (1996)

Bradley, Proportionality in Capital and Non-Capital Sentencing: An Eighth Amendment Enigma, 23 IDAHO LAW REVIEW 195 (1987)

Cassell, Too Severe?: A Defense of the Federal Sentencing Guidelines (And a Critique of Federal Mandatory Minimums), 56 STANFORD LAW REVIEW 1017 (2004)

Chitty, A PRACTICAL TREATISE ON CRIMINAL LAW (1836)

Davis, DISCRETIONARY JUSTICE: A PRELIMINARY INQUIRY (1969)

Dershowitz, Background Paper, FAIR AND CERTAIN PUNISHMENT: REPORT OF THE TWENTIETH CENTURY FUND (1976)

Dubber, Recidivist Statutes as A Rational Punishment, 43 BUFFALO LAW REVIEW 689 (1995)

Farabee, Disparate Departures Under the Federal Sentencing Guidelines: A Tale of Two Districts, 30 CONNECTICUT LAW REVIEW 569 (1998)

Federal Courts Study Committee, REPORT OF THE FEDERAL COURTS STUDY COMMITTEE (1990)

Federal Judicial Center, The Consequences of Mandatory Minimum Prison Terms: A Summary of Recent Findings (1994)

Frankel, CRIMINAL SENTENCES: LAW WITHOUT ORDER (1973)

____, Lawlessness in Sentencing, 41 UNIVERSITY OF CINCINNATI LAW REVIEW 1 (1972)

Freed, Federal Sentencing in the Wake of Guidelines: Unacceptable Limits on the Discretion of Sentencers, 101 YALE LAW JOURNAL 1681 (1992)

Frost, SENTENCING REFORM: EXPERIMENTS IN REDUCING DISPARITY (1982)

Gardner, The Determinate Sentencing Movement and the Eighth Amendment: Excessive Punishment Before and After Rummel v. Estelle, 1980 DUKE LAW JOURNAL 1103

Granucci, "Nor Cruel and Unusual Punishments Inflicted:" The Original Meaning, 57 CALIFORNIA LAW REVIEW 839 (1969)

Hall, THEFT, LAW AND SOCIETY (1952)

Hart, The Aims of the Criminal Law, 23 LAW AND CONTEMPORARY PROBLEMS 401 (1958)

Hatch, The Role of Congress in Sentencing: The United States Sentencing Commission, Mandatory Minimum Sentences, and the Search for a Certain and Effective Sentencing System, 28 WAKE FOREST LAW REVIEW 185 (1993)

Herman & Murphy, Mandatory Minimum Drug Sentences – Can They Be Any Less Draconian? 16 THOMAS M. COOLEY LAW REVIEW 99 (1999)

Kadish, Legal Norm and Discretion in the Police and Sentencing Processes, 75 HARVARD LAW REVIEW 904 (1962)

Kennedy, The State, the Criminal Law, and Racial Discrimination: A Comment, 107 HARVARD LAW REVIEW 1255 (1994)

Klein & Steiker, The Search for Equality in Criminal Sentencing, 2002 SUPREME COURT REVIEW 223 (2002)

Kobil, The Quality of Mercy Strained: Wrestling the Pardoning Power from the King, 69 TEXAS LAW REVIEW 569 (1991)

Levine, The Confounding Boundaries of "Apprendi-land": Statutory Minimums and the Federal Sentencing Guidelines, 29 AMERICAN JOURNAL OF CRIMINAL LAW 377 (2002)

Lindsay, Indeterminate Sentence and the Parole System, 16 JOURNAL OF CRIMINAL LAW & CRIMINOLOGY 9 (1925)

Lowenthal, Mandatory Sentencing Laws: Undermining the Effectiveness of Determinate Sentencing Reform, 81 CALIFORNIA LAW REVIEW 61 (1993)

Luna, Gridland: An Allegorical Critique of Federal Sentencing, 96 JOURNAL OF CRIMINAL LAW & CRIMINOLOGY 25 (2005)

Mackey, Rationality Versus Proportionality: Reconsidering the Constitutional Limits on Criminal Sanctions, 51 TENNESSEE LAW REVIEW 623 (1984)

Marvell & Moody, The Lethal Effects of Three-Strike Laws, 30 JOURNAL OF LEGAL STUDIES 89 (2001)

National Center for State Courts, CLEMENCY: LEGAL AUTHORITY, PROCEDURE, AND STRUCTURE (1977)

Newman, CONVICTION: THE DETERMINATION OF GUILT OR INNOCENCE WITHOUT TRIAL (1966)

Oberdorfer, Mandatory Sentencing: One Judge's Perspective – 2002, 40 AMERICAN CRIMINAL LAW REVIEW 11 (2003)

O'Donnell, Churgin & Curtis, TOWARD A JUST AND EFFECTIVE SENTENCING SYSTEM: AGENDA FOR LEGISLATIVE REFORM (1977)

Ogletree, The Death of Discretion? Reflections on the Federal Sentencing Guidelines, 101 HARVARD LAW REVIEW 1938 (1988)

O'Hear, The Original Intent of Uniformity in Federal Sentencing, 74 UNIVERSITY OF CINCINNATI LAW REVIEW 749 (2006)

Packer, THE LIMITS OF THE CRIMINAL SANCTION (1968)

Payne, Does Inter-Judge Disparity Really Matter? An Analysis of the Effects of Sentencing Reforms in Three Federal District Courts, 17 INTERNATIONAL REVIEW OF LAW AND ECONOMICS 337 (1997)

Pound, CRIMINAL JUSTICE IN AMERICA (1930)

Ristroph, Desert, Democracy, and Sentencing Reform, 96 JOURNAL OF CRIMINAL LAW & CRIMINOLOGY 1293 (2006)

Rubin, THE LAW OF CRIMINAL CORRECTION (2d ed. 1973)

Saris, Below the Radar Screens: Have the Sentencing Guidelines Eliminated Disparity? One Judge's Perspective, 30 SUFFOLK UNIVERSITY LAW REVIEW 1027 (1997)

Schulhofer, Rethinking Mandatory Minimums, 28 WAKE FOREST LAW REVIEW 199 (1993)

Schultz, No Joy in Mudville Tonight: The Impact of "Three Strike" Laws on State and Federal Correctional Policy, Resources, and Crime Control 557 (2000)

Singer, JUST DESERTS: SENTENCING BASED ON EQUALITY AND DESERT (1979)

Sklansky, Cocaine, Race, and Equal Protection, 47 STANFORD LAW REVIEW 1283 (1995)

Spade, Beyond the 100:1 Ratio: Towards a Rational Cocaine Sentencing Policy, 38 ARIZONA LAW REVIEW 1233 (1996)

Sporkin, Hutchinson, & Roberts, Debate: Mandatory Minimums in Drug Sentencing: A Valuable Weapon in the War on Drugs or a Handcuff on Judicial Discretion? 36 AMERICAN CRIMINAL LAW REVIEW 1279 (1999)

Stephen, HISTORY OF THE CRIMINAL LAW OF ENGLAND (1883)

Stewart, Sentencing in the States: The Good, the Bad, and the Ugly, 39 OSGOODE HALL LAW JOURNAL 413 (2001)

Stith & Cabranes, FEAR OF JUDGING: SENTENCING GUIDELINES IN THE FEDERAL COURTS (1998)

_, Judging Under the Federal Sentencing Guidelines, 91 NORTHWESTERN UNIVERSITY LAW REVIEW 1247 (1997)

Tappan, Sentencing Under the Model Penal Code, 23 LAW AND CONTEMPORARY PROBLEMS 528 (1958)

Tonry, SENTENCING MATTERS (1996)

Turnbladh, A Critique of the Model Penal Code Sentencing Proposals, 23 LAW AND CONTEMPORARY PROBLEMS 544 (1958)

United States General Accounting Office, Federal Drug Offenses: Departures from Sentencing Guidelines and Mandatory Minimum Sentences, Fiscal Years 1999-2001, GAO-04-105 (Oct. 2003)[GAO is now known as the United States Government Accountability Office]

United States Sentencing Commission, Guidelines Manual (2012)

_, Report to the Congress: Mandatory Minimum Penalties in the Federal Criminal Justice System (2011)

_, Special Report to the Congress: Cocaine and Federal Sentencing Policy (1997)

_, Special Report to the Congress: Downward Departures from the Federal Sentencing Guidelines (2003)

_, Special Report to the Congress: Mandatory Minimum Penalties in the Federal Criminal Justice System (1991)

Villa, Retooling Mandatory Minimum Sentencing: Fixing the Federal "Statutory Safety Valve" to Act as an Effective Mechanism for Clemency in Appropriate Cases, 21 HAMLINE LAW REVIEW 109 (1997)

Weinstein, Fifteen Years After the Federal Sentencing Revolution: How Mandatory Minimums Have Undermined Effective and Just Narcotics Sentencing, 40 AMERICAN CRIMINAL LAW REVIEW 87 (2003)

Wheeler, Toward a Theory of Limiting Punishment: An Examination of the Eighth Amendment, 24 STANFORD LAW REVIEW 838 (1972)

Whiteside, The Reality of Federal Sentencing: Beyond the Criticism, 91 NORTHWESTERN UNIVERSITY LAW REVIEW 1574 (1997)

Wilkins, Newton & Steer, Competing Sentencing Policies in a "War on Drugs" Era, 28 WAKE FOREST LAW REVIEW 305 (1993)

Zalman, The Rise and Fall of the Indeterminate Sentence, 24 WAYNE LAW REVIEW 45 (1977)

Notes and Comments

Do Judicial "Scarlet Letters" Violate the Cruel and Unusual Punishments Clause of the Eighth Amendment, 16 HASTINGS CONSTITUTIONAL LAW QUARTERLY 115 (1988)

The Eighth Amendment, Becarria, and the Enlightenment: An Historical Justification for the Weems v. United States Excessive Punishment Doctrine, 24 BUFFALO LAW REVIEW 783 (1975)

Interpretation of the Eighth Amendment—Rummel, Solem and the Venerable Case of Weems v. United States, 1984 DUKE LAW JOURNAL 789

Mandatory Minimum Sentences: Exemplifying the Law of Unintended Consequences, 28 FLORIDA STATE UNIVERSITY LAW REVIEW 935 (2001)

Rethinking Mandatory Minimums After Apprendi, 96 NORTHWESTERN UNIVERSITY LAW REVIEW 811 (2002)

The "Safety Valve" Provision: Should the Government Get an Automatic Shut-Off Valve? 2002 UNIVERSITY OF ILLINOIS LAW REVIEW 529

Solem v. Helm: The Supreme Court Extends the Proportionality Requirement to Sentences of Imprisonment, 1984 WISCONSIN LAW REVIEW 1401

United States v. Pho: Reasons and Reasonableness in Post-Booker Appellate Review, 115 YALE LAW JOURNAL 2183 (2006)

The Verdict Is In: Throw Out Mandatory Sentences, 79 American Bar Association Journal 78 (1994).

End Notes

[1] Although others may differ, this report does not classify as mandatory minimum sentencing statutes those statutory proscriptions that call for a mandatory minimum fine unless they also call for a mandatory minimum term of imprisonment.

[2] Commentators have defined mandatory minimums in a number of ways, *see e.g.*, *Mandatory Minimum Sentences Coupled with Multi-Facet Interventions: An Effective Response to Domestic Violence*, 6 UNIVERSITY OF THE DISTRICT OF COLUMBIA LAW REVIEW 51, 68 (2001), *quoting, Determinate Sentencing and Judicial Participation in Democratic Punishment*, 108 HARVARD LAW REVIEW 947 (1995)("mandatory minimums require judges to impose a specified minimum prison term if an offense meets certain statutory criteria"); Lowenthal, *Mandatory Sentencing Laws: Undermining the Effectiveness of Determinate Sentencing Reform*, 81 CALIFORNIA LAW REVIEW 61, 64 (1993) ("mandatory sentencing statutes generally provide that when a specified circumstance exists in connection with the commission of a crime (1) the court must sentence the defendant to prison and (2) the duration of the defendant's incarceration will be substantially longer than it would have been in the absence of the circumstance"); Bernstein, *Discretion Redux—Mandatory Minimums, Federal Judges, and the 'Safety Valve' Provision of the 1994 Crime Act*, 20 UNIVERSITY OF DAYTON LAW REVIEW 765, 768 (1995)(ellipse in the original)("[m]andatory minimums, which are most commonly applied in drug cases, are statutory provisions calling for a sentence of 'no less than ... ' for a given offense (adjusted for criminal record)").

The definition used here – *i.e.*, any statute that effectively requires a federal judge, at a minimum, to sentence a convicted defendant to a term of imprisonment is a mandatory minimum – is designed to avoid exclusion of any provisions that should arguably be listed.

[3] *E.g.*, 18 U.S.C. 3553(e)("*Upon motion of the Government*, the court shall have the authority to impose a sentence below a level established by statute as minimum sentence so as to reflect a defendant's substantial assistance in the investigation or prosecution of another person who has committed an offense ... ")(emphasis added). Prosecutorial discretion is somewhat confined, however, by the courts' authority to accept or reject plea bargains, F.R.Crim.P. 32, and their consideration of relevant but uncharged misconduct under the federal Sentencing Guidelines, U.S.S.G. §1B1.3.

[4] *E.g.*, U.S.Const. Art. II, §2 ("The President ... shall have power to grant reprieves and pardons for offenses against the United States ... ").

[5] Various parts of the report are drawn from the author's earlier reports, principally CRS Report RL30281, *Federal Mandatory Minimum Sentencing Statutes: A List of Citations with Captions, Introductory Comments, and Bibliography*; CRS Report R42386, *Mandatory Minimum Sentencing for Federal Sex Offenses: An Overview*; CRS Report R42100, *Mandatory Minimum Sentencing: Federal Aggravated Identity Theft*; CRS Report R41326, *Federal Mandatory Minimum Sentences: The Safety Valve and Substantial Assistance Exceptions*; CRS Report R41412, *Federal Mandatory Minimum Sentencing: The 18 U.S.C. 924(c) Tack-on in Cases Involving Drugs or Violence*; CRS Report R41461, *Three Strike Mandatory Sentencing (18 U.S.C. 3559(c)): An Overview.*

[6] *E.g.*, 18 U.S.C. 924(c)(1)(A)(" ... any person who, during and in relation to any crime of violence or drug trafficking crime ... for which the person may be prosecuted in a court of the United States uses or carries a firearm ... shall in addition to the punishment provided for such crime ... (i) be sentenced to a term of imprisonment of not less than 5 years ... ").

[7] *E.g.*, 18 U.S.C. 844(f)(1)("Whoever maliciously damages or destroys ... by means of fire or an explosive any ... personal or real property ... owned or possessed by ... the United States ... shall be imprisoned for not less than 5 years and not more than 20 years ... ").

[8] *E.g.*, 18 U.S.C. 2252(b)(1)("Whoever violates ... paragraphs (1), (2), or (3) of subsection (a) [relating to commercial activities with respect child pornography] shall be fined under this title and imprisoned not less than 5 years and not more than 20 years.... ").

[9] "Notwithstanding any other provision of law, in the case of an offense under section 401, 404, or 406 of the Controlled Substances Act (21 U.S.C. 841, 844, 846) or section 1010 or 1013 of the Controlled Substances Import and Export Act (21 U.S.C. 960, 963), the court shall impose a sentence pursuant to guidelines promulgated by the United States Sentencing Commission under section 994 of title 28 without regard to any statutory minimum sentence, if the court finds at sentencing, after the Government has been afforded the opportunity to make a recommendation, that—

"(1) the defendant does not have more than 1 criminal history point, as determined under the sentencing guidelines;

"(2) the defendant did not use violence or credible threats of violence or possess a firearm or other dangerous weapon (or induce another participant to do so) in connection with the offense;

"(3) the offense did not result in death or serious bodily injury to any person;

"(4) the defendant was not an organizer, leader, manager, or supervisor of others in the offense, as determined under the sentencing guidelines and was not engaged in a continuing criminal enterprise, as defined in section 408 of the Controlled Substances Act; and

"(5) not later than the time of the sentencing hearing, the defendant has truthfully provided to the Government all information and evidence the defendant has concerning the offense or offenses that were part of the same course of conduct or of a common scheme or plan, but the fact that the defendant has no relevant or useful other information to provide or that the Government is already aware of the information shall not preclude a determination by the court that the defendant has complied with this requirement," 18 U.S.C. 3553(f).

[10] "Upon motion of the Government, the court shall have the authority to impose a sentence below a level established by statute as a minimum sentence so as to reflect a defendant's substantial assistance in the investigation or prosecution of another person who has committed an offense. Such sentence shall be imposed in accordance with the guidelines and policy statements issued by the Sentencing Commission pursuant to section 994 of title 28, United States Code," 18 U.S.C. 3553(e).

[11] *E.g.,*, 2 U.S.C. 390 ("Every person who, having been subpenaed as a witness under this chapter [relating to Congressional contested elections] to give testimony or to produce documents, willfully makes default, or who, having appeared, refuses to answer any question pertinent to the contested election case, shall be deemed guilty of a misdemeanor punishable by fine of not more than $1,000 nor less than $100 *or* imprisoned for not less than one month nor more than twelve months, *or both*")(emphasis added).

The initial Sentencing Commission report included them within its definition of mandatory minimums, United States Sentencing Commission, *Special Report to the Congress: Mandatory Minimum Penalties in the Federal Criminal Justice System (Commission Report I)*, 4-5 (1991)("Under some statutes, a mandatory prison term is only required when the court otherwise determines to impose a sentence of imprisonment"); the more recent Commission report includes them in its appended list of mandatory minimum statutes with the notation that they "require a minimum period of imprisonment only when the court imposes a term of imprisonment," *Report to the Congress: Mandatory Minimum Penalties in the Federal Criminal Justice System (Commission Report II)*, A-20 (2011). They highlight instances where Congress might have been thought to establish a mandatory minimum but where its treatment of the fine to be imposed may leave its intentions in doubt. *See e.g.,* 18 U.S.C. 242 (Whoever ... willfully subjects any person ... to the deprivation of any rights ... if death results ... shall be fined under this title, *or* imprisoned for any term of years or for life, *or both*..... ")(emphasis added).

[12] *E.g.,* 18 U.S.C. 1651 ("Whoever, on the high seas, commits the crime of piracy as defined by the law of nations, and is afterwards brought into or found in the United States *shall be imprisoned for life*")(emphasis added).

[13] *E.g.*, 18 U.S.C. 1201(a)("Whoever unlawfully seizes, confines, inveigles, decoys, kidnaps, abducts, or carries away and holds for ransom or reward or otherwise any person ... if death of any person results, shall be punished by death or life imprisonment").
Most observers might exclude from this category capital crimes made punishable by death, life imprisonment, *or imprisonment for any term of years*, under the theory that a sentence of imprisonment for zero years is a sentence of "any term of years." Yet this can hardly have been the intent of Congress given the seriousness of the offense to which the sentence attaches.

[14] *E.g.*, 18 U.S.C. 1114 ("Whoever kills ... any officer or employee of the United States ... shall be punished – (1) in the case of murder, as provided under section 1111.... ").

[15] 543 U.S. 220 (2005). *Booker* left the Guidelines in place and essentially intact, but they continue to have a large, rather than a commanding, presence within the federal sentencing scheme, *see e.g., Rita v. United States*, 551 U.S. 338 (2007)(appellate courts may consider a sentence within the accurately identified Guideline range reasonable); *Gall v. United States*, 552 U.S. 38, 49-51 (2007)(sentencing courts must begin by determining the appropriate Guideline range for the case at hand and then consider the other sentencing factors identified in 18 U.S.C. 3553(a); they may not accept a sentence within the Guideline range per se reasonable nor one outside that range per se unreasonable; appellate courts are to review trial court sentences under a deferential abuse of discretion standard).

[16] The Sentencing Commission did not think of its Guidelines as mandatory minimum provisions, *Commission Report I*, 4 (footnote 3 of the Commission's *Report* in brackets) ("'Mandatory minimums,' 'mandatory minimum sentencing provisions,' and related terms refer to statutory provisions requiring the imposition of at least a specified minimum sentence when criteria specified in the relevant statute have been met. [Consistent with the intent of the statutory directive for this Report, only minimums required by statute are considered to be 'mandatory minimums.' Not included in the definitions (and in fact contrasted with mandatory minimums in a later chapter of this Report) are sentences required by the federal sentencing guidelines ...]"). The Sentencing Guidelines, however, are promulgated pursuant to statutory authority and before *Booker* often curtailed the authority of a sentencing court to impose a sentence that did not include a term of imprisonment – upon conviction for violation of a statute which on its face is not a mandatory minimum.

[17] This is particularly so because the Guidelines impose constraints on the option of probation that make a sentence other than incarceration more uncommon than was once the case: "Prior to the [Sentencing Reform Act], the prison to probation ratio in federal criminal sentencing was about sixty to forty. Congress said nothing in the statute about abolishing or even drastically curtailing probation.... The Commission, however, drafted guidelines containing a presumptive sentence of imprisonment for every felony in the United States Code. Near the bottom of the scale of crimes, it established several ranges in which a court could select either prison or probation.... The result is that the incidence of probation since the guidelines has been cut by more than half (15.5%)," Freed, *Federal Sentencing in the Wake of Guidelines: Unacceptable Limits on the Discretion of Sentencers*, 101 YALE LAW JOURNAL 1681, 1706-707 (1992). According to the most recent statistics, the current incidence of probation is 5.6% with an additional 3.0% of offenders sentenced to some mix of confinement and probation, *U.S. Sentencing Commission's 2012 Sourcebook of Federal Sentencing Statistics*, Table 16, available at http://www.ussc.gov/Research_and_Statistics/Annual_Reports_and_Sourcebooks/2012/Table16.pdf.

[18] Blackstone, COMMENTARIES ON THE LAWS OF ENGLAND (1765); CHITTY, A PRACTICAL TREATISE ON CRIMINAL LAW (3D AMER. ED. 1836); STEPHEN, HISTORY OF THE CRIMINAL LAW OF ENGLAND (1883); Rubin, THE LAW OF CRIMINAL CORRECTION (2d ed. 1973).

[19] Frankel, CRIMINAL SENTENCES: LAW WITHOUT ORDER (1973); Frankel, *Lawlessness in Sentencing*, 41 UNIVERSITY OF CINCINNATI LAW REVIEW 1 (1972); O'Donnell, Churgin & Curtis, TOWARD A JUST AND EFFECTIVE SENTENCING SYSTEM: AGENDA FOR LEGISLATIVE REFORM (1977); Stith & Cabranes, FEAR OF JUDGING (1998).

[20] *Harmelin v. Michigan*, 501 U.S. 957, 999 (Kennedy, J. concurring).

[21] Blackstone's summary on the eve of the Revolutionary War marks the evolution of English sentencing law to that point: " ... [T]he court must pronounce that judgment, which the law hath annexed to the crime.... Of these some are capital, which extend to the life of the offender, and consist generally in being hanged by the neck till dead; though in very atrocious crimes other circumstances of terror, pain, or disgrace are superadded: as, in treasons of all kinds, being drawn or dragged to the place of execution; in high treason affecting the king's person or government, embowelling alive, beheading, and quartering; and in murder, a public dissection. And, in case of any treason committed by a female, the judgment is to be burned alive. But the humanity of the English nation has authorized, by a tacit consent, an almost general mitigation of such part of these judgments as savour of torture or cruelty: a sledge or hurdle being usually allowed to such traitors as are condemned to be drawn; and there being very few instances (and those accidental or by negligence) of any person's being embowelled or burned, till previously deprived of sensation by strangling. Some punishments consist in exile or banishment, by abjuration of the realm, or transportation to the American colonies; others in loss of liberty, by perpetual or temporary imprisonment. Some extent to confiscation, by forfeiture of lands, or movables, or both, or of the profits of lands for life: others induce a disability, of holding offices or employments, being heirs, executors, and the like. Some, though rarely, occasion a mutilation or dismembering, by cutting off the hand or ears: others fix a lasting stigma on the offender by slitting the nostrils, or branding the hand or face. Some are merely pecuniary, by stated or discretionary fines: and lastly there are others, that consist principally in their ignominy, though most of them are mixed with some degree of corporal pain; and theses are inflicted chiefly for crimes, which arise from indigence, or which render even opulence disgraceful. Such as whipping, hard labour in the house of correction, the pillory, the stocks, and the ducking stool." 4 Blackstone, COMMENTARIES ON THE LAWS OF ENGLAND 369-70 (1769).

[22] ID. at 390; Kobil, *The Quality of Mercy Strained: Wresting the Pardoning Power From the King*, 69 TEXAS LAW REVIEW 569, 583-89 (1991).

[23] Hall, THEFT, LAW AND SOCIETY, 114-32 (1952); Rubin, *supra* footnote 22 at 180.

[24] 1 Blumstein, Cohen, Martin & Tonry, RESEARCH ON SENTENCING: THE SEARCH FOR REFORM, 58 (1983); Rothman, THE DISCOVERY OF THE ASYLUM: SOCIAL ORDER AND DISORDER IN THE NEW REPUBLIC, 61 (rev.ed. 1990).

[25] The Act of April 30, 1790 declared that "persons ... adjudged guilty of treason against the United States ... shall suffer death," 1 Stat. 112; the same sentence awaited those who committed murder within the exclusive jurisdiction of the United States, 1 Stat. 113, or engaged in piracy, 1 Stat. 113-14, or counterfeiting, 1 Stat. 115.

[26] Rubin, THE LAW OF CRIMINAL CORRECTION, 180-84 (2d ed. 1973).

[27] Zalman, *The Rise and Fall of the Indeterminate Sentence*, 24 WAYNE LAW REVIEW 45 (1977); Lindsay, *Indeterminate Sentence and Parole System*, 16 JOURNAL OF CRIMINAL LAW & CRIMINOLOGY 9 (1925).

[28] Even treason was made punishable by imprisonment at hard labor for not less than five years rather than by death, at the discretion of the court, Rev.Stat. §5332; and the penalty for forgery or counterfeiting of U.S. securities was reduced from death to imprisonment for not more than fifteen years, Rev.Stat. §5414.

[29] Mail robbery, for instance, became punishable by imprisonment at hard labor for not less than five years and not more than ten years; by imprisonment for life for a 2d offense or if the custodian of the mail were wounded or his life placed in jeopardy by the use of dangerous weapons, Rev.Stat. §5472.

[30] As the Joint Committee on Revision of the Laws explained: "The committee has also adopted a uniform method of fixing in all offenses not punishable by death the maximum punishment only, leaving the minimum to the discretion of the trial judge. "The criminal law necessarily subjects to its corrective discipline all who violate its provisions. The weak and the vicious, the first offender and the atrocious criminal, the mere technical transgressor and the expert in crime are alike guilty of the same offense. In the one case the utmost severity of punishment can scarcely provide the protection to which society is entitled; in the other anything except as nominal punishment may effectually prevent the reclamation of the offender. "The argument most frequently urged against leaving the minimum punishments to the discretion of the trial judge is that it affords parties convicted of crime of a heinous character an opportunity to obtain immunity because of the weakness or dishonesty of judges. It has been well said by a distinguished authority upon this subject that— Instances of the former are rare, and of the latter none is believed ever to have existed. The purity of our judiciary is one of things which calumny has as yet left untouched. "This recommendation will be found to be in accordance with the humane spirit of advanced criminal jurisprudence. The early English statutes were proverbially cruel; the gravest crimes and the most trivial offenses alike invoked the penalty of death. Our own crimes act of 1790 reflected this barbarous spirit and denounced the death penalty for thirteen distinct offenses, but this spirit of vindictive retribution has entirely disappeared. We have abolished the punishment of death in all except three cases—treason, murder, and rape—and have provided that even in these cases it may be modified to imprisonment for life; and as humane judges in England availed themselves of the most technical irregularities in pleadings and proceedings as an excuse for discharging prisoners from the cruel rigors of the common law, so jurors here often refuse to convict for offenses attended with extenuating circumstances rather than submit the offender to what in their judgment is the cruel requirement of a law demanding a minimum punishment," S.Rep.No.10, 60th Cong., 1st Sess. 14 (1908).

[31] Act of June 25, 1910, §1 36 Stat. 819, and Act of Jan. 23, 1913, 37 Stat. 650.

[32] Act of March 4, 1925, 43 Stat. 1259.

[33] "The minimum punishment provisions were omitted because of the court's power, under 3651 of this title, to suspend sentence whenever the crime or offense is not punishable by death or life imprisonment, and, also, to conform with policy adopted by the codifiers of the 1909 Criminal Code," H.R.Rep. 304, 80th Cong., 1st Sess. *Reviser's Notes* A16 (1947).

[34] Kadish, *Legal Norm and Discretion in the Police and Sentencing Process*, 75 HARVARD LAW REVIEW 904, 915 (1962).

[35] Davis, DISCRETIONARY JUSTICE: A PRELIMINARY INQUIRY (1969); Packer, THE LIMITS OF THE CRIMINAL SANCTION (1968); Frankel, CRIMINAL SENTENCES: LAW WITHOUT ORDER (1973).

[36] A determinate sentence is a sentence for a fixed period of time, a flat sentence; an indeterminate sentence is one whose duration is not specifically fixed but is determined by prison and/or parole authorities, BLACK'S LAW DICTIONARY 1367 (7th ed. 1999); *see generally*, *Indeterminate Sentencing: An Analysis of Sentencing in America*, 70 SOUTHERN CALIFORNIA LAW REVIEW 1717 (1997); Gardner, *The Determinate Sentencing Movement and The Eighth Amendment: Excessive Punishment Before and After Rummel v. Estelle*, 1980 DUKE LAW JOURNAL 1103, 1104-105; *Do Judicial "Scarlet Letters" Violate the Cruel and Unusual Punishments Clause of the Eighth Amendment?*, 16 HASTINGS CONSTITUTIONAL LAW QUARTERLY 115, 118-19 (1988) (contrasting 7 indeterminate sentencing structure states with 9 determinate sentence states).

[37] Robinson, *A Sentencing System for the 21st Century?*, 66 TEXAS LAW REVIEW 1, 24-5 (1987). Sentencing guidelines do not necessarily circumscribe judicial sentencing discretion; the guidelines may simply be advisory. Sentencing Commissions and sentencing guidelines have become common, *see e.g.*, Ala.Code §§12-25-1 to 12-25-12; Alaska Stat. §12.55.125(c) to (e); Ark.Code Ann. §§16-90-801 to 16-90-804; Conn.Gen.Stat.Ann. §54-

300; Del.Code Ann. tit.11, §§6580 to 6581A; Fla.Stat. Ann. §§921.001 to 921.00265; Ill. Comp.Stat.Ann. ch.730, §§5/5-5-3.1, 5/5/-5-3.2; Kan.Stat.Ann. §§21-6801 to 21-6828; La.Rev. Stat.Ann. §§15:321 to 15:324; Md.Crim.Pro. §§6-201 to 6-216; Mass.Gen.Laws Ann. ch.211E, §§1-4; Mich.Comp.Laws Ann. ch. 777; Minn.Stat.Ann. ch.244 App.; Mo.Ann.Stat. §558.019; N.C.Gen. Stat. §§15A-1340.13 to 1340.17; Ohio Rev. Code ann. §§181.21 to 181.56; Ore.Rev.Stat. §§137.667 to 137.671; Pa.Stat.Ann. tit. 42, §§2151-2156; S.C. Code §§24-26-10 to 24-26-60; Tenn.Code Ann. §§40- 35-101 to 40-35-122; Utah Code Ann. §§63-25a-301 to 63-25a-306; Va.Code §§17.1-800 to 17.1-806, 19.2-298.01; Vt. Stat.Ann. tit. 13, §§5451-5452; Wash.Rev. Code Ann. §§9.94A.401 to 9.94A.702; Wis.Stat.Ann. §973.017.

[38] *Do Judicial "Scarlet Letters" Violate the Cruel and Unusual Punishments Clause of the Eighth Amendment*, 16 HASTINGS CONSTITUTIONAL LAW QUARTERLY 115, 119 n.32 (1988) (listing 33 states with mandatory minimum sentencing structures).

[39] *See e.g.*, Alaska Stat.§§12.55.125 to 12.55.185; Cal.Pen.Code §1170; Colo.Rev.Stat. §§16-11-304, 18-1-105; Ind.Code Ann. §35-50-6-1; Minn.Stat.Ann. §244.05; N.M.Stat.Ann. §§31-18-15, 31-21-10. Note that some of the jurisdictions that have abolished parole as a discretionary means of reducing an offender's term of imprisonment authorize "reentry parole" or terms of "supervised release" under which the offender is subject to supervision after service of his or her full term of imprisonment.

[40] The Sentence Reform Act is chapter II, 98 Stat. 1987, of the Comprehensive Crime Control Act of 1984, 98 Stat. 1976, enacted as title II of P.L. 98-473, 98 Stat. 1837 (1984).

[41] 18 U.S.C. 3651 (1982 ed.).

[42] 18 U.S.C. 4201 to 4218 (1982 ed.).

[43] 28 U.S.C. 991 to 998.

[44] The mandatory minimum applicable when a firearm is used during the course of a federal crime of violence, 18 U.S.C. 924(c), originated in the same legislation as the Sentence Reform Act, P.L. 98-473, 98 Stat. 2138 (1984). The armed career criminal provisions, 18 U.S.C. 924(e), first surfaced in the Firearms Owners Protection Act, P.L. 99-308, 100 Stat. 458 (1986); the mandatory minimums for drug trafficking, 21 U.S.C. 841(b), in the Anti-Drug Abuse Act of 1986, P.L. 99-570, 100 Stat. 3207-2; the mandatory minimums for crack possession, 21 U.S.C. 844, in the Anti-Drug Abuse Act of 1988, P.L. 100-690, 102 Stat. 4370; the three strikes and child pornography provisions, 18 U.S.C. 3559(c) and 18 U.S.C. 2251-2252A, in the Violent Crime Control and Law Enforcement Act of 1994, P.L. 103-322, 108 Stat. 1982, 2037. The drug kingpin mandatory minimum, 21 U.S.C. 848, enacted as part of the original Controlled Substances Act in 1970, P.L. 91-513, 84 Stat. 1265 (1970), and most of the mandatory minimums cited in the appendix predate their more well-known fellows. The safety valve feature of 18 U.S.C. 3553(f) available to nonviolent, first-time drug offenders and passed in 1994, P.L. 103-322, 108 Stat. 1985, might be seen as a break in the trend toward greater use of mandatory minimums even though it does not enhance federal judicial sentencing discretion.

[45] 18 U.S.C. 3553(e).

[46] Section 1007(a) of P.L. 99-570, 100 Stat. 32-07-7 (1986).

[47] U.S.S.G. §5K1.1; *see also*, F.R.Crim.P. 35(b) which authorizes a court to reduce the sentence it imposed upon the defendant upon the government's motion based on the defendant's substantial assistance.

[48] *Melendez v. United States*, 518 U.S. 120, 125-26 (1996)("We believe that §3553(e) requires a government motion requesting or authorizing the district court to impose a sentence below a level established by statute as a[a] minimum sentence before the court may impose such a sentence"); *United States v. Massey*, 663 F.3d 852, 860 (6th Cir. 2011).

[49] *Wade v. United States*, 504 U.S. 181, 186 (1992); *United States v. Gomez*, 705 F.3d 68, 79 (2d Cir. 2013).

[50] *United States v. Motley*, 587 F.3d 1153, 1159 (D.C. Cir. 2009); *United States v. Smith*, 574 F.3d 521, 525 (8th Cir. 2009); *United States v. Doe*, 445 F.3d 202, 207 (2d Cir. 2006).

[51] *Wade v. United States*, 504 at 186.

[52] *United States v. Freemont*, 513 F.3d 884, 889 (8th Cir. 2008)("The district court may review the government's refusal to make a motion in limited circumstances. First, the district court may review the government's decision for an unconstitutional motive.... Second, a district court can compel a §3553(e) motion if the government acknowledges the defendant provided substantial assistance, but refuses to make a motion expressly because the defendant engaged in unrelated misconduct – a reason unrelated to the quality of the defendant's assistance.... Third, the district court may be able to compel a motion if the government acted in bad faith by refusing to make a motion"); but see *United States v. Perez*, 526 F.3d 1135, 1138 (8th Cir. 2008)(citing cases evidencing a split within the circuit over whether bad faith provides a sufficient based to compel a government motion).

[53] *Survey, Question 15. Substantial Assistance*. Only 35% of the respondents disagreed with the statement that "Congress should amend 18 USC §3553(e) to authorize judges to sentence a defendant below the applicable statutory mandatory minimum to reflect a defendant's substantial assistance, even if the government does not make a motion," *Id.*

[54] *Melendez v. United States*, 518 U.S. 120, 126 (1996).

[55] *United States v. Williams*, 687 F.3d 283, 286 (6th Cir. 2012); *United States v. Span*, 682 F.3d 565, 566 (7th Cir. 2012); *United States v. Winebarger*, 664 F.3d 388 (3d Cir. 2011)("Congress's chosen language explicitly indicates that the reduction below the statutory minimum is to 'reflect' a defendant's assistance to the government in investigating and prosecuting other offenders. This language does not give a court carte blanche to sentence a defendant below a statutory minimum sentence based on non-assistance-related factors once it is established that the defendant provided assistance to the government"); *United States v. Burns*, 577 F.3d 887, 894 (8th Cir. 2009)(en banc)("Where a court has authority to sentence below a statutory minimum only by virtue of a government motion under §3553(e), the reduction below the statutory minimum must be based exclusively on assistance-related considerations"); *United States v. Jackson,* 577 F.3d 1032, 1036 (9th Cir. 2009); *United States v. Hood*, 556 F.3d 226, 234 n.2 (4th Cir. 2009), citing *inter alia United States v. Richardson,* 521 F.3d 149, 159 (2d Cir. 2008) and *United States v. Desselle,* 450F.3d 179, 182 (5th Cir. 2006).

[56] U.S.S.G. §5K1.1(a); *United States v. Gabbard*, 586 F.3d 1046, 1051 (6th Cir. 2009), citing *United States v. Richardson*, 521 F.3d at 159.

[57] *Hearing, Testimony of Jeffrey B. Steinback on behalf of the Practitioner's Advisory Group* at 8, quoting *United States v. Brigham*, 977 F.2d 317, 318 (7th Cir. 1992); see also *Hearing, Written Statement of Cynthia Hujar Orr, President of the National Ass'n of Criminal Defense Lawyers* at 3 (defendants "who have little or no information to provide the government, end up with far more severe sentences than leaders of conspiracies who run the operations and know the other participants").

[58] *Survey, Question 15. Substantial Assistance*. Only 24% of the respondents disagreed with the statement that "In determining the extent of a reduction below the statutory mandatory minimum under 18 USC §3553(e) ... the court's consideration should not be limited to the nature of the defendant's substantial assistance but also should include consideration of the factors at 18 USC §3553(a)," *Id.*

[59] "*Retribution or 'Just Desserts.'* Perhaps the most commonly-voiced goal of mandatory minimum penalties is the 'justness' of long prison terms for particular serious offenses.... *Deterrence.* By requiring the imposition of substantial penalties for targeted offenses, mandatory minimums are intended both to discourage the individual sentenced ... from further involvement in crime ... and, by example discourage other potential lawbreakers.... *Incapacitation, Especially of the Serious Offender.* Mandating increased sentence severity aims to protect the public by incapacitating offenders.... *Disparity.* Indeterminate sentencing systems permit substantial latitude in setting the sentence, which in turn can mean that defendants convicted of the same offense are sentenced to widely disparate sentences. *Inducement of Cooperation.* Because they provide specific lengthy sentences, mandatory

minimums encourage offenders to assist in the investigation of criminal conduct by others [in order to take advantage of the escape hatch 18 U.S.C. 3553(e) supplies to those who cooperate with authorities].... *Inducement of Pleas* ... [P]rosecutors express the view that mandatory minimum sentences can be valuable tools in obtaining guilty pleas ... " *Commission Report* 13-4.

[60] *Commission Report* at ii, 11 ("four statutes account for approximately 94 percent of the cases ... 21 U.S.C. 841 [illicit drug trafficking], 21 U.S.C. 844 [illicit drug possession], 21 U.S.C. 960 [drug smuggling], and 18 U.S.C. 924(c)[armed career criminals]").

[61] *Commission Report* at ii. ("[The] lack of uniform application creates unwarranted disparity in sentencing and compromises the potential for the guidelines sentencing system to reduce disparity"). *But see*, Stith & Cabranes, FEAR OF JUDGING, 106 1998)("Our analysis suggests four major conclusions: 1. Inter-judge sentence variation was not as rampant or as 'shameful' in the federal courts under the pre-Guidelines regime as Congress apparently believed. 2. No thorough empirical study has demonstrated a *reduction* in the total amount of disparity under the Guidelines. 3. While reduction of inter-judge disparity is a worthwhile goal ... it is a complex goal, and a myopic focus on this objective can result in a system that too often ignores other, equally important goals of a just sentencing system 4. Important sources of disparity remain in the Guidelines regime"); Farabee, *Disparate Departures Under the Federal Sentencing Guidelines: A Tale of Two Districts*, 30 CONNECTICUT LAW REVIEW 569 (1998)(discussing sentencing disparity under the guidelines between two adjacent federal court districts); Payne, *Does Inter-Judge Disparity Really Matter? An Analysis of the Effects of Sentencing Reforms in Three Federal District Courts*, 17 INTERNATIONAL REVIEW OF LAW AND ECONOMICS 337 (1997) (suggesting that inter-judge disparity exists the guidelines notwithstanding).

[62] *Commission Report I,* iii ("Since the charging and plea negotiation processes are neither open to public review nor generally reviewable by the courts, the honesty and truth in sentencing intended by the guidelines system is compromised"). "There are two basic responses to this critique. First, prosecutors undoubtedly do, through charging decisions and plea bargains, sometimes seek, or agree to, lower than the maximum possible sentences. They have always done that. With respect to charging decisions, the Guidelines themselves do not even attempt to limit the historical practice. Indeed, it is difficult to imagine a system which could eliminate prosecutorial charging discretion. Nonetheless, the Justice Department recognized at the outset ... that unrestrained pre-indictment bargaining over charges would undermine the Guidelines.... Therefore, it issued internal directives that prosecutors are to charge the most serious readily provable offense consistent with the nature of the defendant's conduct.... As for plea bargains after indictment, the primary justification of the relevant conduct guideline is to ensure that prosecutors cannot manipulate sentences by dismissing courts. As long as the judge knows all the facts, the precise charge of which a defendant is convicted is usually of little consequence except to set the statutory maximum sentence.... Thus, in order to really control sentences through plea bargaining, a prosecutor must be willing to hide facts from the court.... The truth is that most prosecutors, most of the time, play the sentencing game straight down the middle. To achieve plea bargains, they will give defendants the benefit of close class on the provability of certain facts, or on the applicability of certain enhancements to the undoubted facts of a given case. But they will not lie and they will not conceal evidence. The consequence is that prosecutors, too, have had their discretion restrained by the Guidelines," Bowman, *The Quality of Mercy Must Be Restrained, and Other Lessons in Learning to Love the Federal, Sentencing Guidelines*, 1996 WISCONSIN LAW REVIEW 679, 727-28.

[63] *Commission Report I,* iii. The disparate impact of the federal sentencing practices, including mandatory minimums, has been the subject to extensive debate; *see e.g.*, Albonetti, *The Effects of the "Safety Valve" Amendment on Length of Imprisonment for Cocaine Trafficking/Manufacturing Offenders: Mitigating the Effects of Mandatory Minimum Penalties and Offender's Ethnicity*, 87 IOWA LAW REVIEW 401 (2002); CRS Report 97-743,

Federal Cocaine Sentencing: Legal Issues, by Paul Starett Wallace Jr. (April 25, 2002); *A "Second Look" at Crack Cocaine Sentencing Policies: One More Try for Federal Equal Protection*, 34 AMERICAN CRIMINAL LAW REVIEW 1211 (1997); Sklansky, *Cocaine, Race, and Equal Protection*, 47 STANFORD LAW REVIEW 1283 (1995).

[64] *Commission Report I,* 26 ("Sentencing guidelines look to an array of indicators to determine offense seriousness, including the offense of conviction, any relevant quantity determinant (*e.g.*, the amount of drugs in a trafficking offense, dollar loss in fraud offense), weapon use, victim injury or death, the defendant's role in the offense, and whether the defendant accepted responsibility for the offense or, on the other hand, obstructed justice. Mandatory minimums, in contrast, typically look to only one (or sometimes two) measurements of offense seriousness.... Thus, for example, whether the defendant was a peripheral participant or the drug ring's kingpin, whether the defendant used a weapon, whether the defendant accepted responsibility or, on the other hand, obstructed justice, have no bearing on the mandatory minimum to which each defendant is exposed"). These arguments would seem to be most persuasive in the case of flat sentence mandatory minimums; in other instances the range between the mandatory minimum and the statutory maximum would seem to provide ample room for the type of distinctions just mentioned.

[65] *Commission Report I,* iii ("While mandatory minimum sentences may increase severity, the data suggest that uneven application may dramatically reduce certainty. The consequences of this bifurcated pattern is likely to thwart the deterrent value of mandatory minimums"). Proponents might suggest that incapacitation and the prospect of minimal punishment were always the principal objectives. Deterrence is at best challenging to judge; the fact that not all possible cases receive mandatory minimum treatment is no reason to abandon incapacitation for those that are ensnared; and the result is one more properly laid to the door of prosecutorial discretion than to mandatory minimums.

[66] *Commission Report I,* iii ("Since the power to determine the charge of conviction rests exclusively with the prosecution for 85 percent of the cases that do not proceed to trial, mandatory minimums transfer sentencing power from the court to the prosecution. To the extent that prosecutorial discretion is exercised with preference to some and not to others, and to the extent that some are convicted of conduct carrying a mandatory minimum penalty while others who engage in the same or similar conduct are not so convicted, disparity is reintroduced"). This presumes that unwarranted disparity existed before the guidelines, that the guidelines have reduced or eliminated it, and that mandatory minimums returned it to the system – three propositions upon which there is no consensus. Even if one accepts all three, the question remains whether disparity, produced by plea agreements that make possible the conviction of other wrongdoers, is unwarranted or appropriately laid to the door of mandatory minimums.

[67] *Commission Report I,* 29 ("The 'Cliff' Effect of Mandatory Minimums. Related to the proportionality problems posed in mandatory minimums already described are the sharp differences in sentence between defendants who fall just below the threshold of a mandatory minimum compared with those whose criminal conduct just meets the criteria of the mandatory minimum penalty. Just as mandatory minimums fail to distinguish among defendants whose conduct and prior records in fact differ markedly, they distinguish far too greatly among defendants who have committed offense conduct of highly comparable seriousness"). Critics might suggest that such cliffs are natural, necessary, and frequently occurring in the law (*e.g.*, the age of majority, alcohol-blood levels, statutes of limitations) or that few cliffs are as high as the one that stands between a crime committed the day before the effective date of the guidelines and one committed the day after.

[68] *Commission Report I,* iv. Critics might note that the perpetual need for self-correction neither inspires great confidence nor dilutes the prospect of disparity.

[69] *Commission Report I,* iv.

[70] *United States Department of Justice: An Analysis of Non-Violent Drug Offenders with Minimal Criminal Histories, reprinted in*, 54 CRIMINAL LAW REPORTER 2101 (1994).

[71] *Commission Report II*, 66 ("The total number of federal cases has almost tripled from 29,011 in fiscal year 1990 to 83, 947 in fiscal year 2010"); *see also*, *Commission Report I*, 51 (noting that 29,011 defendants were sentenced under the Guidelines in fiscal year 1990).

[72] *Commission Report II*, 64 ("In the period from 1992 through 1994, Congress created federal criminal statues penalizing failure to pay child support, carjacking, and domestic violence, and expanded the Hobbs Act to include robbery. In 1996, Congress added laws punishing drug-induced rape and church arsons. In 1998, Congress enacted new laws punishing sexual abuse of children, identity theft, telemarketing fraud, and the theft of cellular phone service").

[73] *E.g.*, P.L. 103-322, §§140006 (mandatory minimum for employing a child to traffic certain controlled substances), 180201 (increasing the mandatory minimum for drug trafficking at a truck stop)(1994), now 21 U.S.C. 861, 849, respectively.

[74] 18 U.S.C. 3553(b)(1)(" ... [T]the court shall impose a sentence of the kind, and within the range, [dictated by the Sentencing Guidelines,] unless the court finds that there exists an aggravating or mitigating circumstance of a kind, or to a degree, not adequately taken into consideration by the Sentencing Commission in formulating the guidelines that should result in a sentence different from that described").

[75] In *United States v. Booker*, 543 U.S. 220 (2005), the Court held that Sixth Amendment right to jury trial precluded mandatory application of the Guidelines, but permitted their discretionary application. Thereafter, it explained that "district court should begin all sentencing proceedings by correctly calculating the applicable Guidelines range.... [T]he district judge should then consider all of the §3553(a) factors to determine whether they support the sentence requested by a party," *United States v. Gall*, 552 U.S. 38, 49-50 (2007). Thereafter, 'the appellate court must review the sentence under the abuse of discretion standard. It must first ensure that the district court committed no significant procedural error, such as failing to calculate (improperly calculating) the Guidelines range ... " *id.* at 51.

[76] *Commission Report II*, 85-6 ("Indeed, Congress enacted many mandatory minimum penalties, together with the then- mandatory guidelines system, as part of its effort in the 1980s to narrow judicial sentencing discretion and curb what it viewed as unduly disparate and lenient sentences.... The Department of Justice has observed that sentencing disparities have increased under the advisory guidelines system because for offenses for which there are no mandatory minimums, sentencing decisions have become largely unconstrained as a matter of law.... After *Booker*, some prosecutors have charged offenses carrying mandatory minimum penalties in order to narrow the sentencing court's discretion").

[77] *Id.* at 87 ("According to the Department of Justice, sentencing reforms in the 1980's, including the enactment and enhancement of many mandatory minimum penalties, helped reduce crime rates. Some prosecutors and police officers report that the certainty of punishment provided by mandatory minimum penalties is critical to law enforcement efforts. Furthermore, some scholars believe that the severity of mandatory minimum penalties increases their deterrent effect by raising the costs of committing crime to would-be offenders").

[78] *Id.* at 88 ("Congressman Asa Hutchinson argued that the strongest justification for mandatory minimum penalties is that they give society the means of expressing its outrage toward certain offenses that are so harmful to the public").

[79] *Id.* at 89 ("Many in the law enforcement community view mandatory minimum penalties as an important investigative tool. The threat of a mandatory minimum penalty gives law enforcement leverage over defendants.... [T]he Department of Justice views mandatory minimum penalties as an essential and critical tool in obtaining cooperation from members of violent street gangs and drug distribution networks").

[80] *Id.* (The Department of Justice contends "that because of the substantial concurrent state and federal jurisdiction in many drug and firearm cases, if a state sentence for one of these

crimes is inappropriately low, the existence of a substantially higher, federal mandatory minimum ensures a sentence that protects the public").

[81] *Id.* at 90-1 ("In the American Bar Association's view, treating unlike offenders identically is as much a blow to rational sentencing policy as is treating similar offenders differently. Many believe that mandatory minimum penalties result in arbitrary and disparate sentences because they rely on certain specified triggering facts to the exclusion of all others.... A majority of judges believe that mandatory minimum penalties contribute to sentencing disparity. In a 2010 Commission survey of United States District Judges on a range of sentencing issues, 52 percent of judges ranked mandatory minimum penalties among the top three factors contributing to sentencing disparity").

[82] *Id.* at 93-4 ("The Department of Justice has stated that there are real and significant excesses in terms of the imprisonment meted out for some offenders under existing mandatory sentencing laws, especially for some non-violent offenders. The Department of Justice explained that mandatory minimum sentencing statutes ... apply to a significant array of serious crimes; and they also, by and large, mandate very severe imprisonment terms. This, in turn, has produced exponential growth in the federal prison population ... and the federal Bureau of Prison[s'] overcapacity has real and detrimental consequences.... For this reason, the Department of Justice suggests some reforms of existing mandatory minimum sentencing statutes are needed ... to eliminate excessive severity in current statutory sentencing laws and to help address the unsustainable growth in the federal prison population").

[83] *Id.* at 95 ("[T]he Judicial Conference has long urged Congress to reconsider the wisdom of mandatory minimum penalties because they block judges from considering the individual circumstances of particular cases. Because mandatory minimum penalties may prevent a judge form considering all (or even most) of the pertinent facts and circumstances of the case (such as offender characteristics), the resulting sentence may be unfair or irrational").

[84] *Id.* at 96-7 ("Mandatory minimums effectively transfer sentencing authority from trial judge to federal prosecutions who may pre-set punishment through creative investigative and charging practices, producing troubling punishment differentials among offenders with similar culpability.... Justice Anthony Kennedy has observed that even though a prosecutor may act in good faith, the trial judge is the one actor in the system most experienced with exercising discretion in a transparent, open and reasoned way. In the Commission's 2010 survey of judges, 66 percent of respondents ranked charging decisions among the top three factors contributing to sentencing disparities").

[85] Id. at 98-9 ("Some scholars ... note that the research conducted by social scientists and public policy analysts has found little evidence to support the argument that mandatory minimums prevent crime.... The American Bar Association has raised a threshold question of whether inducing cooperation is a legitimate sentencing goal. Beyond that threshold question, many observe that the exchange of reduced sentences for information results in 'inverted sentencing,' in which offenders with valuable information – kingpins, organizers, and other highly culpable defendants – can avoid mandatory minimum penalties through charge-bargaining and substantial assistance motions while low- level offenders cannot because they lack such valuable information").

[86] *Id.* at 100 ("The late Chief Justice Rehnquist noted that mandatory minimum penalties fueled the trend toward federalizing crimes because law enforcement elects to pursue charges in federal rather than state courts because of the severe mandatory minimum penalties available under federal law").

[87] *Id.* at 101 ("Some express concerns that mandatory minimum penalties unfairly impact racial minorities and the economically disadvantaged. This may be attributable in part to the fact that the most frequently applied mandatory minimum penalties are for drug offenses, which according to some disproportionately impacts certain racial or ethnic groups").

[88] *United States v. Lopez*, 514 U.S. 549 (1995).

[89] U.S. Const. Amend. X.

[90] U.S. Const. Art. I, §8, cls.10, 17, 14, 3, and 18, respectively.

[91] U.S. Const. Art. I, §8, cl.18; see generally *United States v. Comstock*, 130 S.Ct. 1949 (2010).

[92] E.g., 18 U.S.C. 2241(a)("Whoever, in the special maritime and territorial jurisdiction of the United States ... knowing causes another person to engage in a sexual act – (1) by using force against that other person ... shall be ... imprisoned for any term of years or life ... ").

[93] E.g., 18 U.S.C. 2251(a), (e)("(a) Any person ... who transports any minor in or affecting interstate or foreign commerce ... with the intent that such minor engage in any sexually explicit conduct for the purpose of producing any visual depiction of such conduct.... (e) Any individual who violates ... this section shall be ... imprisoned not less than 15 years ... ").

[94] U.S. Const. Art. I, §8, cl. 3.

[95] *United States v. Lopez*, 514 U.S. 549, 558-59 (1995).

[96] *Id.* at 559.

[97] *Id.* at 561.

[98] *Id.*

[99] *Id.* at 563-64 ("The Government argues that possession of a firearm in a school zone may result in violent crime and that violent crime can be expected to affect the functioning of the national economy in two ways. First, the costs of violent crime are substantial, and, through the mechanism of insurance, those costs are spread throughout the population. Second, violent crime reduces the willingness of individuals to travel to areas within the country that are perceived to be unsafe. The Government also argues that the presence of guns in schools poses a substantial threat to the educational process by threatening the learning environment. A handicapped educational process, in turn, will result in a less productive citizenry. That, in turn, would have an adverse effect on the Nation's economic well-being.... Thus, if we were to accept the Government's arguments, we are hard pressed to posit any activity by an individual that Congress is without power to regulate "); *id.* at 567 ("To uphold the Government's contentions here, we would have to pile inference on inference in a manner that would bid fair to convert congressional authority under the Commerce Clause to a general police power of the sort retained by the States").

[100] *United States v. Morrison*, 529 U.S. 598, 671-18 (2000).

[101] 545 U.S. 1, 22 (2005)(internal citations omitted).

[102] U.S. Const. Art. I, §8, cl. 18.

[103] *McCulloch v. Maryland*, 4 Wheat. (17 U.S.) 316, 421 (1819).

[104] *Sabri v. United States*, 541 U.S. 600, 605 (2004)("*McCulloch v. Maryland* ... establish[es] review for means-ends rationality under the Necessary and Proper Clause").

[105] *United States v. Comstock*, 130 S.Ct. 1949 (2010).

[106] 18 U.S.C. 4248.

[107] *United States v. Comstock*, 130 S.Ct. at 1965.

[108] U.S. Const. Art. II, §2, c. 2.

[109] *E.g.*, SINGLE CONVENTION ON NARCOTIC DRUGS, Mar. 30, 1961, 18 U.S.T. 1407, 520 U.N.T.S. 204; CONVENTION ON PSYCHOTROPIC SUBSTANCES, Feb. 21, 1971, 32 U.S.T. 543, 1019 U.N.T.S. 175.

[110] U.S. Const. Art. I, §8, cl. 10.

[111] U.S. Const. Art. I, §8, cl. 17.

[112] U.S. Const. Art. III, §2; Art. I, §8, cl. 18.

[113] E.g., 18 U.S.C. 2241(c), 2242.

[114] The Eighth Amendment to the United States Constitution states in its entirety, "[e]xcessive bail shall not be required, nor excessive fines imposed, nor cruel and unusual punishments inflicted."

[115] *Woodson v. North Carolina*, 428 U.S. 280, 305-306 (1976); *see also*, *Miller v. Alabama*, 132 S.Ct. 2455, 2463 (2012).

[116] *Miller v. Alabama*, 132 S.Ct. at 2475 (2012).

[117] *Ewing v. California*, 538 U.S. 11, 31-2 (2003).

[118] In *Pervear* v. *Massachusetts*, 72 U.S. (5 Wall.) 475 (1866), the Court held that the clause applied to the federal government and not the states; the first substantive cruel and unusual punishment case apparently did not arrive before the Supreme Court until *Wilkerson* v. *Utah*, 99 U.S. 130 (1878), Mulligan, *Cruel and Unusual Punishment: The Proportionality Rule*, 47 FORDHAM LAW REVIEW 639, 642 (1979).

[119] *See, Wilkerson* v. *Utah*, 99 U.S. 130 (1878) (challenging execution of the death penalty by firing squad); *In re Kemmler*, 136 U.S. 436 (1889) (challenging execution of the death penalty by electrocution).

[120] 144 U.S. 323, 339-40 (1892) (Field, J.)(dissenting); *see also*, 144 U.S. at 371 (Harlan with Brewer, JJ.)(dissenting) ("The judgment before us by which the defendant is confined at hard labor ... for the term of ... fifty-four years ... inflicts punishment, which, in view of the character of the offences committed must be deemed cruel and unusual"). O'Neil, a mail order liquor dealer licensed in New York, was convicted for filling mail orders sent to Vermont where he had no license. The majority opinion disposed of the case on jurisdictional grounds and did not reach the Eighth Amendment question.

[121] 217 U.S. 349, 371 (1910). Weems was convicted of falsifying public documents for which he was sentenced to fifteen years' imprisonment and "accessories" which meant that while imprisoned he would "carry a chain at the ankle, hanging from the wrists, ... [would] be employed at hard and painful labor, and receive no assistance whatsoever from without the institution" and that after release he would forever continue under a form of civil death during which he could not vote or hold public office or receive a pension, could not hold or dispose of property, and would be subject to lifelong probation. 217 U.S. at 364. The Court pointed out that the sentence was more severe than might be imposed for some degrees of homicide, for misprision of treason, inciting rebellion, conspiracy to destroy the government, robbery, larceny, or forgery. 217 U.S. at 380. From the Court's perspective the legislation establishing the sentencing scheme had "no fellow in American legislation.... It is cruel in its excess of imprisonment and that which accompanies and follows imprisonment. It is unusual in its character. Its punishments come under the condemnation of the bill of rights, both on account of their degree and kind." 217 U.S. at 377.

[122] There are a few cases in the interim in which the Court may have applied the proportionality doctrine, sub silentio, because it found no infirmity in the sentences challenged, see e.g., *Graham* v. *West Virginia*, 224 U.S. 616 (1912); *Badders* v. *United States*, 240 U.S. 391 (1916). Statements in *Trop* that might be thought to confirm the doctrine's existence are dicta suggesting the Court's awareness, although not necessarily its endorsement, of the doctrine, *Trop* v. *Dulles*, 356 U.S. 86, 99-100 (1958) ("Since wartime desertion is punishable by death, there can be no argument that the penalty of denationalization is excessive in relation to the gravity of the crime.... Fines, imprisonment and even execution may be imposed depending upon the enormity of the crime.").

[123] 408 U.S. 238 (1972). In *Furman*, the Court found that the Eighth Amendment's cruel and unusual punishments clause, made binding upon the states by the due process clause of the Fourteenth Amendment, precluded imposition of the death penalty at the unguided discretion of the judge or jury.

[124] *Gregg v. Georgia*, 428 U.S. 153, 173 (1976).

[125] *Id.* at 187.

[126] 433 U.S. 583, 597 (1977).

[127] In *Enmund* v. *Florida*, 458 U.S. 782 (1982), the Court held that the death penalty was a disproportionate punishment for a felony murder in which the defendant neither killed nor intended to kill and whose culpability was limited to participation in the predicate felony. On the other hand, defendants who were major participants in the predicate felony and who acted with at least reckless indifference to the risk to human life thereby created might be sentenced to death without breaching the proportionality doctrine, *Tison* v. *Arizona*, 481 U.S. 137 (1982). In both instances, the Court examined the practices in other jurisdictions and the seriousness of the defendant's conduct.

[128] 445 U.S. 263 (1980).

[129] *Id.* at 272-74.

[130] *Id.* at 275. *See also, Hutto* v. *Davis*, 454 U.S. 370, 372-73 (1982), which summarized *Rummel* as follows: "Like the respondent in this case, Rummel argued that the length of his imprisonment was so 'grossly disproportionate' to the crime for which he was sentenced that it violated the ban on cruel and unusual punishment of the Eighth and Fourteenth Amendments. In rejecting that argument, we distinguished between punishments – such as the death penalty – which by their very nature differ from all other forms of conventionally accepted punishments, and punishments which differ from others only in duration. This distinction was based upon two factors. First, this 'Court's Eighth Amendment judgments should neither be nor appear to be merely the subjective views of individual Justices.' And second, the excessiveness of one prison term as compared to another is invariably a subjective determination, there being no clear way to make 'any constitutional distinction between one term of years and a shorter or longer term of years.' Thus, we concluded that 'one could argue without fear of contradiction by any decision of this Court that for crimes concededly classified and classifiable as felonies, ... the length of the sentence actually imposed is purely a matter of legislative prerogative.' Accordingly, we held that Rummel's life sentence did not violate the constitutional ban on cruel and unusual punishment."

[131] 463 U.S. 277 (1983).

[132] *Id.* at 292. Rummel with prior two nonviolent felony convictions was sentenced to life imprisonment for obtaining $120 under false pretenses. Helms, the *Solem* defendant with six prior nonviolent felony convictions was sentenced to life imprisonment for uttering a $100 "no account" check. The Court distinguished *Solem* from *Rummel* on at least two grounds. Solem was ineligible for parole, while Rummel enjoyed the advantage of a fairly liberal early release scheme; in *Solem* the life sentence without possibility of parole was imposed as a matter of judicial discretion, while the life sentence in *Rummel* was required as a matter of legislative policy, *id.* at 300-303.

[133] 428 U.S. 153 (1976).

[134] 428 U.S. 280, 305-306 (1976).

[135] *Id* at 288-301.

[136] *Id.* at 302.

[137] *Woodson's* rejection of mandatory capital punishment seemed to lose none of its force because two members of the five justice majority considered all capital punishment – discretionary or mandatory, guided or unguided – contrary to the demands of the Eighth Amendment. The two justices in question, Brennan and Marshall, subsequently joined in a majority opinion holding a Nevada mandatory death penalty statute unconstitutional for failure to adhere to the individualized capital sentencing doctrine, *Sumner* v. *Shuman*, 483 U.S. 66 (1987).

[138] *See e.g., Roberts* v. *Louisiana*, 431 U.S. 633 (1977); *Lockett* v. *Ohio*, 438 U.S. 586 (1978); *Eddings* v. *Oklahoma*, 455 U.S. 104 (1982); *Skipper* v. *South Carolina*, 477 U.S. 1 (1986); *Hitchcock* v. *Dugger*, 481 U.S. 393 (1987); *Sumner* v. *Shuman*, 483 U.S. 66 (1987).

[139] "The futility of attempting to solve the problems of mandatory death penalty statutes by narrowing the scope of the capital offense stems from our society's rejection of the belief that every offense in a like legal category calls for an identical punishment without regard to the past life and habits of a particular offender," *Roberts* v. *Louisiana*, 428 U.S. at 333; *Sumner* v. *Shuman*, 483 U.S. at 75 n.3.

[140] "We recognize that, in noncapital cases, the established practice of individualized sentences rests not on constitutional commands, but on public policy enacted into statutes," *Lockett* v. *Ohio*, 438 U.S. at 604-605.

[141] 501 U.S. 957 (1991).

[142] *Id.* at 995, quoting *Furman v. Georgia*, 408 U.S. at 306 (Stewart, J.)(concurring).

[143] *Id.* at 995 (citations omitted).

[144] *Id.* at 994.

[145] *Id.* 501 U.S. at 1004.

[146] *Id.* at 1001. Four principles dictate a high proportionality threshold for a plurality of the Court: "The first ... is that the fixing of prison terms for specific crimes involves a substantive penological judgment that, as a general matter, is properly within the province of legislatures, not courts.... The efficacy of any sentencing system cannot be assessed absent agreement on the purposes and objectives of the penal system. And the responsibility for making these fundamental choices and implementing them lies with the legislature.... "The second principle is that the Eighth Amendment does not mandate adoption of any one penological theory. The principles which have guided criminal sentencing ... have varied with the times. The federal and state criminal systems have accorded different weights at different times to the penological goals of retribution, deterrence, incapacitation, and rehabilitation. And competing theories of mandatory and discretionary sentencing have been in varying degrees of ascendancy or decline since the beginning of the Republic. "Third, marked divergences both in underlying theories of sentencing and in the length of prescribed prison terms are the inevitable, often beneficial, result of the federal structure.... State sentencing schemes may embody different penological assumptions, making interstate comparison of sentences a difficult and imperfect enterprise. And even assuming identical philosophies, differing attitudes and perceptions of local conditions may yield different, yet rational, conclusions regarding the appropriate length of prison terms for particular crimes. Thus, the circumstance that a State has the most severe punishment for a particular crime does not by itself render the punishment grossly disproportionate ... Absent a constitutionally imposed uniformity inimical to traditional notions of federalism, some State will always bear the distinction of treating particular offenders more severely than any other State. "The fourth principle ... is that proportionality review by federal courts should be informed by objective factors to the maximum possible extent.... [O]ur decisions recognize that we lack clear objective standards to distinguish between sentences for different terms of years.... Although no penalty is per se constitutional, the relative lack of objective standards concerning terms of imprisonment has meant that outside the context of capital punishment, successful challenges to the proportionality of particular sentences are exceedingly rare," 501 U.S. at 998-1001 (citations omitted).

[147] *Id.* at 1003.

[148] "It is beyond question that the legislature 'has the power to define criminal punishments without giving the courts any sentencing discretion,' *Chapman v. United States*, [500 U.S. 453, 467 (1991)]. Since the beginning of the Republic, Congress and the States have enacted mandatory sentencing schemes. To set aside petitioner's mandatory sentence would require rejection not of the judgment of a single jurist, as in *Solem*, but rather the collective wisdom of the Michigan Legislature and, as a consequence, the Michigan citizenry. We have never invalidated a penalty mandated by a legislature based only on the length of sentence, and, especially with a crime as severe as this one, we should do so only in the most extreme circumstance. "In asserting the constitutionality of this mandatory sentence, I offer no judgment on its wisdom. Mandatory sentencing schemes can be criticized for depriving judges of the power to exercise individual discretion when remorse and acknowledgment of guilt, or other extenuating facts, present what might seem a compelling case for departure from the maximum. On the other hand, broad and unreviewed discretion exercised by sentencing judges leads to the perception that no clear standards are being applied, and that the rule of law is imperiled by sentences imposed for no discernible reason other than the subjective reactions of the sentencing judge. The debate illustrates that, as noted at the outset, arguments for and against particular sentencing schemes are for legislatures to resolve," 501 U.S. at 1006-1007.

[149] 524 U.S. 321 (1998).

[150] *Id.* at 338-40.

[151] 538 U.S. 11 (2003). Ewing was sentenced to life imprisonment, but would be eligible for parole after serving 25 years, *id.* at 16, 20. His case came to the court directly from the

California appellate courts. At the same time but without reaching the merits, the Court disposed of another California three strikes case that reached it by way of habeas review from the Ninth Circuit, *Lockyer v. Andrade*, 538 U.S. 63 (2003). The habeas statute binds the federal courts to any state court interpretation of a constitutional issue unless the decision of the state courts was "contrary to, or involved an unreasonable application of, clearly established federal law, as determined by the Supreme Court of the United States," 28 U.S.C. 2254(d)(1). Relying on *Rummel*, the California courts had rejected Andrade's Eighth Amendment challenge of his sentence under the three strikes law. In doing so, a majority of the Court concluded that the California appellate decision foreclosed federal habeas review, since the California decision was neither contrary to the Court's Eighth Amendment jurisprudence nor unreasonably applied it, 538 U.S. at 74-7.

[152] *Id.* at 16-7.

[153] *Id.* at 20.

[154] *Id.* 31-2 (Scalia, J. concurring in the judgment); *id.* at 32 (Thomas, J. concurring in the judgment).

[155] *Id.* at 20.

[156] *Id.* at 28.

[157] *Id.* at 29. Prior to his three strike triggering conviction for stealing the golf clubs, Ewing had been convicted of: theft in 1984, grand theft auto in 1988, petty theft in 1990, battery in 1992, burglary in January of 1993, possession of drug paraphernalia in February of 1993, appropriating lost property in July of 1993, trespassing and unlawful possession of a firearm in September of 1993, robbery and three counts of burglary in December of 1993, *id.* at 18-9. The four dissenting Justices found the proportionality standard applicable and would have found Ewing's sentence grossly disproportionate to the gravity of his offense consequently in violation of the Eight Amendment, *id.* at 32 (Breyer, J, with Stevens, Souter, and Ginsburg, dissenting).

[158] *Id.* at 30-1.

[159] 536 U.S. 304, 321 (2002).

[160] *Id.* at 314-15.

[161] *Id.* at 315-16

[162] *Id.* at 321 ("Construing and applying the Eighth Amendment in the light of our 'evolving standards of decency,' we therefore conclude that such punishment is excessive and that the Constitution 'places a substantial restriction on the State's power to take the life' of a mentally retarded offender").

[163] 543 U.S. 551, 564-78.

[164] 130 S.Ct. 2011, 2021 (2010).

[165] *Id.*

[166] *Id.* at 2022.

[167] *Id.*

168 Id.

[169] 132 S.Ct. 2455 (2012).

[170] *Id.* at 2461-462.

[171] *Id.* at 2476.

[172] *Id.* at 2466.

[173] *Id.* (internal citations and quotation marks omitted).

[174] U.S.Const. Amends. V, VI.

[175] 397 U.S. 358, 364 (1970).

[176] 42 Pa.Cons.Stat. 9712 (1982), reprinted in *McMillan v. Pennsylvania*, 477 U.S. 79, 81-2 n.1 (1986).

[177] The right to grand jury indictment was not implicated since the Sixth Amendment right to grand jury indictment applies only to federal prosecutions, *Alexander v. Louisiana*, 405 U.S. 625, 633 (1972).

[178] *McMillan v. Pennsylvania*, 477 U.S. 79 (1986).

[179] *Id.* at 84, 93.

[180] *Almendarez-Torres v. United States*, 523 U.S. 224, 247 (1998).

[181] 530 U.S. 466, 476 (2000)(emphasis added).

[182] "Thus, the Court appears to hold that any fact that increases or alters the range of penalties to which a defendant is exposed – which, by definition, must include increases or alterations to either the minimum or maximum penalties – must be proved to a jury beyond a reasonable doubt. In *McMillan*, however, we rejected such a rule to the extent it concerned those facts that increase or alter the minimum penalty to which a defendant is exposed. Accordingly, it is incumbent on the Court not only to admit that it is overruling *McMillan*, but also to explain why such a course of action is appropriate under normal principles of *stare decisis*," 530 U.S. at 533 (O'Connor, with Kennedy, Breyer, JJ., Rehnquist, Ch.J., dissenting).

"[T]his traditional understanding – that a crime includes every fact that is by law a basis for imposing or increasing punishment – continued well into the 20th century, at least until the middle of the century.... I think it clear that the common-law rule would cover the *McMillan* situation of a mandatory minimum sentence.... [A defendant's] expected punishment has increased as a result of the narrowed range and that the prosecution is empowered, by invoking the mandatory minimum, to require the judge to impose a higher punishment than he might wish. The mandatory minimum entitles the government to more than it would otherwise be entitled.... Thus, the fact triggering the mandatory minimum is part of the punishment sought to be inflicted; it undoubtedly enters into the punishment so as to aggravate it, and is an act to which the law affixes punishment. Further ... it is likely that the change in the range available to the judge affects his choice of sentences. Finally, in numerous cases ... the aggravating fact raised the whole range – both the top and bottom. Those courts, in holding that such a fact was an element, did not bother with any distinction between changes in the maximum and the minimum. What mattered was simply the overall increase in the punishment provided by law," 530 U.S. at 518, 521-22 (Thomas, J., concurring); *see also, Rethinking Mandatory Minimums After Apprendi*, 96 NORTHWESTERN UNIVERSITY LAW REVIEW 811 (2002); Levine, *The Confounding Boundaries of "Apprendi-land": Statutory Minimums and the Federal Sentencing* Guidelines, 29 AMERICAN JOURNAL OF CRIMINAL LAW 377 (2002).

[183] *Harris v. United States*, 536 U.S. 545, 568 (2002)("Reaffirming *McMillan* and employing the approach outlined in that case, we conclude that the federal provision at issue, 18 U.S.C. §924(c)(1)(A) (ii), is constitutional. Basing a 2-year increase in the defendant's minimum sentence on a judicial finding of brandishing does not evade the requirements of the Fifth and Sixth Amendments. Congress 'simply took one factor that has always been considered by sentencing courts to bear on punishment ... and dictated the precise weight to be given that factor.' *McMillan*, 477 U.S. at 89-90. That factor need not be alleged in the indictment, submitted to the jury, or proved beyond a reasonable doubt").

Of course, *Harris* was not meant to serve as either an endorsement or condemnation of mandatory minimum sentencing as such: "The Court is well aware that many question the wisdom of mandatory minimum sentencing. Mandatory minimums, it is often said, fail to account for the unique circumstances of offenders who warrant a lesser penalty. These criticisms may be sound, but they would persist whether the judge or the jury found the facts given rise to the minimum," 530 U.S. at 568. *See also*, 530 U.S. at 570-71 (Breyer, J., concurring in part and concurring in the judgment): "I do not mean to suggest my approval of mandatory minimum sentences as a matter of policy. During the past two decades, as mandatory minimum sentencing statutes have proliferated in number and importance, judges, legislators, lawyers, and commentators have criticized those statutes, arguing that they negatively affect the fair administration of the criminal law, a matter concern to judge sand to legislators alike."

"Mandatory minimum statutes are fundamentally inconsistent with Congress' simultaneous effort to create a fair, honest, and rational sentencing system through the use of Sentencing Guidelines. Unlike Guideline sentences, statutory mandatory minimums generally deny the judge the legal power to depart downward, no matter how unusual the special circumstances that call for leniency. They rarely reflect an effort to achieve sentencing proportionality – a key element of sentencing fairness that demands that the law punish a drug 'kingpin' and a 'mule' differently. They transfer sentencing power to prosecutors, who can determine sentences through the charges they decide to bring, and who thereby have reintroduced much of the sentencing disparity that Congress created Guidelines to eliminate. They rarely are based upon empirical study. And there is evidence that they encourage subterfuge leading to more frequent downward departures (on a random basis), thereby making them comparatively ineffective means of guaranteeing tough sentences."

[184] 133 S.Ct. 2151 (2013).

[185] 18 U.S.C. 924(c).

[186] 133 S.Ct. at 2156.

[187] *Id.* at 2155 (internal citations and quotation marks omitted).

[188] *Loving v. United States*, 517 U.S. 748, 757 (1996).

[189] *United States v. Chapman*, 500 U.S. 453, 467 (1991).

[190] *United States v. Kaluna*, 192 F.3d 1188, 1199 (9th Cir. 1999); *United States v. Rasco*, 123 F.3d 222, 226-27 (5th Cir. 1997); *United States v. Washington*, 109 F.3d 335, 338 (7th Cir. 1997); *United States v. Prior*, 107 F.3d 654, 660 (8th Cir. 1997).

[191] *Mistretta v. United States*, 488 U.S. 361 (1989). Mistretta, sentenced under the guidelines to 18 months' imprisonment for conspiracy to distribute cocaine, argued that the guidelines constituted an unconstitutional delegation of Congress's legislative authority and that the service of judges upon the Commission constituted extrajudicial service at odds with the separation of powers doctrine. The Court rejected both arguments concluding "that in creating the Sentencing Commission ... Congress neither delegated excessive legislative power nor upset the constitutionally mandated balance of powers among the coordinate Branches," 488 U.S. at 412.

[192] Codified at 21 U.S.C. 801 to 904, and 21 U.S. 951 to 971, respectively. Schedule I and II are reserved for substances with a high potential for abuse, 21 U.S.C. 812(b)(1), (2). The Maritime Drug Law Enforcement Act applies the prohibitions and mandatory minimums of the Controlled Substances and Controlled Substances Import and Export Act in certain maritime situations, 46 U.S.C. 70501 to 70508.

[193] 21 U.S.C. 841(b)(1); 21 U.S.C. 960(b)(1).

[194] 21 U.S.C. 841(b)(1)(A), (B); 21 U.S.C. 960(b)(1), (2).

[195] *Id.*

[196] *Id.*

[197] 21 U.S.C. 846, 963.

[198] 21 U.S.C. 841(b)(1)(B)(i)("100 grams or more of a mixture or substance containing a detectable amount of heroin") (10 grams = .35 ounces; 1 kilogram (1,000 grams) = 2.2 lbs.). 21 U.S.C. 841(b) and 960(b) use the same thresholds.

[199] 21 U.S.C. 841(b)(1)(B)(ii)("500 grams or more of a mixture or substance containing a detectable amount of- (I) coca leaves, except coca leaves and extracts of coca leaves from which cocaine, ecgonine, and derivatives of ecgonine or their salts have been removed; (II) cocaine, its salts, optical and geometric isomers, and salts of isomers; (III) ecgonine, its derivatives, their salts, isomers, and salts of isomers; or (IV) any compound, mixture, or preparation which contains any quantity of any of the substances referred to in subclauses (I) through (III)").

[200] 21 U.S.C. 841(b)(1)(B)(iii)("28 grams or more of a mixture or substance described in clause (ii) which contains cocaine base").

[201] 21 U.S.C. 841(b)(1)(B)(iv)("10 grams or more of phencyclidine (PCP) or 100 grams or more of a mixture or substance containing a detectable amount of phencyclidine (PCP)").

[202] 21 U.S.C. 841(b)(1)(B)(v)("1 gram or more of a mixture or substance containing a detectable amount of lysergic acid diethylamide (LSD)").

[203] 21 U.S.C. 841(b)(1)(B)(vi)("40 grams or more of a mixture or substance containing a detectable amount of N- phenyl-N- [1- (2-phenylethyl) -4-piperidinyl] propanamide or 10 grams or more of a mixture or substance containing a detectable amount of any analogue of N-phenyl-N-[1-(2-phenylethyl)-4-piperidinyl] propanamide").

[204] 21 U.S.C. 841(b)(1)(B)(viii)("5 grams or more of methamphetamine, its salts, isomers, and salts of its isomers or 50 grams or more of a mixture or substance containing a detectable amount of methamphetamine, its salts, isomers, or salts of its isomers").

[205] 21 U.S.C. 841(b)(1)(B)(vii)("100 kilograms or more of a mixture or substance containing a detectable amount of marihuana, or 100 or more marihuana plants regardless of weight").

[206] 21 U.S.C. 841(b)(1)(A)(i)("1 kilogram grams or more of a mixture or substance containing a detectable amount of heroin") (10 grams = .35 ounces; 1 kilogram (1,000 grams) = 2.2 lbs.). 21 U.S.C. 841(b) and 960(b) use the same thresholds.

[207] 21 U.S.C. 841(b)(1)(A)(ii)("5 kilograms or more of a mixture or substance containing a detectable amount of- (I) coca leaves, except coca leaves and extracts of coca leaves from which cocaine, ecgonine, and derivatives of ecgonine or their salts have been removed; (II) cocaine, its salts, optical and geometric isomers, and salts of isomers; (III) ecgonine, its derivatives, their salts, isomers, and salts of isomers; or (IV) any compound, mixture, or preparation which contains any quantity of any of the substances referred to in subclauses (I) through (III)").

[208] 21 U.S.C. 841(b)(1)(A)(iii)("280 grams or more of a mixture or substance described in clause (ii) which contains cocaine base").

[209] 21 U.S.C. 841(b)(1)(A)(iv)("100 grams or more of phencyclidine (PCP) or 1 kilogram grams or more of a mixture or substance containing a detectable amount of phencyclidine (PCP)").

[210] 21 U.S.C. 841(b)(1)(A)(v)("10 grams or more of a mixture or substance containing a detectable amount of lysergic acid diethylamide (LSD)").

[211] 21 U.S.C. 841(b)(1)(A)(vi)("400 grams or more of a mixture or substance containing a detectable amount of N- phenyl-N- [1- (2-phenylethyl) -4-piperidinyl] propanamide or 10 grams or more of a mixture or substance containing a detectable amount of any analogue of N-phenyl-N-[1-(2-phenylethyl)-4-piperidinyl] propanamide").

[212] 21 U.S.C. 841(b)(1)(A)(viii)("50 grams or more of methamphetamine, its salts, isomers, and salts of its isomers or 500 grams or more of a mixture or substance containing a detectable amount of methamphetamine, its salts, isomers, or salts of its isomers").

[213] 21 U.S.C. 841(b)(1)(A)(vii)("1000 kilograms or more of a mixture or substance containing a detectable amount of marihuana, or 1000 or more marihuana plants regardless of weight").

[214] 21 U.S.C. 841(b)(1)(C)("In the case of a controlled substance in schedule I or II, gamma hydroxybutyric acid (including when scheduled as an approved drug product for purposes of section 3(a)(1)(B) of the Hillory J. Farias and Samantha Reid Date-Rape Drug Prohibition Act of 2000), or 1 gram of flunitrazepam, except as provided in subparagraphs (A), (B), and (D), such person ... if death or serious bodily injury results from the use of such substance shall be sentenced to a term of imprisonment of not less than twenty years or more than life, a fine not to exceed the greater of that authorized in accordance with the provisions of title 18 or $1,000,000 if the defendant is an individual or $5,000,000 if the defendant is other than an individual, or both. If any person commits such a violation after a prior conviction for a felony drug offense has become final, such person shall be sentenced to a term of imprisonment of not more than 30 years and if death or serious bodily injury results from the use of such substance shall be sentenced to life imprisonment, a fine not to exceed the greater of twice that authorized in accordance with the provisions of title 18 or $2,000,000 if the defendant is an individual or $10,000,000 if the defendant is other than an individual, or both ... ").

[215] 21 U.S.C. 848(c)("For purposes of subsection (a) of this section, a person is engaged in a continuing criminal enterprise if - (1) he violates any provision of this subchapter or subchapter II of this chapter the punishment for which is a felony, and (2) such violation is a part of a continuing series of violations of this subchapter or subchapter II of this chapter -

(A) which are undertaken by such person in concert with five or more other persons with respect to whom such person occupies a position of organizer, a supervisory position, or any other position of management, and (B) from which such person obtains substantial income or resources").

216 21 U.S.C. 848(a).

217 21 U.S.C. 848(e)(1)("In addition to the other penalties set forth in this section- (A) any person engaging in or working in furtherance of a continuing criminal enterprise, or any person engaging in an offense punishable under section 841(b)(1)(A) or section 960(b)(1) of this title who intentionally kills or counsels, commands, induces, procures, or causes the intentional killing of an individual and such killing results, shall be sentenced to any term of imprisonment, which shall not be less than 20 years, and which may be up to life imprisonment, or may be sentenced to death; and (B) any person, during the commission of, in furtherance of, or while attempting to avoid apprehension, prosecution or service of a prison sentence for, a felony violation of this subchapter or subchapter II of this chapter who intentionally kills or counsels, commands, induces, procures, or causes the intentional killing of any Federal, State, or local law enforcement officer engaged in, or on account of, the performance of such officer's official duties and such killing results, shall be sentenced to any term of imprisonment, which shall not be less than 20 years, and which may be up to life imprisonment, or may be sentenced to death").

218 21 U.S.C. 848(b), (s)("Any person who engages in a continuing criminal enterprise shall be imprisoned for life ... if - (1) such person is the principal administrator, organizer, or leader of the enterprise or is one of several such principal administrators, organizers, or leaders; and (2)(A) the violation referred to in subsection (c)(1) of this section involved at least 300 times the quantity of a substance described in subsection 841(b)(1)(B) of this title [or at least 200 times the quantity of methamphetamine described in that section] or (B) the enterprise, or any other enterprise in which the defendant was the principal or one of several principal administrators, organizers, or leaders, received $10 million dollars in gross receipts [or $5 million in the case of methamphetamine trafficking] during any twelve-month period of its existence for the manufacture, importation, or distribution of a substance described in section 841(b)(1)(B) of this title").

219 21 U.S.C. 960a ("Whoever engages in conduct that would be punishable under section 841(a) of this title if committed within the jurisdiction of the United States, or attempts or conspires to do so, knowing or intending to provide, directly or indirectly, anything of pecuniary value to any person or organization that has engaged or engages in terrorist activity ... or terrorism ... shall be sentenced to a term of imprisonment of not less than twice the minimum punishment under section 841(b)(1), and not more than life, a fine in accordance with the provisions of title 18, or both").

220 21 U.S.C. 844(a)(".... Any person who violates this subsection may be sentenced to a term of imprisonment of not more than 1 year, and shall be fined a minimum of $1,000, or both, except that if he commits such offense after a prior conviction under this subchapter or subchapter II of this chapter, or a prior conviction for any drug, narcotic, or chemical offense chargeable under the law of any State, has become final, he shall be sentenced to a term of imprisonment for not less than 15 days but not more than 2 years, and shall be fined a minimum of $2,500, except, further, that if he commits such offense after two or more prior convictions under this subchapter or subchapter II of this chapter, or two or more prior convictions for any drug, narcotic, or chemical offense chargeable under the law of any State, or a combination of two or more such offenses have become final, he shall be sentenced to a term of imprisonment for not less than 90 days but not more than 3 years, and shall be fined a minimum of $5,000 ... ").

221 21 U.S.C. 861(f), (b), (c).

222 21 U.S.C. 859. The same is true using children to traffic, 21 U.S.C. 861(a), (b), (c).

223 21 U.S.C. 860 ("(a) Any person who violates section 841(a)(1) of this title ... by distributing, possessing with intent to distribute, or manufacturing a controlled substance in or on, or

within one thousand feet of, the real property comprising a public or private elementary, vocational, or secondary school or a public or private college, junior college, or university, or a playground, or housing facility owned by a public housing authority, or within 100 feet of a public or private youth center, public swimming pool, or video arcade facility, is (except as provided in subsection (b) of this section) subject to.... Except to the extent a greater minimum sentence is otherwise provided by section 841(b) of this title, a person shall be sentenced under this subsection to a term of imprisonment of not less than one year. The mandatory minimum sentencing provisions of this paragraph shall not apply to offenses involving 5 grams or less of marihuana. (b) Any person who violates section 841(a)(1) of this title by distributing, possessing with intent to distribute, or manufacturing a controlled substance in or on, or within one thousand feet of, ... or within 100 feet of a public or private youth center, public swimming pool, or video arcade facility, after a prior conviction under subsection (a) of this section has become final is punishable.... Except to the extent a greater minimum sentence is otherwise provided by section 841(b) of this title, a person shall be sentenced under this subsection to a term of imprisonment of not less than three years ... ").

[224] *United States v. Capers*, 708 F.3d 1286, 1297 (11th Cir. 2013); *United States v. Mancuso*, 718 F.3d 780, 791 (9th Cir. 2013); *United States v. Tovar*, 719 F.3d 376, 389 (5th Cir. 2013).

[225] *United States v. Sanders*, 668 F.3d 1298, (11th Cir. 2012)("Although [for the mandatory minimums to apply] the jury must determine the quantity and type of drug involved, nothing in the statute, the Constitution, or Apprendi requires the government to prove that the defendant had knowledge of the particular drug type or quantity for which a sentence is enhanced under §841(b)"); see also, *McPhearson v. United States*, 675 F.3d 553, 561 (6th Cir. 2012); *United States v. Betancourt*, 586 F.3d 303, 308 (5th Cir. 2009); *United States v. Branham* , 515 F.3d 1268, 1275-276 (D.C.Cir. 2008).

[226] *United States v. Tovar*, 719 F.3d 376, 388 (5th Cir. 2013); *United States v. Duenas*, 691 F.3d 1070 (9th Cir. 2012); *United States v. Thompson*, 686 F.3d 575, 583 (8th Cir. 2012).

[227] *United States v. Berry*, 717 F.3d 823, 830 n.3 (10th Cir. 2013); *see also, United States v. Bagby*, 696 F.3d 1074, 1081 (10th Cir. 2012)("Dominion or control may be exercised personally or through others who have an adequate tie to the defendant"); *United States v. Duenas*, 691 F.3d at 1084 (internal citations and quotations marks omitted)("An individual constructive possesses drugs when he or she exercises dominion and control over them. Constructive possession may be established by direct or circumstantial evidence that the defendant had the power to dispose of the drug, the ability to produce the drug, or that the defendant had the exclusive control or dominion over property on which contraband narcotics are found. It may also be demonstrated by a defendant's participation in a joint venture by which he shares authority with others to exercise dominion and control over the drug").

[228] *United States v. Capers*, 708 F.3d at 1301; *United States v. Finch*, 630 F.3d 1057, 1061 (8th Cir. 2011) ("Circumstantial evidence such as drug quantity, packaging material, and the presence of cash may be used to establish intent to distribute.... This Court has set forth factors from which an intent to distribute a controlled substance may be inferred. Most significant is the presence of a firearm").

[229] *United States v. Cortes-Caban*, 691 F.3d 1, 23-4 (1st Cir. 2012)(holding that corrupt police officers who planted drugs on a suspect evidenced an intent to distribute).

[230] *Burgess, v. United States*, 553 U.S. 124, 126 (2008).

[231] *United States v. Dyke*, 718 F.3d 1282, 1292 (10th Cir. 2013).

[232] 21 U.S.C. 851.

[233] *United States v, Isaac*, 655 F.3d 148, 155-57 (3d Cir. 2011)(citing cases on either side of the divide).

[234] *Commission Report II*, 356 ("Congress should mitigate the cumulative impact of criminal history by reassessing both the scope and severity of the recidivist provisions at 21 U.S.C. §§841 and 960. The mandatory minimum penalties provided in those provisions are double

(from five to ten years of imprisonment, and from ten to 20 years of imprisonment) if the offender has a prior conviction for a 'felony drug offense.' An offender with two or more prior drug felonies is subject to a mandatory minimum term of life imprisonment. This doubling of the mandatory minimum penalties, and the mandatory minimum term of life imprisonment, are sometimes viewed as disproportionate and excessively severe in individual cases and far exceed the more graduated, proportional increases provided by the guidelines for such prior conduct").

[235] Id. ("In addition, Congress should more finely tailor their scope to reduce inconsistent application of these provisions. This could be accomplished by amending the current definition of 'felony drug offenses' that triggers the heightened mandatory minimum penalties. Among other possible changes, Congress might consider incorporating the particular state's classification of an offense as a 'felony' or 'misdemeanor' to better reflect the state's judgment concerning the serious of the prior offense, or by excluding simple possession offenses form the definition of 'prior drug offense'").

[236] 21 U.S.C. 856, 963.

[237] *Id.*

[238] 18 U.S.C. 2.

[239] *United States v. Stallworth*, 656 F.3d 721, 728 (7th Cir. 2011); *United States v. Hunt*, 656 F.3d 906, 912 (9th Cir. 2011).

[240] *United States v. Johnson*, 719 F.3d 660, 666 (8th Cir. 2013); *United States v. Tavera*, 719 F.3d 705, 713 (6th Cir. 2013)("Where drugs are involved, the government must show an agreement to violate drug laws, intent to join the conspiracy, and participation in the conspiracy"); *United States v. Capers*, 708 F.3d 1286, 1299 (11th Cir. 2013).

[241] *United States v. Johnson*, 719 F.3d at 666; *United States v. Duenas*, 691 F.3d 1070, 1085 (9th Cir. 2012); *United States v. Lee*, 687 F.3d 935, 943 (8th Cir. 2012).

[242] *United States v. Johnson*, 719 F.3d at 666; *United States v. Lee*, 687 F.3d at 943; *United States v. Vasquez*, 677 F.3d 685, 963-64 (5th Cir. 2012).

[243] *United States v. Capers*, 708 F.3d 1286, 1306 (11th Cir. 2013) *United States v. Vasquez*, 677 F.3d at 695.

[244] *United States v. Lee*, 687 F.3d 935, 940 (8th Cir. 2012); *see also*, *United States v. Isaac*, 655 F.3d 148, 154 (3d Cir. 2011); *United States v. Moore*, 651 F.3d 20, 80 (D.C.Cir. 2011).

[245] 21 U.S.C. 848(e); *United States v. Hager*, 721 F.3d 167, 179-80 (4th Cir. 2013), citing, *United States v. Aguilar*, 585 F.3d 652, 657 (2d Cir. 2009)(internal citations and quotation marks omitted)("There are three prongs to this statue. The first prong covers those who intentionally kill someone while engaged in a CCE. The second prong concerns the one who intentionally kills another while working in furtherance of a CCE. And, the third prong envelops that person who intentionally kills another while engaged in an offense punishable under section 841(b)(1)(A) ... or section 960(b)(1)"). *Hager* and *Aguilar* describe 21 U.S.C. 848(e)(1)(A). Section 848(e)(1)(B) establishes the same 20 year mandatory minimum for a killing of a police officer in the line of duty when committed in furtherance or to avoid punishment for any violation of the Controlled Substances or Controlled Substances Import and Export Acts.

[246] H.Rept. 103-460, at 4 (1994); *United States v. Carillo-Ayala*, 713 F.3d 82, 88 (11th Cir. 2013).

[247] 18 U.S.C. 3553(f)("Notwithstanding any other provision of law, in the case of an offense under section 401, 404, or 406 of the Controlled Substances Act (21 U.S.C. 841, 844, 846) or section 1010 or 1013 of the Controlled Substances Import and Export Act (21 U.S.C. 960, 963), the court shall impose a sentence pursuant to guidelines promulgated by the United States Sentencing Commission under section 994 of title 28 without regard to any statutory minimum sentence, if the court finds at sentencing.... ").

[248] *United States v. Phillips*, 382 F.3d 489, 499-500 (5th Cir. 2004); *United States v. Koons*, 300 F.3d 985, 993 (8th Cir. 2002); *United States v. Kakatin*, 214 F.3d 1049, 1050-51 (9th Cir. 2000); *United States v. Anderson*, 200 F.3d 1344, 1346-348 (11th Cir. 2000); *United States v. McQuilkin*, 78 F.3d 105, 108 (3d Cir. 1996). One Commission witness indicated that "in

districts where substantial portions of towns and cities fall within protected zones, prosecutors can, and some do, charge violations of 21 U.S.C. §860 for the purpose of preventing safety valve relief for offenders who would otherwise qualify," *Hearings, Statement of Michael Nachmanoff, Federal Public Defender for E.D. Va.* at 31.

[249] *United States v. Gamboa-Cardenas*, 508 F.3d 491, 496-503 (9th Cir. 2007).

[250] *United States v. Foote*, 705 F.3d 305, 306 (8th Cir. 2013); *United States v. Rodriguez*, 676 F.3d 183, 191 (D.C.Cir. 2012); *United States v. Aidoo*, 670 F.3d 600, 606-607 (4th Cir. 2012); *United States v. Pena*, 598 F.3d 289, 292 (6th Cir. 2010); *United States v. Larios*, 593 F.3d 82, 89 (1st Cir. 2010); *United States v. Altamirano-Quintero*, 511 F.3d 1087, 1098 (10th Cir. 2007); *United States v. Olivas-Ramirez*, 487 F.3d 512, 516-17(7th Cir. 2007); *United States v. Mejia- Pimental*, 477 F.3d 1100, 1104 (9th Cir. 2007).

[251] 18 U.S.C. 3553(f)(1)("the defendant does not have more than 1 criminal history point, as determined under the sentencing guidelines").

[252] 18 U.S.C. 3553(f)(2)("the defendant did not use violence or credible threats of violence or possess a firearm or other dangerous weapon (or induce another participant to do so) in connection with the offense").

[253] 18 U.S.C. 3553(f)(4)("the defendant was not an organizer, leader, manager, or supervisor of others in the offense, as determined under the sentencing guidelines and was not engaged in a continuing criminal enterprise, as defined in section 408 of the Controlled Substances Act").

[254] 18 U.S.C. 3553(f)(5)("not later than the time of the sentencing hearing, the defendant has truthfully provided to the Government all information and evidence the defendant has concerning the offense or offenses that were part of the same course of conduct or of a common scheme or plan, but the fact that the defendant has no relevant or useful other information to provide or that the Government is already aware of the information shall not preclude a determination by the court that the defendant has complied with this requirement").

[255] 18 U.S.C. 3553(f)(3)("the offense did not result in death or serious bodily injury to any person").

[256] U.S.S.G. §§4A1.1(a), (b), (d); 4A1.2(d). *United States v. Yepez*, 704 F.3d 1087, 1089-90 (9th Cir. 2012)(a federal crime committed while the offender is on state probation is no less so because a state court subsequently terminates the probationary term as of the time it was originally ordered (i.e., before the federal crime was committed)).

[257] U.S.C.G. §§4A1.1(c); 4A1.2.

[258] U.S.S.G. §4A1.2(h).

[259] U.S.S.G. §4A1.2(i).

[260] U.S.S.G. §4A1.2(g). Sentences imposed by general and special courts martial are counted, *id.*

[261] U.S.S.G. §§4A1.2(j); 4A1.2, cmt. n.6.

[262] U.S.S.G. §4A1.2(c).

[263] The full list includes: "fish and game violations, hitchhiking, juvenile status offenses and truancy, local ordinance violations (except those violations that are also violations under state criminal law), loitering, minor traffic infractions (e.g., speeding), public intoxication, [and] vagrancy," U.S.S.G. §4A1.2(c)(2).

[264] Again, the full list consists of: "careless or reckless driving, contempt of court, disorderly conduct or disturbing the peace, driving without a license or with a revoked or suspended license, false information to a police officer, gambling, hindering or failure to obey a police officer, insufficient funds check, leaving the scene of an accident, non-support, prostitution, resisting arrest, [and] trespassing," U.S.S.G. §4A1.2(c)(1).

[265] U.S.S.G. §4A1.2(c)(1), (c)(2). The Sentencing Guidelines suggest a number of factors to assist in the determination of whether an unlisted offense may be consider "similar" for purposes of section 4A1.2(c): " (i) a comparison of punishments imposed for the listed and unlisted offenses; (ii) the perceived seriousness of the offense as indicated by the level of punishment; (iii) the elements of the offense; (iv) the level of culpability involved; and (v)

the degree to which the commission of the offense indicates a likelihood of recurring criminal conduct, U.S.S.G. §4A1.2, cmt. n.12(A). *See e.g.*, *United States v. Foote*, 705 F.3d 305, 307-308 (8th Cir. 2013)(possession of small amount of marijuana punishable by a small fine is not a similar offense to a similarly fined traffic offense); *United States v. Burge*, 683 F.3d 829, (7th Cir. 2012)(abandonment of a llama in violation of state wildlife code is sufficient similar to fish and game violations); *United States v. DeJesus-Concepcion*, 607 F.3d 303, 305-306 (2d Cir. 2010) (third degree unauthorized use of a vehicle is not a similar offense to careless or reckless driving); *United States v. Calderon Espinosa*, 569 F.3d 1005, 1008 (9th Cir. 2009)(offense of loitering for drug activities is loitering "by whatever name it is known"); *United States v. Russell*, 564 F.3d 200, 206 (3d Cir. 2009)(misdemeanor marijuana possession is not similar to public intoxication); *United States v. Pando*, 545 F.3d 682, 684 (8th Cir. 2008)(driving while intoxicated is not similar to careless or reckless driving, citing U.S.S.G. §4A1.2, cmt. n.5); *United States v. McKenzie*, 539 F.3d 15, 17-18 (1st Cir. 2008)(shoplifting is not similar to "insufficient funds check"); *United States v. Garrett*, 528 F.3d 525, 527-29 (7th Cir. 2008)(bail jumping is similar to contempt of court); *United States v. Sanchez-Cortez*, 530 F.3d 357, 359-60 (5th Cir. 2008)(military AWOL offense was not similar to truancy); *United States v. Cole*, 418 F.3d 592, 599- 600 (6th Cir. 2005)(underage (over 18 but under 21) possession of alcohol was similar to a juvenile status offense).

266 *Survey, Question 2. Safety Valve*. Only 22% disagreed and another 12% were neutral, *Id.*

267 *Id.* Asked whether the criterion should be expanded to include offenders with 4, 5 or 6 criminal history points, only 22% agreed; 60% disagreed; and 18% were neutral, *Id.*

268 *Hearing, Statement of Michael Nachmanoff, Federal Public Defender for E.D. Va.* at 30-31 ("In fiscal year 2009, only 5,447 (35%) of defendants subject to a mandatory minimum qualified for the safety valve, while 10,085 (65%) did not. Yet, 83.2% of all drug trafficking offenses involved no weapon, 94.1% of drug trafficking defendants played no aggravated role or a mitigated role, 51.4% had zero to one criminal history points, and another 11.7% had two to three criminal history points. By requiring no more than one criminal history point, the safety valve excludes many offenders who were not involved in any violence and whose role in the offense was not serious. The safety valve does not distinguish between high- and low-level offenders based on role in the offense, but instead distinguishes among low- level offenders who differ little from each other, i.e., by one criminal history point"); *Statement of Jay Rorty, American Civil Liberties Union* at 4.

269 *Commission Report II*, 355 (2011).

270 U.S.S.G. §5C1.2, cmt., n.4.

271 *United States v. Denis*, 560 F.3d 872, 873 (8th Cir. 2009); *United States v. Figueroa-Encarnacion*, 343 F.3d 23, 34 (1st Cir. 2003); *United States v. Sarabia*, 297 F.3d 983, 989 (10th Cir. 2002).

272 *United States v. Ochoa*, 643 F.3d 1153, 1158 (8th Cir. 2011); *United States v. Jackson*, 552 F.3d 908, 909-10 (8th Cir. 2009), citing in accord *United States v. Matias*, 465 F.3d 169, 173-74 (5th Cir. 2006); *United States v. Herrera,* 446 F.3d 283, 287 (2d Cir. 2006); *United States v. McLean*, 409 F.3d 492, 501 (1st Cir. 2005); *United States v. Gomez,* 431 F.3d 818, 820-22 (D.C.Cir. 2005); *United States v. Stewart,* 306 F.3d 295, 327 n.19 (6th Cir. 2002), but noting in apparent disagreement *United States v. Zavalza-Rodriguez*, 379 F.3d 1182, 1186-187 (10th Cir. 2004).

273 *United States v. Stewart*, 306 F.3d 295, 326 (6th Cir. 2002).

274 18 U.S.C. 3553(f)(2). *United States v. Sandoval-Sianuqui*, 632 F.3d 438, 443 (8th Cir. 2011)(the disqualifying violence or threat of violence extends to efforts to avoid detection or conviction). *But see*, *United States v. Carillo- Ayala*, 713 F.3d 82, 91 (11th Cir. 2013)("At least one of our sister circuits appears to hold that imposition of the enhancement under [U.S.S.G] §2D1.1(b)(1)[(enhancement under the drug conviction guideline for *possession* of a dangerous weapon without explicitly requiring that it be *possessed in connection* with the offense)] necessarily precludes safety valve relief ... See *United States v. Ruiz*, 621 F.3d

390, 397 (5th Cir. 2010).... We hold that not all defendants who receive the enhancement under §2D1.1(b)(1) are precluded from relief under subsection (a)(2) of the safety valve. Where 'a firearm was possessed' by the defendant personally, and yet the defendant also seeks the protection of the safety valve, the district court must determine whether the facts of the case show that a 'connection' between the firearm and the offense, though possible, is not probable").

[275] *United States v. Carillo-Ayala*, 713 F.3d at 92; *United States v. Jackson*, 552 F.3d 908, 910 (8th Cir. 2009); *United States v. Stark,* 499 F.3d 72, 80 (1st Cir. 2007); *United States v. Stewart*, 306 F.3d 295, 327 (6th Cir. 2002).

[276] U.S.S.G. §5c1.2, cmt. n.2; §1B1.1, cmt. n.1(L).

[277] The Eleventh Circuit in a nonbinding opinion seems to have come to same conclusion, *United States v. Valencia- Vergara*, 264 Fed.Appx. 832, 836 (11th Cir. 2008)("The district court did not clearly err in denying Valencia-Vergara a reduction under the safety valve provisions. The evidence shows that both he and one of his codefendants sustained second and third degree burns on their bodies, for which they had to be treated at a hospital").

[278] Cf., *United States v. Grimmett*, 150 F.3d 958, 960-61(8th Cir. 1998).

[279] U.S.S.G. §5C1.2, cmt. n.5 ("'Organizer ... supervisor of others in the offense, as determined under the sentencing guidelines' as used in subsection (a)(4), means a defendant who receives an adjustment for an aggravating role under §3B1.1 (Aggravating Role)"). E.g., *United States v. Gonzalez-Mendoza*, 584 F.3d 726, 729 (7th Cir. 2009); *United States v. Bonilla-Filomeno,* 579 F.3d 852, 858 (8th Cir. 2009); *United States v. Nobari*, 574 F.3d 1065, 1083-84 (9th Cir. 2009); *United States v. Rendon*, 354 F.3d 1320, 1333 (11th Cir. 2003).

[280] See U.S.S.G. §3B1.2 (Mitigating Role).

[281] *United States v. Ceballos*, 605 F.3d 468, 472 (8th Cir. 2010); *United States v. Altamirano-Quintero*, 511 F.3d 1087, 1096 (10th Cir. 2007), citing *United States v. Montes*, 381 F.3d 631, 635-36 (7th Cir. 2004); *United States v. Johnson*, 375 F.3d 1300, 1302-303 (11th Cir. 2004); *United States v. Salgado*, 250 F.3d 438, 459 (6th Cir. 2001); *United States v. Cruz*, 156 F.3d 366, 371 (2d Cir. 1998); *United States v. Miller*, 151 F.3d 957, 958 (9th Cir. 1998); *United States v. Sabir*, 117 F.3d 750, 753 (3d Cir. 1997).

[282] *United States v. DeLaTorre*, 599 F.3d 1198, 1206 (10th Cir. 2010).

[283] *United States v. Cervantes*, 519 F.3d 1254, 1257 (10th Cir. 2008)(" In making this determination, we join the First, Second, Fourth, Fifth, Seventh, and Ninth Circuits in ruling that a probation officer is not the government for the purposes of the safety valve,"), citing *United States v. Wood*, 378 F.3d 342, 351 (4th Cir. 2004); *Emezuo v. United States*, 357 F.3d 703, 706 n.2(7th Cir. 2004); *United States v. Contreras*, 136 F.3d 1245, 1246 (9th Cir. 1998); *United States v. Jimenez Martinez*, 83 F.3d 488, 495-66 (1st Cir. 1996); *United States v. Rodriguez*, 60 F.3d 193, 195-96 (5th Cir. 1995); and *United States v. Smith*, 174 F.3d 52, 56 (2d Cir. 1999).

[284] *United States v. Milkintas,* 470 F.3d. 1339, 1345 (11th Cir. 2006), citing *United States v. O'Dell*, 247 F.3d 655, 675 (6th Cir. 2001); *United States v. Ortiz*, 136 F.3d 882, 884 (2d Cir. 1997); *United States v. Flanagan,* 80 F.3d 143, 146- 47 (5th Cir. 1996); and *United States v. Ivester*, 75 F.3d 182, 185-86 (4th Cir. 1996).

[285] *United States v. Rodriguez*, 676 F.3d 183, 190-91 (D.C.Cir. 2012)("The provision does not distinguish between defendants who provide the authorities only with truthful information and those who provide false information before finally telling the truth"); *United States v. Wu*, 668 F.3d 882, 888 (7th Cir. 2011)("Here, in contrast, the district court denied the reduction. It believed that Wu's credibility had been undermined by inconsistencies in his statements and his ultimate retraction"); *United States v. Padilla-Colon*, 578 F.3d 23, 31-2 (1st Cir. 2009)("Inconsistencies between statements made during the proffer and statements made to the authorities on other occasions are not necessarily disqualifying. But the court may legitimately consider such inconsistencies in deciding on the truthfulness of the proffer"); *United States v. Mejia-Pimental*, 477 F.3d 1100, 1108 (9th Cir. 2007)("The

district court therefore erred, as a matter of law, in finding Mejia-Pimental ineligible for safety valve relief on the basis of the lies and delays that preceded his final proffer"); *United States v. Jeffers*, 329 F.3d 94, 99-100 (2d Cir. 2003)("[A] sentencing court may not disqualify a defendant at the threshold from eligibility for safety valve relief based solely on his commission of perjury at trial, where the defendant otherwise fulfills the statutory criteria under 18 U.S.C. §3553(f)(1)-(5). To do so would contradict the plain language of the statute and contravene the statutory deadline for full compliance with its criteria at the time of the commencement of the sentencing hearing. A court may, of course, consider the relevance of the prior perjury or other obstructive behavior in making a factual finding as to whether the defendant has made a complete and truthful proffer in compliance with 18 U.S.C. §3553(f)(5)").

[286] 18 U.S.C. 924(e).

[287] 18 U.S.C. 924(c).

[288] See *United States v. O'Brien*, 560 U.S. 218, 2172 (2010)("The Court must interpret, once again, §924(c) of Title 18 of the United States Code"). Other decisions include: *Alleyne v. United States*, 133 S.Ct. 2151 (2013); *United States v. Abbott*, 131 S.Ct. 18 (2010); *Dean v . United States*, 556 U.S. 568 (2009); *Watson v. United States*, 552 U.S. 74 (2007); *Harris v. United States*, 536 U.S. 545 (2002); *Castillo v. United States*, 530 U.S. 120 (2000); *Mascarello v. United States*, 524 U.S. 125 (1998); *United States v. Gonzales*, 520 U.S. 1 (1997); *Bailey v. United States,* 516 U.S. 137 (1995); *Smith v. United States*, 508 U.S. 223 (1993); *Deal v. United States*, 508 U.S. 129 (1993).

[289] E.g., P.L. 90-618, 82 Stat. 1223 (1968), 18 U.S.C. 924(c)(1970 ed.); P.L. 91-644, §13, 84 Stat. 1889 (1971), 18 U.S.C. 924(c) (1976 ed.); P.L. 98-473, §1005, 98 Stat. 2138 (1984), 18 U.S.C. 924(c) (1982 ed.)(Supp. II); P.L. 99-308, 100 Stat. 457 (1986), 18 U.S.C. 924(c) (1982 ed.)(Supp. IV); P.L. 100-690, §6460, 102 Stat. 4373 (1988), 18 U.S.C. 924(c) (1988 ed.); P.L. 101-647, §1101,104 Stat. 4829 (1990), 18 U.S.C. 924(c) (1988 ed.)(Supp. II); P.L. 105-386, §1, 112 Stat. 3469 (1998), 18 U.S.C. 924(c) (2000 ed.); P.L. 109-92, §6(b), 119 Stat. 2102 (2005), 18 U.S.C. 924(c)(2000 ed.)(Supp. V).

[290] 18 U.S.C. 924(c)(1), (5).

[291] 18 U.S.C. 921(a)(3), (4) ("(3) The term 'firearm' means (A) any weapon (including a starter gun) which will or is designed to or may readily be converted to expel a projectile by the action of an explosive; ... (C) any firearm muffler or firearm silencer; or (D) any destructive device.... (4) The term 'destructive device' means - (A) any explosive, incendiary, or poison gas - (i) bomb, (ii) grenade, (iii) rocket having a propellant charge of more than four ounces, (iv) missile having an explosive or incendiary charge of more than one-quarter ounce, (v) mine, or (vi) device similar to any of the devices described in the preceding clauses ... "); *United States v. York*, 600 F.3d 347, 354 (5th Cir. 2010) (Molotov cocktail constitutes a "firearm" for purposes of section 924(c)).

[292] *United States v. Cooper*, 714 F.3d 873, 881 (5th Cir. 2013).

[293] *United States v. Garrido*, 596 F.3d 613, 617 (9th Cir. 2010)("Possession of a toy or replica gun cannot sustain a conviction under §924(c)"); *United States v. Roberson*, 459 F.3d 39, 47 (1st Cir. 2006).

[294] 18 U.S.C. 924(c)(1), (5).

[295] 18 U.S.C. 924(c)(1970 ed.).

[296] *Bailey v. United States*, 516 U.S. 137, 143 (1995)(emphasis in the original)(Section 924(c) "requires evidence sufficient to show an *active employment* of the firearm by the defendant, a use that makes the firearm an operative factor in relation to the predicate offense.... '[U]se' must connote more than mere possession of a firearm by a person who commits a drug offense").

[297] 18 U.S.C. 924(c)(2000 ed.). *United States v. Gurka*, 605 F.3d 40, 43 (1st Cir. 2010).

[298] 18 U.S.C. 924(c)(2), referring to 21 U.S.C. 801-904; 21 U.S.C. 951-971; and 46 U.S.C. 70501-70507; respectively.

[299] 18 U.S.C. 924(c)(3).

[300] 543 U.S. 1 (2004). 18 U.S.C. 16 provides that, "the term 'crime of violence' means - (a) an offense that has as an element the use, attempted use, or threatened use of physical force against the person or property of another, or (b) any other offense that is a felony and that, by its nature, involves a substantial risk that physical force against the person or property of another may be used in the course of committing the offense".

[301] *Leocal v. Ashcroft*, 543 U.S. 1, 9 (2004)(emphasis added).

[302] *Id.* at 10 (emphasis added)(quoting, *United States v. Doe*, 960 F.2d 221, 225 (1st Cir. 1992) ("The reckless disregard in §16 relates not to the general conduct or to the possibility that harm will result from a person's conduct, but to the risk that the use of physical force against another might be *required* in committing a crime.... The ordinary meaning of this term.... 'calls to mind a tradition of crimes that involve the possibility of more closely related, *active* violence'").

[303] *Id.*

[304] *United States v. Andrews*, 442 F.3d 996, 1002 (7th Cir. 2006)(bank robbery (18 U.S.C. 2113); *United States v. Jones*, 418 F.3d 726, 729 (7th Cir. 2005)(attempted bank robbery (18 U.S.C. 2113); *United States v. Green*, 521 F.3d 929, 932- 33 (8th Cir. 2008)(kidnapping (18 U.S.C. 1201); *United States v. Frye*, 489 F.3d 201, 208-209 (5th Cir. 2007)(carjacking (18 U.S.C. 2119); *United States v. Munro*, 394 F.3d 865, 870-71 (10th Cir. 2005)(attempted seduction of a minor by computer (18 U.S.C. 2422(b); *United States v. Acosta*, 470 F.3d 132, 135-36 (2d Cir. 2006)(deprivation of civil rights under color of law resulting in injury or involving a dangerous weapon (statutory sentencing factors)(18 U.S.C. 242); *United States v. Pospisil*, 186 F.3d 1023, 1031 (8th Cir. 1999)(interfering with fair housing rights (42 U.S.C. 3631); *United States v. Acosta*, 470 F.3d at 136-37(conspiracy to oppress the enjoyment of civil rights (18 U.S.C. 241); *United States v. Turner*, 501 F.3d 59, 67-68 (1st Cir. 2007)(Hobbs Act conspiracy (robbery or extortion)); *United States v. Desena*, 287 F.3d 170, 181 (2d Cir. 2002))(conspiracy to assault in aid of racketeering (18 U.S.C. 1959); *United States v. Khan*, 461 F.3d 477, 489-90 (4th Cir. 2006)(conspiracy to violate the Neutrality Act (18 U.S.C. 960); *id.* at 490 (4th Cir. 2006)(conspiracy to provide material support to a terrorist organization (18 U.S.C. 2339B); *United States v. Ayala*, 601 F.3d 256, 266-67 (4th Cir. 2010)(RICO conspiracy with 18 U.S.C. 1959 predicates), quoting *United States v. Elder*, 88 F.3d 127, 129 (2d Cir. 1996)("[A] conspiracy 'is itself a crime of violence when its objectives are violent crimes'"); *United States v. Ivezaj*, 568 F.3d 88, 95-96 (2d Cir. 2009)(RICO conspiracy with loan sharking and extortionate predicates); *United States v. Juvenile Male*, 118 F.3d 1344, 1350 (9th Cir. 1997)(RICO conspiracy with Hobbs Act predicates).

[305] *United States v. Serafin*, 562 F.3d 1105, 1107-1116 (10th Cir. 2009)("[T]he danger from an unregistered short- barreled rifle is inherent to its use, not merely in its possession. Although Serafin clearly disregarded the law by possessing an illegal short-barreled rifle, we must confine the scope of §924(c)(3)(B) to active, violent crimes which pose a substantial risk that force may be used during the course of the offense"), citing among others *United States v. Hull*, 456 F.3d 133, 140 (3d Cir. 2006) (possession of an unregistered pipe bomb [included within the definition of firearm in 18 U.S.C. 921(a)(3), (4)] was not a crime of violence under 18 U.S.C. 16); *Henry v. Bureau of Immigration & Customs Enforcement*, 493 F.3d 303, 309 (3d Cir. 2007)(possession of an unregistered pipe bomb with the intent to use was a crime of violence under section 16); *United States v. Jennings*, 195 F.3d 795, 798 (5th Cir. 1999)(possession of a pipe bomb [without reference to intent] was a crime of violence under section 16); *United States v. Diaz-Diaz*, 327 F.3d 410, 413-14 (5th Cir. 2003)(possession of an unregistered short-barreled firearm was not a crime of violence under section 16; "apparently reversing its contrary holding in *United States v. Rivas-Palacios*, 244 F.3d 396 (5th Cir. 2001)").

[306] *United States v. Perez*, 661 F.3d 568, 576 (11th Cir. 2011); *United States v. Brown*, 669 F.3d 10, 29-30 (1st Cir. 2012); *but see*, *United States v. Angilau*, 717 F.3d 781, 788 (10th Cir. 2013)("Thus, the elements of §924(c) are (1) using or carrying a firearm (2) during and in

relation to (3) any federal crime of violence.... We need not decide whether some form of scienter is also a required element because it would not affect our analysis").

307 *United States v. Renteria*, 720 F.3d 1245, 1255 (10th Cir. 2013); *United States v. Eller*, 670 F.3d 762, 765 (7th Cir. 2012); *United States v. Parish*, 606 F.3d 480, 490 (8th Cir. 2010); *United States v. Pena*, 586 F.3d 105, 113 (1st Cir. 2009); *United States v. Jeffers*, 570 F.3d 557, 565 (4th Cir. 2009); *United States v. London*, 568 F.3d 553, 559 (5th Cir. 2009); *United States v. Lopez-Garcia*, 565 F.3d 1306, 1322 (11th Cir. 2009).

308 *United States v. Renteria*, 720 F.3d at 1255; *United States v. Eller*, 670 F.3d at 765; *United States v. Pena*, 586 F.3d at 113; *United States v. Penney*, 576 F.3d 297, 315 (1st Cir. 2009).

309 *United States v. Renteria*, 720 F.3d at 1255; *see also*, *United States v. Brown*, 715 F.3d 985, 993-94 (6th Cir. 2013); *United States v. Gill*, 685 F.3d 606, 611 (6th Cir. 2012); *United States v. Johnson*, 677 F.3d 138, 143 (3d Cir. 2012); *United States v. Eller*, 670 F.3d at 766; *United States v. London*, 568 F.3d at 559; *United States v. Lopez-Garcia*, 565 F.3d at 1322; *United States v. Perry*, 560 F.3d 246, 254 (4th Cir. 2009); see also *United States v. Chavez*, 549 F.3d 119, 130 (2d Cir. 2008)(noting after quoting the factors that, "while no conviction would lie for a drug dealer's innocent possession of a firearm, ... a drug dealer may be punished under §924(c)(1)(A) where the charged weapon is readily accessible to protect drugs, drug proceeds, or the drug dealer himself"); but see *United States v. Hector*, 474 F.3d 1150, 1157 (9th Cir. 2007)(internal citations omitted)("Although the Fifth Circuit has developed a non-exclusive list of factors ... we have concluded that this approach is not particularly helpful in close cases.... In our most recent case addressing the 'in furtherance question," we reiterated the importance of the factual inquiry. We declined once again to adopt a checklist approach to deciding this issue and held that it is the totality of the circumstances, coupled with a healthy dose of a jury's common sense when evaluating the facts in evidence, which will determine whether the evidence suffices to support a conviction").

310 *Watson v. United States,* 552 U.S. 74 (2007).

311 *United States v. Gurka*, 605 F.3d 40, 44 (1st Cir. 2010)("We join the three circuits holding *Watson* does not affect the prong of 18 U.S.C. §924(c)(1)(A) concerned with 'possession in furtherance'), citing in accord, *United States v. Gardner*, 602 F.3d 97, 103 (2d Cir. 2010); *United States v. Mahan*, 586 F.3d 1185, 1189 (9th Cir. 2009); *see also*, *United States v. Miranda*, 666 F.3d 1280, 1282-284 (11th Cir. 2012); *United States v. Dickerson*, 705 F.3d 683, 688-90 (7th Cir. 2013).

312 *Bailey v. United States*, 516 U.S. 137, 143 (1995); *United States v. Haynes*, 582 F.3d 686, 704 (7th Cir. 2009)); *United States v. Combs,* 369 F.3d 925, 932 (6th Cir. 2004).

313 *Smith v. United States*, 508 U.S. 223, 228 (1993); *Bailey v. United States,* 516 U.S. 137, 148 (1995).

314 *United States v. Cox*, 324 F.3d 77, 82 (2d Cir. 2003).

315 *Watson v. United States*, 552 U.S. at 78.

316 *Muscarello v. United States,* 524 U.S. 125, 126 (1998)("The question before us is whether the phrase 'carries a firearm' is limited to the carrying of firearms on the person. We hold that it is not so limited. Rather, it also applies to a person who knowingly possesses and carries a firearm in a vehicle, including locked in a glove compartment or trunk of a car, which the person accompanies"); *United States v. Franklin*, 561 F.3d 398, 403 (5th Cir. 2009); *United States v. Winder*, 557 F.3d 1129, 1138-139 (10th Cir. 2009); *United States v. Robinson*, 390 F.3d 853, 878 (6th Cir. 2005); *United States v. Williams*, 344 F.3d 365, 370 (3d Cir. 2003).

317 *United States v. Mashek*, 606 F.3d 922, 930 (8th Cir. 2010), quoting *Smith v. United States*, 508 U.S. 223, 238 (1993); *United States v. Roberson*, 459 F.3d 39, 48 (1st Cir. 2006); *United States v. Combs,* 369 F.3d 925, 933 (6th Cir. 2004); *United States v. Williams*, 344 F.3d 365, 371 (3d Cir. 2003).

318 *United States v. Burkley*, 513 F.3d 1183, 1189-190 (10th Cir,. 2008)("A firearm is carried during and in relation to the underlying crime when the defendant avails himself of the weapon and ... the weapon plays an integral role in the underlying offense.... Thus, the

government must prove that the defendant intended the firearm to be available for use in the offense").

[319] 18 U.S.C. 924(c)(1)(A)(ii), (iii).

[320] *Dean v. United States*, 129 S.Ct. 1849, 1853 (2009).

[321] *Alleyne v. United States*, 133 S.Ct. 2151, 2163 (2013)("Because the finding of brandishing increased the penalty to which the defendant was subjected, it was an element, which had to be found by the jury beyond a reasonable doubt"). *Alleyne* overruled *Harris* which had held that brandishing was a sentencing factor that might be entrusted to the judge to find by a preponderance of the evidence (*Harris v. United States*, 535 U.S. 545, 556 (2002)).

[322] 18 U.S.C. 924(c)(4)("For purposes of this subsection, the term 'brandish' means, with respect to a firearm, to display all or part of the firearm, or otherwise make the presence of the firearm known to another person, in order to intimidate that person, regardless of whether the firearm is directly visible to that person"); *United States v. Carter*, 560 F.3d 1107, 1114 (9th Cir. 2009).

[323] *United States v. Bowen*, 527 F.3d at 1075 (10th Cir. 2008).

[324] 18 U.S.C. 924(c)(1)(emphasis added)("(A) Except to the extent that a greater minimum sentence is otherwise provided by this subsection or by any other provision of law, any person who, during and in relation to any crime of violence or drug trafficking crime (including a crime of violence or drug trafficking crime that provides for an enhanced punishment if committed by the use of a deadly or dangerous weapon or device) for which the person may be prosecuted in a court of the United States, uses or carries a firearm, or who, in furtherance of any such crime, possesses a firearm, shall, in addition to the punishment provided for such crime of violence or drug trafficking crime - *(i) be sentenced to a term of imprisonment of not less than 5 years; (ii) if the firearm is brandished, be sentenced to a term of imprisonment of not less than 7 years; and (iii) if the firearm is discharged, be sentenced to a term of imprisonment of not less than 10 years ... "*).

[325] 18 U.S.C. 924(c)(1)(" ... (B) If the firearm possessed by a person convicted of a violation of this subsection - (i) is a short-barreled rifle, short-barreled shotgun, or semiautomatic assault weapon, the person shall be sentenced to a term of imprisonment of not less than 10 years; or (ii) is a machinegun or a destructive device, or is equipped with a firearm silencer or firearm muffler, the person shall be sentenced to a term of imprisonment of not less than 30 years ... ").

[326] 18 U.S.C. 924(c)(1)(" ... (C) In the case of a second or subsequent conviction under this subsection, the person shall - (i) be sentenced to a term of imprisonment of not less than 25 years; and (ii) if the firearm involved is a machinegun or a destructive device, or is equipped with a firearm silencer or firearm muffler, be sentenced to imprisonment for life").

[327] *United States v. Burwell*, 690 F.3d 500, 510-11 (D.C.Cir. 2012)(citing cases evidencing a split).

[328] *Castillo v. United States*, 530 U.S. 120, 121 (2000).

[329] *United States v. O'Brien*, 130 U.S. 2169, 2180 (2010).

[330] *United States v. Rivera-Rivera,* 555 F.3d 277, 291 (1st Cir. 2009); *United States v. Mejia*, 545 F.3d 179, 207-208 (2d Cir. 2008). This is true even after *Alleyne*, because the Court continues to recognize a recidivist exception to the *Apprendi* rule, *see e.g., Alleyne v. United States*, 133 S.Ct. 2151, 2160 n.1 ("In *Almendarez-Torres v. United States*, 523 U.S. 224 (1998), we recognized a narrow exception to this general rule for the fact of a prior conviction. Because the parties do not contest that decision's vitality, we do not revisit it for purposes of our decision today").

[331] 18 U.S.C. 924(c)(1976 ed.).

[332] *United States v. Shabazz*, 564 F.3d 280, 289 (3d Cir. 2009), citing in accord *United States v. Johnson*, 507 F.3d 793, 798 (2d Cir. 2007); *United States v. Dare*, 425 F.3d 634, 642 (9th Cir. 2005); *United States v. Avery*, 295 F.3d 1158, 1170 (10th Cir. 2002); *United States v. Cristobal*, 293 F.3d 134, 147 (4th Cir. 2002); *United States v. Sandoval*, 241 F.3d 549, 551

(7th Cir. 2001); *United States v. Pounds*, 230 F.3d 1317, 1319 (11th Cir. 2000); *United States v. Silas*, 227 F.3d 244, 246 (5th Cir. 2000).

333 18 U.S.C. 924(c)(1)(D)(i).

334 18 U.S.C. 924(c)(1)(D)(ii).

335 *United States v. Chavez*, 549 F.3d 119, 135 (2d Cir. 2008); *United States v. Hatcher*, 501 F.3d 931, 933 (8th Cir. 2007); *United States v. Franklin*, 499 F.3d 578, 584-85 (6th Cir. 2007); *United States v. Roberson*, 474 F.3d 432, 436 (7th Cir. 2007).

336 *United States v. Sandstrom*, 594 F.3d 634, 658 (8th Cir. 2010)("... [M]ultiple underlying offenses support multiple §924(c) convictions"); *United States v. Catalan-Roman*, 585 F.3d 453, 472 (1st Cir. 2009); *United States v. Penny*, 576 F.3d 297, 316 (6th Cir. 2009)("[W]hen two separate predicate offenses for triggering §924(c)(1) are charged and proved, a defendant may be convicted and sentenced for two separate crimes, even if both offenses were committed in the course of the same event"); *United States v. Looney*, 532 F.3d 392, 396 (5th Cir. 2008).

337 *Deal v. United States*, 508 U.S. 129, 132 (1993); *United States v. Washington,* 714 F.3d 962, 969-70 (6th Cir. 2013)(noting, however, that the stacking should be governed by the rule of lenity, so that for example, the 25-year mandatory minimums for second offenses should be stacked starting with a7-year brandishing sentence rather than a 10-year discharge sentence); *see also*, *United States v. Phaknikone*, 605 F.3d 1099, 1101, 1111-112 (11th Cir. 2010)(the defendant was charged with, and convicted for, a string of 15 armed bank robberies for which he received a sentenced of 2005 months (167 years); the court observed that, "Phaknikone also argues that, because each count under section 924 was charged in a single indictment, the district court erroneously applied the higher mandatory minimum of 25 years of imprisonment for second or subsequent conviction, 18 U.S.C. §924(c)(1)(C), to six of his seven convictions. We long ago rejected this argument"); *United States v. Beltran-Moreno*, 556 F.3d 913, 915 (9th Cir. 2009)("In this case, the defendants pled guilty to various drug offenses that, taken together, imposed a mandatory minimum sentence of ten years. They also pled guilty to two §9254(c) charges, the first of which required a mandatory minimum sentence of five years and the second of which required an additional sentenced of twenty-five years. Because the statute does not allow any of these sentences to run concurrently, the mandatory minimum sentence for both defendants is forty years in prison"); *United States v. Watkins*, 509 F.3d 277, 282 (6th Cir. 2007) ("Finally, the district court sentenced Watkins to an additional 7 years for brandishing a firearm during the first robbery, in violation of 18 U.S.C. §924(c), and to 25 years for each count of using or brandishing a firearm during the other five robberies. The length of the firearm sentences are predetermined by §924(c)(1)(C)(i). Pursuant to §924(c)(1(D)(ii), the court then ordered that each of the §924(c) gun convictions run consecutively to the underlying offenses").

338 *United States v. Almany*, 598 F.3d 238, 241-42 (6th Cir. 2010); *United States v. Whitley*, 529 F.3d 150, 153-56 (2d Cir. 2008).

339 *Abbott v. United States*, 131 S.Ct. 18, 23 (2010).

340 *Id.*

341 18 U.S.C. 924(c)(5)("Except to the extent that a greater minimum sentence is otherwise provided under this subsection, or by any other provision of law, any person who, during and in relation to any crime of violence or drug trafficking crime (including a crime of violence or drug trafficking crime that provides for an enhanced punishment if committed by the use of a deadly or dangerous weapon or device) for which the person may be prosecuted in a court of the United States, uses or carries armor piercing ammunition, or who, in furtherance of any such crime, possesses armor piercing ammunition, shall, in addition to the punishment provided for such crime of violence or drug trafficking crime or conviction under this section - (A) be sentenced to a term of imprisonment of not less than 15 years; and (B) if death results from the use of such ammunition - (i) if the killing is murder (as defined in section 1111), be punished by death or sentenced to a term of

imprisonment for any term of years or for life; and (ii) if the killing is manslaughter (as defined in section 1112), be punished as provided in section 1112").

342 18 U.S.C. 929("(a)(1) Whoever, during and in relation to the commission of a crime of violence or drug trafficking crime (including a crime of violence or drug trafficking crime which provides for an enhanced punishment if committed by the use of a deadly or dangerous weapon or device) for which he may be prosecuted in a court of the United States, uses or carries a firearm and is in possession of armor piercing ammunition capable of being fired in that firearm, shall, in addition to the punishment provided for the commission of such crime of violence or drug trafficking crime be sentenced to a term of imprisonment for not less than five years. (2) For purposes of this subsection, the term "drug trafficking crime" means any felony punishable under the Controlled Substances Act (21 U.S.C. 801 et seq.), the Controlled Substances Import and Export Act (21 U.S.C. 951 et seq.), or chapter 705 of title 46. "(b) Notwithstanding any other provision of law, the court shall not suspend the sentence of any person convicted of a violation of this section, nor place the person on probation, nor shall the terms of imprisonment run concurrently with any other terms of imprisonment, including that imposed for the crime in which the armor piercing ammunition was used or possessed").

343 *Pinkerton v. United States*, 328 U.S. 640, 646 (1946); *Salinas v. United States*, 522 U.S. 52, 63 (1997).

344 *United States v. Min*, 704 F.3d 314, 324 n.9 (4th Cir. 2013)("As members of the conspiracy, all of the defendants including Phun, were legally responsible for the possession of firearms, which was a reasonably foreseeable act by their coconspirators in furtherance of that conspiracy"); *United States v. Walker*, 673 F.3d 649, 655 (7th Cir. 2012); *United States v. Merlino,* 592 F.3d 22, 29 (1st Cir. 2010); *United States v. Carter*, 560 F.3d 1107, 1113 (9th Cir. 2009).

345 *United States v. Bowen,* 527 F.3d 1065, 1078 (10th Cir. 2008)(internal citations omitted)("[A]iding and abetting liability allows a jury to hold an aider and abettor responsible for a substantive offense to the same extent as a principal, even though his act was not the cause of the substantive harm. Acts committed in furtherance of the commission of a crime by another constitute 'abetting'.... To be liable for aiding and abetting, a defendant must (1) willfully associate himself with the criminal venture, and (2) seek to make the venture succeed through some action of his own.... One need not participate in an important aspect of a crime to be liable as an aider and abettor; participation of 'relatively slight moment' is sufficient. Even mere 'words or gestures of encouragement' constitute affirmative acts capable of rendering one liable under this theory").

346 *Id. See also*, *United States v. Rosemond*, 695 F.3d 1151, (10th Cir. 2012)("Aiding and abetting in the use of a firearm during a crime of violence under 18 U.S.C. §924(c) requires proof that the defendant (1) knew his cohort used a firearm in the underlying crime and (2) knowingly and actively participated in that underlying crime"); *United States v. Figueroa-Cartagena*, 612 F.3d 69, 83-4 (1st Cir. 2010)("The indictment alleged that she aided and abetted Alberto and Gabriel in their use and carriage of a firearm during the carjacking. To secure a conviction on that count, the government had to prove that Neliza knew to a practical certainty that her confederates would carry or use a firearm and that she willingly took some step to facilitate the carrying or use"); *United States v. Gomez*, 580 F.3d 94, 104 (2d Cir. 2009).

347 U.S. Const. Amend. II.

348 *District of Columbia v. Heller*, 554 U.S. 570, 628-29 (2008)(internal citations omitted)("The inherent right of self- defense has been central to the Second Amendment right.... [Moreover,] [u]nder any of the standards of scrutiny that we have applied to enumerated constitutional rights, banning from the home [a handgun,] the most preferred firearm in the nation to keep and use for protection of one's home and family, would fail constitutional muster"); *see also*, *McDonald v. City of Chicago*, 130 S.Ct. 3020, 3044 (2010)("[T]he

Second Amendment protects a personal right to keep and bear arms for lawful purposes, most notably for self-defense within the home").

349 *District of Columbia v. Heller*, 554 U.S. at 626-27.

350 *United States v. Bryant*, 711 F.3d 364, 368-70 (2d Cir. 2013), citing in accord, *United States v. Potter*, 630 F.3d 1260, 1261 (9th Cir. 2011); and *United States v. Jackson*, 555 F.3d 635, 636 (7th Cir. 2009).

351 U.S. Const. Amend. V.

352 *United States v. Dixon*, 509 U.S. 688, 696 (1993); *United States v. Mahdi*, 598 F.3d 883, 887 (D.C.Cir. 2010); *United States v. Hall*, 551 F.3d 257, 266 (4th Cir. 2009).

353 *Blockburger v. United States*, 284 U.S. 299, 304 (1932); *United States v. Mahdi*, 598 F.3d at 888; *United States v. Sandstrom*, 594 F.3d 634, 654 (8th Cir. 2010); *United States v. Beltran-Moreno*, 556 F.3d 913, 916 (9th Cir. 2009).

354 *United States v. Angilau*, 717 F.3d 781, 788-89 (10th Cir. 2013); *United States v. Sandstrom*, 594 F.3d at 658); *United States v. Catalan-Roman*, 585 F.3d 453, 472 (1st Cir. 2009); *United States v. Penny*, 576 F.3d 297, 316 (6th Cir. 2009); *United States v. Looney*, 532 F.3d 392, 396 (5th Cir. 2008).

355 *United States v. Diaz*, 592 F.3d 467, 470-75 (3d Cir. 2010), citing in accord *United States v. Rodriguez*, 525 F.3d 85, 1119 (1st Cir. 2008); *United States v. Batiste*, 309 F.3d 274, 279 (5th Cir. 2002); *United States v. Anderson*, 59 F.3d 1323, 1326-327 (D.C. Cir. 1995); *United States v. Cappas*, 29 F.3d 1187, 1195 (7th Cir. 1994); *United States v. Taylor*, 13 F.3d 986, 992-994 (6th Cir. 1994); *United States v. Lindsay*, 985 F.2d 666, 676 (2d Cir. 1993); *United States v. Hamilton*, 953 F.2d 1344, 1346 (11th Cir. 1992); *United States v. Smith*, 924 F.2d 889, 894-95 (9th Cir. 1991); *United States v. Henning*, 906 F.3d 1392, 1399 (10th Cir. 1990), and to the contrary, *United States v. Lucas*, 932 F.2d 1210, 1222-223 (8th Cir. 1991); *United States v. Camps*, 32 F.3d 108-109 (4th Cir. 1994).

356 *Rutledge v. United States*, 517 U.S. 292, 306-307 (1996); *United States. Sandstrom*, 594 F.3d at 654; *United States v. Catalan-Roman*, 585 F.3d 453, 472 (1st Cir. 2009).

357 *United States v. Catalan-Roman*, 585 F.3d at 472.

358 United States Sentencing Commission, *Results of Survey of United States District Judges: January 2010 through March 2010, Question 1. Mandatory Minimums* (June 2010), available at http://www.ussc.gov/Judge_Survey/2010/ JudgeSurvey_201006.pdf.

359 *Commission Report II*, 364-65.

360 18 U.S.C. 924(e)(1)("In the case of a person who violates section 922(g) of this title and has three previous convictions by any court referred to in section 922(g)(1) of this title for a violent felony or a serious drug offense, or both, committed on occasions different from one another, such person shall be fined under this title and imprisoned not less than fifteen years, and, notwithstanding any other provision of law, the court shall not suspend the sentence of, or grant a probationary sentence to, such person with respect to the conviction under section 922(g)"). The ACCA is not to be confused with the federal three strikes statute, 18 U.S.C. 3559(c), which establishes a mandatory term of life imprisonment upon a third serious violent felony conviction, or with its two strike counterpart in 18 U.S.C. 3559(e), relating to mandatory life imprisonment for repeated child sex offenders.

361 The other disqualified categories cover fugitives, drug addicts, mental defectives, unlawful aliens, dishonorably discharged members of the armed forces, individuals who have renounced their U.S. citizenship, those under a domestic violence restraining order, and those convicted of misdemeanor domestic violence, 18 U.S.C. 922(g)(2)-(9).

362 18 U.S.C. 924(e)(1).

363 *United States v. Martin*, 526 F.3d 926, 938-39 (6th Cir. 2008)(internal citations omitted).

364 *United States v. Ross*, 569 F.3d 821, 823 (8th Cir. 2009).

365 *United States v. Tucker*, 603 F.3d, 260, 266 (4th Cir. 2010)("Here, the district court relied on the PSR's [Probation Service's Presentence Report] recitation of the facts about the burglaries, but the PSR relied on the police incident report, which is not allowed ...");

United States v. Sneed, 600 F.3d 1326, 1332-333(11th Cir. 2010), each citing *Shepard v. United States*, 544 U.S. 13 (2005).

366 *Custis v. United States*, 511 U.S. 485, 487 (1994)("a defendant has no such right (with the sole exception of convictions obtained in violation of the right to counsel) to collaterally attack prior convictions"); *United States v. Greer*, 607 F.3d 559, 565 (8th Cir. 2010); *United States v. Dean*, 604 F.3d 169, 174-75 (4th Cir. 2010); *United States v. Covington*, 565 F.3d 1336, 1345 (11th Cir. 2009); *United States v. Buie*, 547 F.3d 401, 403-404 (2d Cir. 2008); *United States v. Goodman*, 519 F.3d 310, 318 (6th Cir. 2008); *United States v. Krejcarek*, 453 F.3d 1290, 1297 10th Cir. 2006).

367 18 U.S.C. 924(e)(2)(A)("the term 'serious drug offense' means – (i) an offense under the Controlled Substances Act (21 U.S.C. 801 et seq.), the Controlled Substances Import and Export Act (21 U.S.C. 951 et seq.), or chapter 705 of title 46, for which a maximum term of imprisonment of ten years or more is prescribed by law; or (ii) an offense under State law, involving manufacturing, distributing, or possessing with intent to manufacture or distribute, a controlled substance (as defined in section 102 of the Controlled Substances Act (21 U.S.C. 802), for which a maximum term of imprisonment of ten years or more is prescribed by law").

368 *United States v. Rodriquez*, 533 U.S. 377, 380 (2008).

369 *United States v. Rodriquez*, 533 U.S. at 390; *United States v. Mayer*, 560 F.3d 948, 963(9th Cir. 2009).

370 *United States v. Buie*, 547 F.3d 401, 404 (2d Cir. 2008); *United States v. Williams*, 508 F.3d 724, 728 (4th Cir. 2007); *United States v. Henton*, 473 F.3d 467, 470 (7th Cir. 2004).

371 *McNeill v. United States*,131 S.Ct. 2218, 2221-222 (2011).

372 *United States v. Williams*, 499 F.3d 1004, 1009 (D.C. Cir. 2007).

373 *Begay v. United States*, 553 U.S. 137, 141 (2008).

374 18 U.S.C. 924(e)(2)(B)("the term 'violent felony' means any crime punishable by imprisonment for a term exceeding one year, or any act of juvenile delinquency involving the use or carrying of a firearm, knife, or destructive device that would be punishable by imprisonment for such term if committed by an adult, that—(i) has as an element the use, attempted use, or threatened use of physical force against the person of another; or (ii) is burglary, arson, or extortion, involves use of explosives, or otherwise involves conduct that presents a serious potential risk of physical injury to another").

375 18 U.S.C. 924(e)(2)(B)(i).

376 *Johnson v. United States*, 130 S.Ct. 1265, 1271 (2010); *United States v. Forrest*, 611 F.3d 908, 910 (8th Cir. 2010); *United States v. Ramon Silva*, 608 F.3d 663, 669 (10th Cir. 2010); *United States v. Hughes*, 602 F.3d 669, 673-74 (5th Cir. 2010).

377 *Johnson v. United States*, 130 S.Ct. at 1272.

378 18 U.S.C. 924(e)(2)(B)(ii).

379 *Begay v. United States*, 553 U.S. 137, 144-45 (2008); *Chambers v. United States*, 555 U.S. 122, 128 (2009); *United States v. Alexander*, 609 F.3d 1250, 1254-255 (11th Cir. 2010).

380 *United States v. Sykes*, 131 S.Ct. 2267, 2276 (2011).

381 *Begay v. United States*, 533 U.S. at 139; *Chambers v. United States*, 555 U.S. at 130.

382 *United States v. Sykes*, 131 S.Ct. at 2272, quoting, *James v. United States*, 550 U.S. 192, 202 (2007)("[W]e consider whether the elements of the [prior] offense are of the type that would justify its inclusion within the residual provision, without inquiring into the specific conduct of this particular offender ").

383 *Descamps v. United States*, 133 S.Ct. 2276, 2283 (2013)("We granted certiorari to resolve a Circuit split on whether the modified categorical approach applies to statutes like §459 that contain a single, 'indivisible' set of elements sweeping more broadly than the corresponding generic offense. We hold that it does not").

384 *United States v. Lopez*, 516 U.S. 549, 558-59 (1995); *United States v. Morrison*, 529 U.S. 598, 609 (2000).

385 *United States v. Lopez*, 514 U.S. at 552.

386 18 U.S.C. 922(g).

387 *United States v. Vallejo*, 373 F.3d 855, 860-61 (7th Cir. 2004), *citing in accord, United States v. Thompson*, 361 F.3d 918, 922 (6th Cir. 2004); *United States v. Leathers*, 354 F.3d 955, 599 (8th Cir. 2003); *United States v. Dunn*, 345 F.3d 1285, 1297 (11th Cir. 2003); *United States v. Darrington,* 351 F.3d 632, 634 (5th Cir. 2003).

388 *United States v. Moore*, 666 F.3d 313, 316-17 (4th Cir. 2012), summarizing holdings from the Second, Third, Fifth, Sixth, Seventh, Eighth, Ninth, Tenth and Eleventh Circuits ("We begin our analysis by noting the unanimous result reached by every court of appeals that §922(g)(1) is constitutional, both on its face and as applied. The basis for the various decisions by our sister circuits has varied, but all have uniformly rejected challenges to §922(g)(1) usually based at least in part on the 'presumptively lawful' language in *Heller*").

389 *United States v. Rozier*, 598 F.3d 768, 771-72 (11th Cir. 2010)(holding section 922(g)(1) a permissible limitation of the defendant's Second Amendment right and upholding his sentence under section 924(e)).

390 *Almendarez-Torres v. United States*, 523 U.S. 224, 247 (1998).

391 *Apprendi v. New Jersey*, 530 U.S. 466, 476 (2000)(emphasis added), quoting dicta in *Jones v. United States*, 526 U.S. 227, 243 n.6 (1999).

392 *Blakely v. Washington*, 542 U.S. 296, 301 (2004)("Other than the fact of a prior conviction, any fact that increases the penalty for a crime beyond the prescribed statutory maximum must be submitted to a jury, and proved beyond a reasonable doubt"), quoting *Apprendi v. New Jersey*, 530 U.S. at 490; *United States v. Booker*, 543 U.S. 220, 231 (2005), quoting the same passage from *Apprendi.*

393 *Shepard v. United States*, 544 U.S. 13, 16 (2005)("We hold that ... a later court determining the character of an admitted burglary is generally limited to examining the statutory definition, charging document, written plea agreement, transcript of plea colloquy, and any explicit factual finding by the trial judge to which the defendant assented").

394 *Id.* at 27 (Thomas, J. concurring in part and concurring in the judgment).

395 *Alleyne v. United States*, 133 S.Ct. 2151, 2160 n.1 ("In *Almendarez-Torres v. United States*, 523 U.S. 224 (1998), we recognized a narrow exception to this general rule for the fact of a prior conviction. Because the parties do not contest that decision's vitality, we do not revisit it for purposes of our decision today").

396 *United States v. Walker*, 720 F.3d 705, 708 n.2 (8th Cir. 2013); *United States v. Overstreet*, 713 F.3d 627, 635 (11th Cir. 3013)*; United States v. Anderson*, 695 F.3d 390, 398 (6th Cir. 2012); *United States v. Charlton*, 600 U.S. 43, 55 (1st Cir. 2010)("This court normally is bound by a Supreme Court precedent unless and until the Court itself disavows that precedent. For that reason, we recently have rejected a parade of similarly sculpted challenges to the continued vitality of *Almendarez-Torres* in the context of the ACCA. We reiterate those holdings today"); *United States v. Rozier*, 598 F.3d 768, 771-72 (11th Cir. 2010)("Rozier argues that because these prior convictions were not included within the indictment, nor proven to a jury, any sentence over the 120-month maximum of §924(a)(2) is unconstitutional. This argument runs contrary to the established law of the Supreme Court and this Circuit. See *Almendarez-Torres v. United States*"); *United States v. Jones*, 574 F.3d 546, 553-54 (8th Cir. 2009); *United States v. Salahuddin*, 509 F.3d 858, 863 (7th Cir. 2007); *United States v. Coleman*, 451 F.3d 154, 159-60 (3d Cir. 2006).

397 U.S. Const. Amend. VIII ("Excessive bail shall not be required, nor excessive fines imposed, nor cruel and unusual punishments inflicted").

398 *Graham v. Florida,* 130 S.Ct. 2011, 2021 (2010); *Harmelin v. Michigan*, 501 U.S. 957, 1001 (1991)(Kennedy, J. concurring in part and concurring in the judgment); *Ewing v. California*, 538 U.S. 11, 21 (2003)(opinion of O'Connor, J.).

399 *Harmelin v. Michigan*, 501 U.S. at 994.

400 *Ewing v. California*, 538 U.S. at 30-1.

401 *Roper v. Simmons,* 543 U.S. 551, 560 (2005).

402 *Graham v. Florida,* 130 S.Ct. at 2034.

403 *United States v. Helm*, 502 F.3d 366, (5th Cir. 2007), citing in accord, *United States v. Cardoza*, 129 F.3d 6, 18 (1st Cir. 1997); *United States v. Rudolph*, 970 F.2d 467, 469-70 (8th Cir. 1992); *United States v. Crittendon*, 883 F.2d 326, 331 (4th Cir. 1989); *United States v. Pedigo*, 879 F.2d 1315, 1320 (6th Cir. 1989); *United States v. Dombrowski*, 877 F.2d 520, 526 (7th Cir. 1989); *United States v. Baker,* 850 F.2d 1365, 1372 (9th Cir. 1988); see also *United States v. Lyons*, 403 F.3d 1248, 1256-257 (11th Cir. 2005).

404 *United States v. Jones*, 574 F.3d 546, 552-53 (8th Cir. 2009); *United States v. Salahuddin*, 509 F.3d 858, 863-64 (7th Cir. 2007); *United States v. Wilks*, 464 F.3d 1240, 1243 (11th Cir. 2006).

405 *United States v. Scott*, 610 F.3d 1009, 1017 (8th Cir. 2010)("Scott argues that the Eighth Amendment prohibits enhancing his sentence based on his previous felony drug convictions because he was a juvenile when he committed those crimes.... [W]e have upheld the use of juvenile court adjudications to enhance subsequent sentences for adult convictions.... The U.S. Supreme Court cases that Scott cites, *Roper* and Graham, do not change this result. These decisions established constitutional limits on certain sentences for offenses committed by juveniles. However, Scott was twenty-five years old at the time he committed the conspiracy offense in this case. Neither *Roper* nor *Graham* involved the use of prior offenses committed as a juvenile to enhance an adult conviction, as here.... the Court's analysis in *Graham* was limited to defendants sentenced to life in prison without parole for crimes committed as juveniles. The Court in *Graham* did not call into question the constitutionality of using prior convictions, juvenile or otherwise, to enhance the sentence of a convicted adult. Therefore, we affirm the constitutionality of Scott's life sentence under 21 U.S.C. §841(b)(1)(A)").

406 U.S. Const. Amend. V.

407 *United States v. Dixon*, 509 U.S. 688, 696 (1993); *North Carolina v. Pearce*, 395 U.S. 711, 717 (1969).

408 *Blockburger v. United States*, 284, U.S. 299, 304 (1932); *United States v. Dixon*, 509 U.S. at 696 (1993); *United States v. Faulds*, 612 F.3d 566, 569 (7th Cir. 2010); *United States v. Ayala*, 601 F.3d 256, 265 (4th Cir. 2010); *United States v. Mahdi*, 598 F.3d 883, 888 (D.C. Cir. 2010).

409 *United States v. Keesee*, 358 F.3d 1217, 1220 (9th Cir. 2004); *United States v. Studifin*, 240 F.3d 415, 419 (4th Cir. 2001); *United States v. Bates*, 77 F.3d 1101, 1106 (8th Cir. 1996); *United States v. Wallace*, 889 F.2d 580, 584 (5th Cir. 1989).

410 United States Sentencing Commission, *Results of Survey of United States District Judges: January 2010 through March 2010, Question 1. Mandatory Minimums* (June 2010), available at http://www.ussc.gov/Judge_Survey/2010/ JudgeSurvey_201006.pdf.

411 Protection of Children Against Sexual Exploitation Act of 1977, P.L. 95-225, §2(a), 92 Stat. 7 (1978), 18 U.S.C. 2251, 2252 (1976 ed.)(Supp.II).

412 *18 U.S.C. 2241 (aggravated sexual assault)*: Sexual Abuse Act of 1986, P.L. 99-646, §87(b), 100 Stat. 3620 (1986). *18 U.S.C. 2251A(buying and selling a child for pornographic production)*: Child Pornography and Obscenity Enforcement Act of 1988, Title VII N of the Anti-Drug Abuse Act of 1988, P.L. 100-690, §7512(a), 102 Stat. 4486 (1988). *18 U.S.C. 2245 (federal sex offenses resulting in death)*: Federal Death Penalty Act of 1994, Title VI, of the Violent Crime Control and Law Enforcement Act of 1994, P.L. 103-322, §60010(a)(2), 108 Stat. 1972 (1994). *18 U.S.C. 2252A(child pornography (real and virtual)*: Child Pornography Prevention Act of 1996, Div. A, Title I, of the Act Making Omnibus Consolidated Appropriations for the Fiscal Year Ending September 30, 1997, and for Other Purposes, P.L. 104-208, §101(a), 110 Stat. 3009-28 (1996). *18 U.S.C. 3559(e)(mandatory life imprisonment for repeat sex offenders)*: Protection of Children from Sexual Predators Act of 1988), P.L. 105-314, §501, 112 Stat. 2980 (1998). *18 U.S.C. 1591(sex trafficking)*: Trafficking Victims Protection Act of 2000, §112(a), P.L. 106-386, 114 Stat. 1487 (2000). *18 U.S.C. 2422(b)(enticement to child prostitution), 2423(a)(travel to engage in illicit sexual purposes)*: Prosecutorial Remedies and Other Tools to End the

Exploitation of Children Today Act (PROTECT Act) of 2003, §§103(a)(2)(B), (a)(2)(C), P.L. 108-21, 117 Stat. 653 (2003). *18 U.S.C. 2242 (sexual abuse)*: Adam Walsh Child Protection and Safety Act of 2006, §§205, 207(2), P.L. 109-248, 120 Stat. 613, 615 (2006).

[413] See, e.g., 18 U.S.C. 2241(a)("Whoever, in the special maritime and territorial jurisdiction of the United States or in a Federal prison, or in any prison, institution, or facility in which persons are held in custody by direction of or pursuant to a contract or agreement with the head of any Federal department or agency, knowingly causes another person to engage in a sexual act ..."); a similar jurisdiction phrase occurs in each of chapter 109A's criminal provisions, 18 U.S.C. 2241(b), (c); 2242; 2243; 2244.

[414] 18 U.S.C. 7(3).

[415] *Jurisdiction Over Federal Areas Within the States: Report of the Interdepartmental Committee for the Study of Jurisdiction Over Federal Areas Within the States* (April 1956).

[416] 18 U.S.C. 7(9).

[417] 18 U.S.C. 3261-3267. Those employed by or accompanying the federal government are also subject to criminal liability for misconduct that would constitute a violation of chapter 77 (relating to peonage, slavery, and trafficking in persons) or chapter 117 (relating to transportation for illegal sexual purposes) if committed within the territorial jurisdiction of the United States, 18 U.S.C. 3271-3272.

[418] 18 U.S.C. 7(1), (2), (8). There is jurisdiction with respect to misconduct aboard an aircraft under comparable circumstances, 18 U.S.C. 7(5); 49 U.S.C. 46506.

[419] 18 U.S.C. 3299 ("Notwithstanding any other law, an indictment may be found or an information instituted at any time without limitation for any offense under section 1201 involving a minor victim, and for any felony under chapter 109A, 110 (except for section 2257 and 2257A), or 117, or section 1591").

[420] *United States v. Gouveia*, 467 U.S. 180, 192 (1984), citing *United States v. Marion*, 404 U.S. 307, 322-24 (1971), and *United States v. Lovasco*, 431 U.S. 783, 788-90 (1977)("[A]pplicable statutes of limitations protect against the prosecution's bringing stale criminal charges against any defendant, and, beyond that protection, the Fifth Amendment requires the dismissal of an indictment, even if it is brought within the statute of limitations, if the defendant can prove that the Government's delay in bringing the indictment was a deliberate device to gain an advantage over him and that it caused him actual prejudice in presenting his defense ").

[421] 18 U.S.C. 2241(a), (b).

[422] 18 U.S.C. 2241(c).

[423] 18 U.S.C. 2242. There is considerable overlap between section 2242 and subsection 2241(a) as well as subsection 2241(b).

[424] 18 U.S.C. 2244(b).

[425] 18 U.S.C. 3559(e).

[426] 18 U.S.C. 2246 ("As used in this chapter ... (2) the term 'sexual act' means - (A) contact between the penis and the vulva or the penis and the anus, and for purposes of this subparagraph contact involving the penis occurs upon penetration, however slight; (B) contact between the mouth and the penis, the mouth and the vulva, or the mouth and the anus; (C) the penetration, however slight, of the anal or genital opening of another by a hand or finger or by any object, with an intent to abuse, humiliate, harass, degrade, or arouse or gratify the sexual desire of any person ...").

[427] 18 U.S.C. 2246 ("As used in this chapter ... (2) the term 'sexual act' means ... (D) the intentional touching, not through the clothing, of the genitalia of another person who has not attained the age of 16 years with an intent to abuse, humiliate, harass, degrade, or arouse or gratify the sexual desire of any person").

[428] 18 U.S.C. 2246 ("As used in this chapter ... (3) the term 'sexual contact' means the intentional touching, either directly or through the clothing, of the genitalia, anus, groin, breast, inner thigh, or buttocks of any person with an intent to abuse, humiliate, harass, degrade, or arouse or gratify the sexual desire of any person").

[429] 18 U.S.C. 2241("(a) By Force or Threat.—Whoever ... knowingly causes another person to engage in a sexual act (1) by using force against that other person; or (2) by threatening or placing that other person in fear that any person will be subjected to death, serious bodily injury, or kidnapping; or attempts to do so, shall be fined under this title, imprisoned for any term of years or life, or both. (b) By Other Means.—Whoever ... knowingly - (1) renders another person unconscious and thereby engages in a sexual act with that other person; or (2) administers to another person by force or threat of force, or without the knowledge or permission of that person, a drug, intoxicant, or other similar substance and thereby - (A) substantially impairs the ability of that other person to appraise or control conduct; and (B) engages in a sexual act with that other person; or attempts to do so, shall be fined under this title, imprisoned for any term of years or life, or both ...").

[430] *Id.* Federal crimes punishable by a maximum term of imprisonment of 1 year or more are classified as felonies, 18 U.S.C. 3559(a). Absent a specific countervailing provision, defendants convicted of a felony are subject to a fine of not more than $250,000 (not more than $500,000 for an organization), 18 U.S.C. 3571.

[431] *United States v. White Bull*, 646 F.3d 1082, 1087 (8th Cir. 2011).

[432] 18 U.S.C. 2241(c)("Whoever ... knowingly engages in a sexual act with another person who has not attained the age of 12 years, or knowingly engages in a sexual act under the circumstances described in subsections (a) and (b) with another person who has attained the age of 12 years but has not attained the age of 16 years (and is at least 4 years younger than the person so engaging), or attempts to do so, shall be fined under this title and imprisoned for not less than 30 years or for life. If the defendant has previously been convicted of another Federal offense under this subsection, or of a State offense that would have been an offense under either such provision had the offense occurred in a Federal prison, unless the death penalty is imposed, the defendant shall be sentenced to life in prison").

[433] *United States v. DeCoteau*, 630 F3d. 1091, 1097-98 (8th Cir. 2011).

[434] 18 U.S.C. 2241(c).

[435] *United States v. Villarreal*, 707 F.3d 942, 960 (8th Cir. 2013); *United States v. DeMarce*, 564 F.3d 989, 998 (8th Cir. 2009).

[436] 18 U.S.C. 2241(d).

[437] *United States v. Juvenile Male*, 211 F.3d 1169, 1171-172 (9th Cir. 2000); *United States v. Ransom*, 942 F.2d 775, 776-78 (10th Cir. 1991).

[438] *United States v. Farley*, 607 F.3d 1294, 1336-345 (11th Cir. 2010).

[439] *United States v. DeMarce*, 564 F.3d 989, 1000 (8th Cir. 2009).

[440] *United States v. Robertson*, 606 F.3d 943, 951 (8th Cir. 2010).

[441] 18 U.S.C. 2242, 7(9), 3261-3267.

[442] 18 U.S.C. 2242.

[443] *Id.* ("Whoever, in the special maritime and territorial jurisdiction of the United States or in a Federal prison, or in any prison, institution, or facility in which persons are held in custody by direction of or pursuant to a contract or agreement with the head of any Federal department or agency, knowingly—(1) causes another person to engage in a sexual act by threatening or placing that other person in fear (other than by threatening or placing that other person in fear that any person will be subjected to death, serious bodily injury, or kidnapping); or (2) engages in a sexual act with another person if that other person is—(A) incapable of appraising the nature of the conduct; or (B) physically incapable of declining participation in, or communicating unwillingness to engage in, that sexual act; or attempts to do so, shall be fined under this title and imprisoned for any term of years or for life").

[444] *United States v. Papakee*, 573 F.3d 569, 573-75 (intoxicated); *United States v. Fasthorse*, 639 F.3d 1182, 1184 (9th Cir. 2011)(asleep), citing *United States v. Smith*, 606 F.3d 1270, 1281 (10th Cir. 2010), and *United States v. Peters*, 277 F.3d 963, 967-68 (7th Cir. 2002).

[445] *United States v. Betone*, 636 F.3d 384, 387-88 (8th Cir. 2011).

[446] 18 U.S.C. 2244.

[447] 18 U.S.C. 2244(a)(5)("Whoever, in the special maritime and territorial jurisdiction of the United States or in a Federal prison, or in any prison, institution, or facility in which persons are held in custody by direction of or pursuant to a contract or agreement with the head of any Federal department or agency, knowingly engages in or causes sexual contact with or by another person, if so to do would violate ... (5) subsection (c) of section 2241 of this title had the sexual contact been a sexual act, shall be fined under this title and imprisoned for any term of years or for life").

[448] 18 U.S.C. 2244.

[449] The defendant may be sentenced to death, if convicted of a capital offense, 18 U.S.C. 3559(e)(1).

[450] 18 U.S.C. 3559(e)(2)(D); *United States v. Doss*, 630 F.3d 1181, 1195 (9th Cir. 2011).

[451] 18 U.S.C. 3559(e)(2)(A).

[452] *Id.*

[453] 18 U.S.C. 3559(e)(2)(B)("[T]he term 'State sex offense' means an offense under State law that is punishable by more than one year in prison and consists of conduct that would be a Federal sex offense if, to the extent or in the manner specified in the applicable provision of this title - (i) the offense involved interstate or foreign commerce, or the use of the mails; or (ii) the conduct occurred in any commonwealth, territory, or possession of the United States, within the special maritime and territorial jurisdiction of the United States, in a Federal prison, on any land or building owned by, leased to, or otherwise used by or under the control of the Government of the United States, or in the Indian country (as defined in section 1151)").

[454] *United States v. Doss*, 630 F.3d 1181, 1197 (9th Cir. 2011).

[455] *United States v. Gallenardo*, 579 F.3d 1076, 1085-86 (9th Cir. 2009)("Gallenardo contends that his prior state conviction for felony sexual assault is not within 18 U.S.C. §3559(e)'s purview because his conduct did not involve interstate or foreign commerce.... the plain and unambiguous language of 18 U.S.C. §3559(e) undermines Gallenardo's argument. Section 3559(e)(2)(B) provides that a state sex offense qualifies as a predicate offense if the conduct 'would be' a Federal sex offense 'if it had involved interstate or foreign commerce' or 'if it occurred within federal jurisdiction'"); see also *United States v. Rosenbohm*, 564 F.3d 820, 823-25 (7th Cir. 2009).

[456] *United States v. Gallenardo*, 579 F.3d 1076, 1083-85 (9th Cir. 2009); *United States v. Moore*, 567 F.3d 187, 190-91 (6th Cir. 2009).

[457] 18 U.S.C. 3559(e)(3).

[458] See, e.g., Hamilton, *The "Licentiousness" in Religious Organizations and Why It Is Not Protected Under Religious Liberty Constitutional Provisions*, 18 WILLIAM & MARY BILL OF RIGHTS JOURNAL 953, 969 n.72 (2010); Dubler, *Immoral Purposes: Marriage and the Genus of Illicit Sex*, 115 YALE LAW JOURNAL 756,761 (2005); Friedman, *Name Robbers: Privacy, Blackmail, and Assorted Matters in Legal History*, 30 HOFSTRA LAW REVIEW 1093, 1118 (2002).

[459] 18 U.S.C. 2422(b)("Whoever, using the mail or any facility or means of interstate or foreign commerce, or within the special maritime and territorial jurisdiction of the United States knowingly persuades, induces, entices, or coerces any individual who has not attained the age of 18 years, to engage in prostitution or any sexual activity for which any person can be charged with a criminal offense, or attempts to do so, shall be fined under this title and imprisoned not less than 10 years or for life") (Note that the subsection proscribes the same conduct when committed within the special maritime and territorial jurisdiction of the United States).

[460] *United States v. Berk*, 652 F.3d 132, 138 (1st Cir. 2011), citing in accord *United States v. Cochran*, 534 F.3d 631, 633 (7th Cir. 2008); *United States v. Thomas*, 410 F.3d 1235, 1245 (10th Cir. 2005); *United States v. Brand*, 467 F.3d 179, 201-02 (2d Cir. 2006); and *United States v. Meek*, 366 F.3d 705, 718 (9th Cir. 2004); see also *United States v. Young*, 613 F.3d 735, 742 (8th Cir. 2010).

[461] *United States v. Berk*, 652 F.3d 132, 140 (1st Cir. 2011); *United States v. Chambers*, 642 F.3d 588, 592 (7th Cir. 2011); *United States v. Lanzon*, 639 F.3d 1293, 1299 (11th Cir. 2011); *United States v. Hart*, 635 F.3d 850, 855 (6th Cir. 2011); *United States v. Douglas*, 626 F.3d 161, 164 (2d Cir. 2010).

[462] *United States v. Berk*, 652 F.3d 132, 140 (1st Cir. 2011); *United States v. Chambers*, 642 F.3d 588, 592 (7th Cir. 2011); *United States v. Lanzon*, 639 F.3d 1293, 1299 (11th Cir. 2011); *United States v. Douglas*, 626 F.3d 161, 164 (2d Cir. 2010); *United States v. Hofus*, 598 F.3d 1171, 1174 (9th Cir. 2010).

[463] *United States v. Berk*, 652 F.3d 132, 140 (1st Cir. 2011)("Section 2422(b) criminalizes an intentional attempt to achieve a mental state—a minor's assent—regardless of the accused's intentions vis-a-vis the actual consummation of sexual activities with the minor"); see also *United States v. Berg*, 640 F.3d 239, 252 (7th Cir. 2011), citing in accord *United States v. Lee*, 603 F.3d 904, 914 (11th Cir. 2010); *United States v. Brand*, 467 F.3d 179, 202 (2d Cir. 2006); *United States v. Thomas*, 410 F.3d 1235, 1244 (10th Cir. 2005); and *United States v. Patten*, 397 F.3d 1100, 1103 (8th Cir. 2005).

[464] *United States v. Berk*, 652 F.3d 132, 140 (1st Cir. 2011); *United States v. Lanzon*, 639 F.3d 1293, 1299 (11th Cir. 2011); *United States v. Douglas*, 626 F.3d 161, 164 (2d Cir. 2010); *United States v. Nestor*, 574 F.3d 159, 160-62 (3d Cir. 2009).

[465] *United States v. Lanzon*, 639 F.3d 1293, 1299 (11th Cir. 2011)("[A]n actual minor victim is not required for an attempt conviction under §2422(b)"); see also, *United States v. Nestor*, 574 F.3d 159, 161 (3d Cir. 2009).

[466] *United States v. Brucker*, 646 F.3d 1012, 1018-19 (7th Cir. 2011); *United States v. Hart*, 635 F.3d 850, 858-59 (6th Cir. 2011); *United States v. Farley*, 607 F.3d 1294, 1336-345 (11th Cir. 2010).

[467] *United States v. Orr*, 622 F.3d 864, 868-70 (7th Cir. 2010); *United States v. Young*, 613 F.3d 735, 746-48 (8th Cir. 2010); *United States v. Gagliardi*, 506 F.3d 140, 149-50 (2d Cir. 2007).

[468] *United States v. Hart*, 635 F.3d 850, 858 (6th Cir. 2011).

[469] *United States v. Brucker*, 646 F.3d 1012, 1016-18 (7th Cir. 2011); *United States v. Hughes*, 632 F.3d 956, 960-61 (6th Cir. 2011).

[470] *United States v. Hart*, 635 F.3d 850, 856-58 (6th Cir. 2011); *United States v. Farley*, 607 F.3d 1294, 1324 (11th Cir. 2010); *United States v. Gagliardi*, 506 F.3d 140, 149-50 (2d Cir. 2007); *United States v. Gagliardi*, 506 F.3d 140, 145-47 (2d Cir. 2007).

[471] *United States v. Brucker*, 646 F.3d 1012, 1016, 1019 (7th Cir. 2011)("For in making the sentencing guidelines advisory [in *Booker*], the Court did not authorize courts to sentence below the minimums proscribed not by the guidelines but by constitutional federal statutes.... We have rejected separation of powers challenges to mandatory minimum sentences, and we see no reason to revisit that holding here"); *United States v. Hughes*, 632 F.3d 956, 961 (6th Cir. 2011); *United States v. Gagliardi*, 506 F.3d 140, 148-49 (2d Cir. 2007).

[472] 18 U.S.C. 2423(a)("A person who knowingly transports an individual who has not attained the age of 18 years in interstate or foreign commerce, or in any commonwealth, territory or possession of the United States, with intent that the individual engage in prostitution, or in any sexual activity for which any person can be charged with a criminal offense, shall be fined under this title and imprisoned not less than 10 years or for life").

[473] 18 U.S.C. 2423(e).

[474] 18 U.S.C. 2423(b), (c), and (d), respectively. Attempts or conspiracies to violate any of these are also punishable by imprisonment for not more than 30 years, 18 U.S.C. 2423(e).

[475] *United States v. Broxmeyer*, 616 F.3d 120, 128 (2d Cir. 2010); see also *United States v. Bonty*, 383 F.3d 575, 578 (7th Cir. 2004).

[476] *United States v. Daniels*, 653 F.3d 399, 409-10 (6th Cir. 2011), citing in accord *United States v. Cox*, 577 F.3d 833, 838 (7th Cir. 2009); *United States v. Jones*, 471 F.3d 535, 539 (4th Cir.

2006); *United States v. Griffith*, 284 F.3d 338, 351 (2d Cir. 2002); and *United States v. Taylor*, 239 F.3d 994, 997 (9th Cir. 2001).

477 *United States v. Hoffman*, 626 F.3d 993, 996 (8th Cir. 2010)("The illicit behavior must be one of the purposes motivating ... the interstate transportation of the minor, but need not be the dominant purpose"); *United States v. Bonty*, 383 F.3d 575, 578 (7th Cir. 2004)("The government need only prove that a significant or compelling purpose the trip— not the dominant purpose—was to commit aggravated assault"); *United States v. Hayward*, 359 F.3d 631, 638 (3d Cir. 2004)("Hayward points to no case in which any Court of Appeals required a jury instruction that criminal sexual activity must be the dominant purpose of interstate travel to support a conviction under 18 U.S.C. §2423(a). The Government relies on decisions by the First, Second, Fifth, Sixth, Seventh, and Tenth Circuits, in which criminal sexual activity was one of a number of multiple motives for interstate travel.... Similarly in this case, the District Court's charge that 'a significant or motivating purpose of the travel across state or foreign boundaries was to have the individual transported engage in illegal sexual activity. In other words, the illegal sexual activity must not have been merely incidental to the trip' was not in error").

478 18 U.S.C. 2241(c)("Whoever crosses a State line with intent to engage in a sexual act with a person who has not attained the age of 12 years ... or attempts to do so, shall be fined under this title and imprisoned for not less than 30 years or for life. If the defendant has previously been convicted of another Federal offense under this subsection, or of a State offense that would have been an offense under either such provision had the offense occurred in a Federal prison, unless the death penalty is imposed, the defendant shall be sentenced to life in prison"); e.g., *United States v. King*, 604 F.3d 125, 146 (3d Cir. 2010)(uphold a conviction and 30-year sentence under the travel prong of subsection 2241(c)); *United States v. Farley*, 607 F.3d 1294, 1336-345 (11th Cir. 2010)(reversing a lower court ruling which had held the mandatory minimum sentencing provision of subsection 2241(c) unconstitutionally disproportionate).

479 18 U.S.C. 2241(c).

480 18 U.S.C. 2241(d)("In a prosecution under subsection (c) of this section, the Government need not prove that the defendant knew that the other person engaging in the sexual act had not attained the age of 12 years").

481 18 U.S.C. 1591(a)(1), (a)(2).

482 18 U.S.C. 1591(2)("if the offense was not so effected, and the person recruited, enticed, harbored, transported, provided, or obtained had attained the age of 14 years but had not attained the age of 18 years at the time of such offense, by a fine under this title and imprisonment for not less than 10 years or for life").

483 18 U.S.C. 1591(b)(1)("[I]f the offense was effected by means of force, threats of force, fraud, or coercion described in subsection (e)(2), or by any combination of such means, or if the person recruited, enticed, harbored, transported, provided, or obtained had not attained the age of 14 years at the time of such offense, by a fine under this title and imprisonment for any term of years not less than 15 or for life").

484 18 U.S.C. 1591(a)(1)("Whoever knowingly - (1) in or affecting interstate or foreign commerce, or within the special maritime and territorial jurisdiction of the United States, recruits, entices, harbors, transports, provides, obtains, or maintains by any means a person ... knowing, or in reckless disregard of the fact, that means of force, threats of force, fraud, coercion described in subsection (e)(2), or any combination of such means will be used to cause the person to engage in a commercial sex act, or that the person has not attained the age of 18 years and will be caused to engage in a commercial sex act, shall be punished as provided in subsection (b).

485 18 U.S.C. 1591(a)(2)("Whoever knowingly ... (2) benefits, financially or by receiving anything of value, from participation in a venture which has engaged in an act described in violation of paragraph (1), knowing, or in reckless disregard of the fact, that means of force, threats of force, fraud, coercion described in subsection (e)(2), or any combination of such

means will be used to cause the person to engage in a commercial sex act, or that the person has not attained the age of 18 years and will be caused to engage in a commercial sex act, shall be punished as provided in subsection (b)").

486 *United States v. Todd*, 627 F.3d 329, 333 (9th Cir. 2010); *United States v. Evans*, 476 F.3d 1176, 1178-179 (11th Cir. 2007).

487 *United States v. Anderson*, 560 F.3d 275, 280 (5th Cir. 2009); *United States v. Evans*, 476 F.3d 1176, 1179-180 (11th Cir. 2007).

488 *United States v. Evans*, 476 F.3d 1176, 1180 n.2 (11th Cir. 2007).

489 *United States v. Brooks*, 610 F.3d 1186, 1195 (9th Cir. 2010)("§1591(a) plainly requires proof that the defendant knew that the victim was under the age of eighteen years at the time of crime ...").

490 18 U.S.C. 1591(c)("In a prosecution under subsection (a)(1) in which the defendant had a reasonable opportunity to observe the person so recruited, enticed, harbored, transported, provided, obtained or maintained, the Government need not prove that the defendant knew that the person had not attained the age of 18 years").

491 18 U.S.C. 2245 ("A person who, in the course of an offense under this chapter, or section 1591, 2251, 2251A, 2260, 2421, 2422, 2423, or 2425, murders an individual, shall be punished by death or imprisoned for any term of years or for life").

492 18 U.S.C. 1111 (murder within the special maritime and territorial jurisdiction of the United States), 1118 (murder by federal prisoners).

493 18 U.S.C. 2251(e).

494 18 U.S.C. 2251(e)("Any individual who violates, or attempts or conspires to violate, this section shall be fined under this title and imprisoned not less than 15 years nor more than 30 years, but if such person has one prior conviction under this chapter, section 1591, chapter 71, chapter 109A, or chapter 117, or under section 920 of title 10 (article 120 of the Uniform Code of Military Justice), or under the laws of any State relating to aggravated sexual abuse, sexual abuse, abusive sexual contact involving a minor or ward, or sex trafficking of children, or the production, possession, receipt, mailing, sale, distribution, shipment, or transportation of child pornography, such person shall be fined under this title and imprisoned for not less than 25 years nor more than 50 years, but if such person has 2 or more prior convictions under this chapter, chapter 71, chapter 109A, or chapter 117, or under section 920 of title 10 (article 120 of the Uniform Code of Military Justice), or under the laws of any State relating to the sexual exploitation of children, such person shall be fined under this title and imprisoned not less than 35 years nor more than life. Any organization that violates, or attempts or conspires to violate, this section shall be fined under this title. Whoever, in the course of an offense under this section, engages in conduct that results in the death of a person, shall be punished by death or imprisoned for not less than 30 years or for life").

495 *Id.*

496 18 U.S.C. 2256(1).

497 18 U.S.C. 2251(a), (b), (c), (d).

498 *United States v. Fletcher*, 634 F.3d 395, 400-405 (7th Cir. 2011); *United States v. Heath*, 624 F.3d 884, 886 (8th Cir. 2010); *United States v. Humphrey*, 608 F.3d 955, 957-62 (6th Cir. 2010); *United States v. Malloy*, 568 F.3d 166, 171 (4th Cir. 2009); *United States v. Griffith*, 284 F.3d 338, 349 (2d Cir. 2002); but see *United States v. United States District Court*, 858 F.2d 534, 543 (9th Cir. 1988)("A defendant may avoid conviction only showing, by clear and convincing evidence, that he did not know, and could not reasonable have learned, that the actor or actress was under 18 years of age").

499 18 U.S.C. 2256(5) 'visual depiction' includes undeveloped film and videotape, data stored on computer disk or by electronic means which is capable of conversion into a visual image, and data which is capable of conversion into a visual image that has been transmitted by any means, whether or not stored in a permanent format").

[500] 18 U.SC. 2256(2)(A)("Except as provided in subparagraph (B), 'sexually explicit conduct' means actual or simulated - (i) sexual intercourse, including genital-genital, oral-genital, anal-genital, or oral-anal, whether between persons of the same or opposite sex; (ii) bestiality; (iii) masturbation; (iv) sadistic or masochistic abuse; or (v) lascivious exhibition of the genitals or pubic area of any person").

[501] *United States v. Johnson*, 639 F.3d 433, 439-40 (8th Cir. 2011)("In determining whether images are "lascivious," we have referred to the criteria listed in *United States v. Dost*, 636 F.Supp. 828, 832 (S.D. Cal. 1986), aff'd sub nom., *United States v. Wiegand*, 812 F.2d 1239 (9th Cir. 1987). The factors in *Dost* included (1) whether the focal point of the picture is on the minor's genitals or pubic area; (2) whether the setting of the picture is sexually suggestive; (3) whether the minor is depicted in unnatural poses or inappropriate attire considering the minor's age; (4) whether the minor is fully or partially clothed or is nude; (5) whether the picture suggests sexual coyness or a willingness to engage in sexual activity; and (6) whether the image is intended to elicit a sexual response in the viewer.... However, while we consider these criteria, they are 'neither definitive nor exhaustive"); see also *United States v. Steen*, 634 F.3d 822, 826-27 (5th Cir. 2011); *United States v. Brown*, 579 F.3d 672, 680-83 (6th Cir. 2009); *United States v. Overton*, 573 F.3d 679, 686-90 (9th Cir. 2009); *United States v. Rivera*, 546 F.3d 245, 250 (2d Cir. 2008); *United States v. Frabizio*, 459 F.3d 80, 87 (1st Cir. 2006).

[502] 18 U.S.C. 2251("(a) Any person who employs, uses, persuades, induces, entices, or coerces any minor to engage in, or who has a minor assist any other person to engage in ... with the intent that such minor engage in, any sexually explicit conduct for the purpose of producing any visual depiction of such conduct or for the purpose of transmitting a live visual depiction of such conduct, shall be punished as provided under subsection (e), if such person knows or has reason to know that such visual depiction will be transported or transmitted using any means or facility of interstate or foreign commerce.... (e) Any individual who violates, or attempts or conspires to violate, this section shall.... "); see, e.g., *United States v. Coutentos*, 651 F.3d 809, 823 (8th Cir. 2011)("To convict Coutentos of producing child pornography under 18 U.S.C. §2251(a) and (d)(2000), the government must have established that (1) at a time when K.C. or S.Z., or both, were under eighteen years of age; (2) Coutentos used, persuaded, or induced K.C. or S.Z., or both, to engage in sexually explicit conduct; (3) Coutentos voluntarily and intentionally did this for the purpose of producing at least one visual depiction of such conduct; and (4) at least one those depictions was produced using a camera that had been shipped and transported in interstate or foreign commerce. See §2251(a). The elements are the same to prove attempted sexual exploitation of a minor except that the attempt charge requires only that Coutentos attempted to produce a visual depiction and that he carried out some act which was a substantial step toward that production. See §2251").

[503] 18 U.S.C. 2251(a)("Any person who employs, uses, persuades, induces, entices, or coerces any minor to engage in, or who has a minor assist any other person to engage in, or who transports any minor in or affecting interstate or foreign commerce, or in any Territory or Possession of the United States, with the intent that such minor engage in, any sexually explicit conduct for the purpose of producing any visual depiction of such conduct or for the purpose of transmitting a live visual depiction of such conduct, shall be punished as provided under subsection (e), if such person knows or has reason to know that such visual depiction will be transported or transmitted using any means or facility of interstate or foreign commerce or in or affecting interstate or foreign commerce or mailed, if that visual depiction was produced or transmitted using materials that have been mailed, shipped, or transported in or affecting interstate or foreign commerce by any means, including by computer, or if such visual depiction has actually been transported or transmitted using any means or facility of interstate or foreign commerce or in or affecting interstate or foreign commerce or mailed").

[504] *United States v. Culver*, 598 F.3d 740, 746-47 (11th Cir. 2010); *United States v. McCloud*, 590 F.3d 560, 568 (8th Cir. 2009); *United States v. Malloy*, 568 F.3d 166, 179-80 (4th Cir. 2009).

[505] *United States v. Malloy*, 568 F.3d 166, 180 (4th Cir. 2009); *United States v. Rivera*, 546 F.3d 245, 254-55 (2d Cir. 2008); *United States v. Polk*, 546 F.3d 74, 74-8 (1st Cir. 2008); *United States v. Paton*, 535 F.3d 829, 837-38 (8th Cir. 2008).

[506] 18 U.S.C. 2251(b)("Any parent, legal guardian, or person having custody or control of a minor who knowingly permits such minor to engage in, or to assist any other person to engage in, sexually explicit conduct for the purpose of producing any visual depiction of such conduct or for the purpose of transmitting a live visual depiction of such conduct shall be punished as provided under subsection (e) of this section, if such parent, legal guardian, or person knows or has reason to know that such visual depiction will be transported or transmitted using any means or facility of interstate or foreign commerce or in or affecting interstate or foreign commerce or mailed, if that visual depiction was produced or transmitted using materials that have been mailed, shipped, or transported in or affecting interstate or foreign commerce by any means, including by computer, or if such visual depiction has actually been transported or transmitted using any means or facility of interstate or foreign commerce or in or affecting interstate or foreign commerce or mailed"); see, e.g., *United States v. O'Connor*, 650 F.3d 839, 857-58 (2d Cir. 2011); *United States v. Paige*, 604 F.3d 1268, 1270 (11th Cir. 2010).

[507] Section 2251A is discussed in a later section of this report.

[508] 18 U.S.C. 2251(c)("(1) Any person who, in a circumstance described in paragraph (2), employs, uses, persuades, induces, entices, or coerces any minor to engage in, or who has a minor assist any other person to engage in, any sexually explicit conduct outside of the United States, its territories or possessions, for the purpose of producing any visual depiction of such conduct, shall be punished as provided under subsection (e). (2) The circumstance referred to in paragraph (1) is that - (A) the person intends such visual depiction to be transported to the United States, its territories or possessions, by any means, including by using any means or facility of interstate or foreign commerce or mail; or (B) the person transports such visual depiction to the United States, its territories or possessions, by any means, including by using any means or facility of interstate or foreign commerce or mail"); see, e.g., United States v. Deverso, 518 F.3d 1250, 1257 (11th Cir. 2008).

[509] *United States v. Rowe*, 414 F.3d 271, 278 (2d Cir. 2005).

[510] 18 U.S.C. 2251(d)("(1) Any person who, in a circumstance described in paragraph (2), knowingly makes, prints, or publishes, or causes to be made, printed, or published, any notice or advertisement seeking or offering - (A) to receive, exchange, buy, produce, display, distribute, or reproduce, any visual depiction, if the production of such visual depiction involves the use of a minor engaging in sexually explicit conduct and such visual depiction is of such conduct; or (B) participation in any act of sexually explicit conduct by or with any minor for the purpose of producing a visual depiction of such conduct; shall be punished as provided under subsection (e)").

[511] 18 U.S.C. 2251(d)("... (2) The circumstance referred to in paragraph (1) is that - (A) such person knows or has reason to know that such notice or advertisement will be transported using any means or facility of interstate or foreign commerce or in or affecting interstate or foreign commerce by any means including by computer or mailed; or (B) such notice or advertisement is transported using any means or facility of interstate or foreign commerce or in or affecting interstate or foreign commerce by any means including by computer or mailed").

[512] *United States v. Rowe*, 414 F.3d 271, 277 (2d Cir. 2005).

[513] 18 U.S.C. 2251A(a)("Any parent, legal guardian, or other person having custody or control of a minor who sells or otherwise transfers custody or control of such minor, or offers to sell or otherwise transfer custody of such minor either- (1) with knowledge that, as a consequence of the sale or transfer, the minor will be portrayed in a visual depiction engaging in, or assisting another person to engage in, sexually explicit conduct; or (2) with intent to

promote either - (A) the engaging in of sexually explicit conduct by such minor for the purpose of producing any visual depiction of such conduct; or (B) the rendering of assistance by the minor to any other person to engage in sexually explicit conduct for the purpose of producing any visual depiction of such conduct; shall be punished by imprisonment for not less than 30 years or for life and by a fine under this title, if any of the circumstances described in subsection (c) of this section exist"). Subsection 2251A(b) contains similar provisions and penalties relating to those who acquire or seek to acquire custody or control of a child for purposes of producing child pornography.

514 18 U.S.C. 2256(7).

515 *United States v. Block*, 635 F.3d 721, 723 (5th Cir. 2011).

516 *United States v. Buculei*, 262 F.3d 322, 331 (4th Cir. 2001).

517 *United States v. Frank*, 599 F.3d 1221, 1234 (11th Cir. 2010)("Frank argues that there was insufficient evidence that he 'purchas[ed] ... a minor,' as required by 18 U.S.C. §2241A(b), because (1) the term 'purchase' requires that a defendant purchase a minor from a third party, rather than from the minor herself; and (2) the phrase 'purchase[] or otherwise obtain[] custody or control' requires that purchase must be a form of control, which Frank argues is only achieved through 'sexual slavery,' such as forced prostitution or captivity for the purpose of producing child pornography. We disagree").

518 18 U.S.C. 2251A(c)("the circumstances referred to in subsections (a) and (b) are that - (1) in the course of the conduct described in such subsections the minor or the actor traveled in or was transported in or affecting interstate or foreign commerce; (2) any offer described in such subsections was communicated or transported using any means or facility of interstate or foreign commerce or in or affecting interstate or foreign commerce by any means including by computer or mail; or (3) the conduct described in such subsections took place in any territory or possession of the United States").

519 18 U.S.C. 2252(a)(1), (2), (3). 18 U.S.C. 2252(b)(1)("Whoever violates, or attempts or conspires to violate, paragraph (1), (2), or (3) of subsection (a) shall be fined under this title and imprisoned not less than 5 years and not more than 20 years, but if such person has a prior conviction under this chapter, section 1591, chapter 71, chapter 109A, or chapter 117, or under section 920 of title 10 (article 120 of the Uniform Code of Military Justice), or under the laws of any State relating to aggravated sexual abuse, sexual abuse, or abusive sexual conduct involving a minor or ward, or the production, possession, receipt, mailing, sale, distribution, shipment, or transportation of child pornography, or sex trafficking of children, such person shall be fined under this title and imprisoned for not less than 15 years nor more than 40 years").

520 *Id.*

521 18 U.S.C. 2252(a)(4), (b)(2).

522 18 U.S.C. 2252(b)(1). 18 U.S.C. 2252(b)(2)("Whoever violates, or attempts or conspires to violate, paragraph (4) of subsection (a) shall be fined under this title or imprisoned not more than 10 years, or both, but if such person has a prior conviction under this chapter, chapter 71, chapter 109A, or chapter 117, or under section 920 of title 10 (article 120 of the Uniform Code of Military Justice), or under the laws of any State relating to aggravated sexual abuse, sexual abuse, or abusive sexual conduct involving a minor or ward, or the production, possession, receipt, mailing, sale, distribution, shipment, or transportation of child pornography, such person shall be fined under this title and imprisoned for not less than 10 years nor more than 20 years").

523 18 U.S.C. 2252(a)("Any person who - (1) knowingly transports or ships using any means or facility of interstate or foreign commerce or in or affecting interstate or foreign commerce by any means including by computer or mails, any visual depiction, if - (A) the producing of such visual depiction involves the use of a minor engaging in sexually explicit conduct; and (B) such visual depiction is of such conduct ... shall be punished as provided in subsection (b) of this section").

524 18 U.S.C. 2252(b)(1).

[525] *United States v. Chambers*, 441 F.3d 438, 449 (6th Cir. 2006).
[526] *United States v. Sims*, 428 F.3d 945, 957 (10th Cir. 2005).
[527] *United States v. X-Citment Video, Inc.*, 513 U.S. 64, 78 (1994).
[528] *United States v. Lewis*, 605 F.3d 395, 403 (6th Cir. 2010).
[529] *United States v. Polanco*, 451 F.3d 308, 310 (3d Cir. 2006).
[530] *United States v. Chambers*, 441 F.3d 438, 450 (6th Cir. 2006).
[531] *United States v. Osborne*, 551 F.3d 718, 721 (7th Cir. 2009).
[532] 18 U.S.C. 2252(a)("Any person who ... (2) knowingly receives, or distributes, any visual depiction using any means or facility of interstate or foreign commerce or that has been mailed, or has been shipped or transported in or affecting interstate or foreign commerce, or which contains materials which have been mailed or so shipped or transported, by any means including by computer, or knowingly reproduces any visual depiction for distribution using any means or facility of interstate or foreign commerce or in or affecting interstate or foreign commerce or through the mails, if - (A) the producing of such visual depiction involves the use of a minor engaging in sexually explicit conduct; and (B) such visual depiction is of such conduct ... shall be punished as provided in subsection (b) of this section"); 18 U.S.C. 2252(b)(1).
[533] *United States v. Schwarte*, 645 F.3d 1022, 1032 (8th Cir. 2011). After the events in *Schwarte* occurred, Congress expanded the subsection's jurisdictional reach by adding transportation and transmissions "affecting interstate or foreign commerce," P.L. 110-358, 103(b), 122 Stat. 4003 (2008).
[534] *United States v. Winkler*, 639 F.3d 692, 696 (5th Cir. 2011), citing inter alia, *United States v. Dobbs*, 629 F.3d 1199, 1201, 1207 (10th Cir. 2011)(emphasis in the original)("[T]he lack of a search-and-creation pattern ... when combined with the absence of any evidence establishing that the defendant ever saw the images, forefends any view that *knowing* receipt could have been found by the jury"); *United States v. Kuchinski*, 469 F.3d 853, 861-62 (9th Cir. 2006)"Citing the fact that there was no evidence the defendant was a sophisticated computer user, that he tried to get access to the cache files, or that he knew of the cache's existence"); *United States v. Bass*, 411 F.3d 1198 (10th Cir. 2005)("In *Bass*, the court relied on the fact that the defendant used software specifically aimed at eliminating the digital residue of his illicit activities to determine that the defendant did knowingly receive the files stored in his internet cache").
[535] E.g., *United States v. Winkler*, 639 F.3d 692, 699 (5th Cir. 2011)("Those facts speak to a pattern of child pornography receipt and possession that could also have caused a rational jury to conclude that Winkler knowing received the files in Count One. In sum, this is not the exceptional case in which the government has persisted in bringing a criminal prosecution against the unknowing victim of a computer's inner workings").
[536] *United States v. Szymanski*, 631 F.3d 794, 798-99 (6th Cir. 2011); *United States v. Pires*, 642 F.3d 1, 8 (1st Cir. 2011); *United States v. McNealy*, 625 F.3d 858, 870 (5th Cir. 2010), all citing *United States v. X-Citement Video, Inc.*, 513 U.S. 64, 70-3 (1994).
[537] *United States v. Pires,* 642 F.3d 1, 9 (1st Cir. 2011); see also, *United States v. MacEwan*, 445 F.3d 237, 244 (3d Cir. 2006)("[B]ecause of the very interstate nature of the Internet, once a user submits a connection request to a website server or an image is transmitted from the website server back to the user the data has traveled in interstate commerce").
[538] *United States v. Pires,* 642 F.3d 1, 8 (1st Cir. 2011)(internal citations omitted)("To prove attempt, the government must show both that the accused intended to commit the underlying substantive offense (here, knowing receipt of child pornography) and that he took a substantial step toward committing that crime. But this does not mean that the government bore a burden to prove each element of the underlying offense. While the underlying offense in this case requires the receipt of images of real-life minors engaged in sexually explicit conduct, the government in an attempt case has no burden to prove that the appellant knew that the downloaded file actually contained such images. Rather, the

government is required to prove that the appellant believed that the received file contained such images"); *United States v. Dobbs*, 629 F.3d 1199, 1208-209 (10th Cir. 2011).

[539] *United States v. Linngren*, 652 F.3d 868, 870-71 (8th Cir. 2011); United States v. Becker, 625 F.3d 1309, 1310-313 (10th Cir. 2010)

[540] 18 U.S.C. 2252(a)(3), (b)(1).

[541] 18 U.S.C. 2252(b)(1).

[542] 18 U.S.C. 2252(a)(3)("Any person who ... (A) in the special maritime and territorial jurisdiction of the United States, or on any land or building owned by, leased to, or otherwise used by or under the control of the Government of the United States, or in the Indian country as defined in section 1151 of this title, knowingly sells or possesses with intent to sell any visual depiction ... shall be punished as provided in subsection (b) of this section").

[543] 18 U.S.C. 2252(a)(3)("Any person who ... (B) knowingly sells or possesses with intent to sell any visual depiction that has been mailed, shipped, or transported using any means or facility of interstate or foreign commerce, or has been shipped or transported in or affecting interstate or foreign commerce, or which was produced using materials which have been mailed or so shipped or transported using any means or facility of interstate or foreign commerce, including by computer, if - (i) the producing of such visual depiction involves the use of a minor engaging in sexually explicit conduct; and (ii) such visual depiction is of such conduct ... shall be punished as provided in subsection (b) of this section").

[544] 18 U.S.C. 2252(b)(2).

[545] 18 U.S.C. 2252(a)(4)("Any person who ... either (A) in the special maritime and territorial jurisdiction of the United States, or on any land or building owned by, leased to, or otherwise used by or under the control of the Government of the United States, or in the Indian country as defined in section 1151 of this title, knowingly possesses, or knowingly accesses with intent to view, 1 or more books, magazines, periodicals, films, video tapes, or other matter which contain any visual depiction; or (B) knowingly possesses, or knowingly accesses with intent to view, 1 or more books, magazines, periodicals, films, video tapes, or other matter which contain any visual depiction that has been mailed, or has been shipped or transported using any means or facility of interstate or foreign commerce or in or affecting interstate or foreign commerce, or which was produced using materials which have been mailed or so shipped or transported, by any means including by computer, if - (i) the producing of such visual depiction involves the use of a minor engaging in sexually explicit conduct; and (ii) such visual depiction is of such conduct; shall be punished as provided in subsection (b) of this section").

[546] 18 U.S.C. 2252(b)(2); *United States v. Stults*, 575 F.3d 834, 844-45 (9th Cir. 2009); *United States v. McCutchen*, 419 F.3d 1122, 1125 (10th Cir. 2005).

[547] *United States v. Stults*, 575 F.3d 834, 846 (9th Cir. 2009); *United States v. McCutchen*, 419 F.3d 1122, 1125 (10th Cir. 2005); cf., *United States v. Rezin*, 322 F.3d 443, 447-48 (7th Cir. 2003).

[548] *United States v. Stults*, 575 F.3d 834, 845 (9th Cir. 2009).

[549] *Id.*

[550] 18 U.S.C. 2252(b).

[551] 18 U.S.C. 2252(c)("It shall be an affirmative defense to a charge of violating paragraph (4) of subsection (a) that the defendant - (1) possessed less than three matters containing any visual depiction proscribed by that paragraph; and (2) promptly and in good faith, and without retaining or allowing any person, other than a law enforcement agency, to access any visual depiction or copy thereof - (A) took reasonable steps to destroy each such visual depiction; or (B) reported the matter to a law enforcement agency and afforded that agency access to each such visual depiction").

[552] Compare 18 U.S.C. 2252 (1994 ed. & Supp. II), with 18 U.S.C. 2252A (1994 ed. Supp. II); see also, U.S. Department of Justice, *Criminal Resource Manual* §1969 (2000)("Title 18

U.S.C. §2252A is identical to 18 U.S.C. §2252.... "), available at http://www.justice.gov/usao/eousa/foia_reading_room/ usam/title9/crm01969.htm.

[553] Then, as now, the prohibitions of subsection 2252A(a) reached "any visual depiction, including any photograph, film, video, picture, or computer or computer-generated image or picture, whether made or produced by electronic, mechanical, or other means, of sexually explicit conduct, where - (A) the production of such visual depiction involves the use of a minor engaging in sexually explicit conduct; (B) such visual depiction is a digital image, computer image, or computer-generated image that is, or is indistinguishable from, that of a minor engaging in sexually explicit conduct; or (C) such visual depiction has been created, adapted, or modified to appear that an identifiable minor is engaging in sexually explicit conduct," 18 U.S.C. 2256(8). The Supreme Court in *Ashcroft v. Free Speech Coalition*, 535 U.S. 234, 256 (2002) found an earlier version of paragraph 2256(8)(B)("appears to be a minor") overbroad and impermissible under the First Amendment. It found the language in then paragraph 2256(8)(D)("conveys the impression") overbroad as well, *id.* at 258. Congress subsequently amended paragraph 2256(8)(B) and repealed paragraph 2256(8)(D), P.L. 108-21, §§502(a)(1), 502(a)(3), 117 Stat. 678 (2003).

[554] 18 U.S.C. 2252A(b)(1).

[555] 18 U.S.C. 2252A(b)(1), (b)(2).

[556] 18 U.S.C. 2252A(g)("(1) Whoever engages in a child exploitation enterprise shall be fined under this title and imprisoned for any term of years not less than 20 or for life. (2) A person engages in a child exploitation enterprise for the purposes of this section if the person violates section 1591, section 1201 if the victim is a minor, or chapter 109A (involving a minor victim), 110 (except for sections 2257 and 2257A), or 117 (involving a minor victim), as a part of a series of felony violations constituting three or more separate incidents and involving more than one victim, and commits those offenses in concert with three or more other persons").

[557] 18 U.S.C. 2252A(a)(1), (b)(1).

[558] 18 U.S.C. 2252A(b)(1)("Whoever violates, or attempts or conspires to violate, paragraph (1), (2), (3), (4), or (6) of subsection (a) shall be fined under this title and imprisoned not less than 5 years and not more than 20 years, but, if such person has a prior conviction under this chapter, section 1591, chapter 71, chapter 109A, or chapter 117, or under section 920 of title 10 (article 120 of the Uniform Code of Military Justice), or under the laws of any State relating to aggravated sexual abuse, sexual abuse, or abusive sexual conduct involving a minor or ward, or the production, possession, receipt, mailing, sale, distribution, shipment, or transportation of child pornography, or sex trafficking of children, such person shall be fined under this title and imprisoned for not less than 15 years nor more than 40 years").

[559] *United States v. Wright*, 625 F.3d 583, 590-601 (9th Cir. 2010).

[560] *United States v. Tenuto*, 593 F.3d 695, 698-99 (7th Cir. 2010).

[561] 18 U.S.C. 2252A(c).

[562] 18 U.S.C. 2252A(c)("It shall be an affirmative defense to a charge of violating paragraph (1), (2), (3)(A), (4), or (5) of subsection (a) that - (1)(A) the alleged child pornography was produced using an actual person or persons engaging in sexually explicit conduct; and (B) each such person was an adult at the time the material was produced; or (2) the alleged child pornography was not produced using any actual minor or minors. "No affirmative defense under subsection (c)(2) shall be available in any prosecution that involves child pornography as described in section 2256(8)(C). A defendant may not assert an affirmative defense to a charge of violating paragraph (1), (2), (3)(A), (4), or (5) of subsection (a) unless, within the time provided for filing pretrial motions or at such time prior to trial as the judge may direct, but in no event later than 14 days before the commencement of the trial, the defendant provides the court and the United States with notice of the intent to assert such defense and the substance of any expert or other specialized testimony or evidence upon which the defendant intends to rely. If the defendant fails to comply with this subsection, the court shall, absent a finding of extraordinary circumstances that prevented

timely compliance, prohibit the defendant from asserting such defense to a charge of violating paragraph (1), (2), (3)(A), (4), or (5) of subsection (a) or presenting any evidence for which the defendant has failed to provide proper and timely notice"). 18 U.S.C. 2256(8)(C)(" 'child pornography' means any visual depiction, including any photograph, film, video, picture, or computer or computer-generated image or picture, whether made or produced by electronic, mechanical, or other means, of sexually explicit conduct, where ... (C) such visual depiction has been created, adapted, or modified to appear that an identifiable minor is engaging in sexually explicit conduct").

[563] 18 U.S.C. 2252A("(a) Any person who ... (2) knowingly receives or distributes—(A) any child pornography that has been mailed, or using any means or facility of interstate or foreign commerce shipped or transported in or affecting interstate or foreign commerce by any means, including by computer; or (B) any material that contains child pornography that has been mailed, or using any means or facility of interstate or foreign commerce shipped or transported in or affecting interstate or foreign commerce by any means, including by computer ... shall be punished as provided in subsection (b). (b)(1) Whoever violates, or attempts or conspires to violate paragraph ... (2) ... shall be ... imprisoned not less than 5 years ...").

[564] *Id.*

[565] 18 U.S.C. 2252A(b)(1)("Whoever violates, or attempts or conspires to violate, paragraph (1), (2), (3), (4), or (6) of subsection (a) shall be fined under this title and imprisoned not less than 5 years and not more than 20 years, but, if such person has a prior conviction under this chapter, section 1591, chapter 71, chapter 109A, or chapter 117, or under section 920 of title 10 (article 120 of the Uniform Code of Military Justice), or under the laws of any State relating to aggravated sexual abuse, sexual abuse, or abusive sexual conduct involving a minor or ward, or the production, possession, receipt, mailing, sale, distribution, shipment, or transportation of child pornography, or sex trafficking of children, such person shall be fined under this title and imprisoned for not less than 15 years nor more than 40 years").

[566] *United States v. Pruitt*, 638 F.3d 763, 766 (11th Cir. 2011).

[567] *Id.*

[568] *United States v. Bauer*, 626 F.3d 1004, 1007-1008 (8th Cir. 2010).

[569] *Id.*

[570] *United States v. Dudeck*, 657 F.3d 424, 428-29 (6th Cir. 2011), citing in accord *United States v. Muhlenbruch*, 634 F.3d 987, 1003-04 (8th Cir. 2011); *United States v. Bobb*, 577 F.3d 1366, 1373-375 (11th Cir. 2009); *United States v. Miller*, 527 F.3d 54,72 (3d Cir. 2008).

[571] *United States v. Ehle*, 640 F.3d 689, 694-95 (6th Cir. 2011); *United States v. Overton*, 573 F.3d 679, 695 (9th Cir. 2009).

[572] *United States v. Dudeck*, 657 F.3d 424, 430 (6th Cir. 2011)("[W]hile possession of child pornography is generally a lesser-included offense of receipt of child pornography, conviction under both statutes is permissible if separate conduct is found to underlie the two offenses"); *United States v. Bobb*, 577 F.3d 1366, 1375 (11th Cir. 2009); *United States v. Overton*, 573 F.3d 679, 695 (9th Cir. 2009).

[573] *United States v. Dudeck*, 657 F.3d 424, 431 (6th Cir. 2011),

[574] 18 U.S.C. 2252A("(a) Any person who ... (3) knowingly - (A) reproduces any child pornography for distribution through the mails, or using any means or facility of interstate or foreign commerce or in or affecting interstate or foreign commerce by any means, including by computer; or (B) advertises, promotes, presents, distributes, or solicits through the mails, or using any means or facility of interstate or foreign commerce or in or affecting interstate or foreign commerce by any means, including by computer, any material or purported material in a manner that reflects the belief, or that is intended to cause another to believe, that the material or purported material is, or contains - (i) an obscene visual depiction of a minor engaging in sexually explicit conduct; or (ii) a visual depiction of an actual minor engaging in sexually explicit conduct ... shall be punished as provided in subsection (b)"); 18 U.S.C. 2252A(b)(1).

[575] 18 U.S.C. 2252A(a)(3)(A), (a)(3)(B).
[576] *United States v. Williams*, 553 U.S. 285, 292-307 (2008).
[577] *Id.* at 294.
[578] *Id.* at 295.
[579] *Id.*
[580] *Id.* at 296.
[581] *Id.*
[582] 18 U.S.C. 2252A(c)(emphasis added)("It shall be an affirmative defense to a charge of violating paragraph (1), (2), *(3)(A)*, (4), or (5) of subsection (a) that - (1)(A) the alleged child pornography was produced using an actual person or persons engaging in sexually explicit conduct; and (B) each such person was an adult at the time the material was produced; or (2) the alleged child pornography was not produced using any actual minor or minors").
[583] 18 U.S.C. 2252A(a)(4), (b)(1).
[584] 18 U.S.C. 2252A("(a) Any person who ... (4) ... (A) in the special maritime and territorial jurisdiction of the United States, or on any land or building owned by, leased to, or otherwise used by or under the control of the United States Government, or in the Indian country (as defined in section 1151), knowingly sells or possesses with the intent to sell any child pornography ... shall be punished as provided in subsection (b)").
[585] 18 U.S.C. 2252A("(a) Any person who ... (4) ... (B) knowingly sells or possesses with the intent to sell any child pornography that has been mailed, or shipped or transported using any means or facility of interstate or foreign commerce or in or affecting interstate or foreign commerce by any means, including by computer, or that was produced using materials that have been mailed, or shipped or transported in or affecting interstate or foreign commerce by any means, including by computer ... shall be punished as provided in subsection (b)").
[586] 18 U.S.C. 2252A(c).
[587] 18 U.S.C. 2252A("(a) Any person who ... (6) knowingly distributes, offers, sends, or provides to a minor any visual depiction, including any photograph, film, video, picture, or computer generated image or picture, whether made or produced by electronic, mechanical, or other means, where such visual depiction is, or appears to be, of a minor engaging in sexually explicit conduct ... for purposes of inducing or persuading a minor to participate in any activity that is illegal ... shall be punished as provided in subsection (b)"); 18 U.S.C. 2252A(b)(1).
[588] 18 U.S.C. 2252A(b)(1).
[589] 18 U.S.C. 2252A("(a) Any person who ... (6) knowingly ... offers ... to a minor any visual depiction ... where such visual depiction is, or appears to be, of a minor engaging in sexually explicit conduct - (A) that has been mailed, shipped, or transported using any means or facility of interstate or foreign commerce or in or affecting interstate or foreign commerce by any means, including by computer; (B) that was produced using materials that have been mailed, shipped, or transported in or affecting interstate or foreign commerce by any means, including by computer; or (C) which distribution, offer, sending, or provision is accomplished using the mails or any means or facility of interstate or foreign commerce, for purposes of inducing or persuading a minor to participate in any activity that is illegal ... shall be punished as provided in subsection (b)").
[590] 18 U.S.C. 2252A(c)("It shall be an affirmative defense to a charger of violating paragraph (a), (2), (3)(A), (4), or (5) of subsection (a) that ...").
[591] 18 U.S.C. 2252A(a)(5), (b)(1).
[592] 18 U.S.C. 2252A(b)("... (2) Whoever violates, or attempts or conspires to violate, subsection (a)(5) shall be fined under this title or imprisoned not more than 10 years, or both, but, if such person has a prior conviction under this chapter, chapter 71, chapter 109A, or chapter 117, or under section 920 of title 10 (article 120 of the Uniform Code of Military Justice), or under the laws of any State relating to aggravated sexual abuse, sexual abuse, or abusive

sexual conduct involving a minor or ward, or the production, possession, receipt, mailing, sale, distribution, shipment, or transportation of child pornography, such person shall be fined under this title and imprisoned for not less than 10 years nor more than 20 years").

[593] 18 U.S.C. 2252A("(a) Any person who ... (5) ... (A) in the special maritime and territorial jurisdiction of the United States, or on any land or building owned by, leased to, or otherwise used by or under the control of the United States Government, or in the Indian country (as defined in section 1151), knowingly possesses, or knowingly accesses with intent to view, any book, magazine, periodical, film, videotape, computer disk, or any other material that contains an image of child pornography ... shall be punished as provided in subsection (b)").

[594] 18 U.S.C. 2252A("(a) Any person who ... (5) ... (B) knowingly possesses, or knowingly accesses with intent to view, any book, magazine, periodical, film, videotape, computer disk, or any other material that contains an image of child pornography that has been mailed, or shipped or transported using any means or facility of interstate or foreign commerce or in or affecting interstate or foreign commerce by any means, including by computer, or that was produced using materials that have been mailed, or shipped or transported in or affecting interstate or foreign commerce by any means, including by computer ... shall be punished as provided in subsection (b)").

[595] 18 U.S.C. 2252A(c)("It shall be an affirmative defense to a charge of violating paragraph ... (5) of subsection (a) that - (1)(A) the alleged child pornography was produced using an actual person or persons engaging in sexually explicit conduct; and (B) each such person was an adult at the time the material was produced; or (2) the alleged child pornography was not produced using any actual minor or minors").

[596] 18 U.S.C. 2252A(g)(1).

[597] 18 U.S.C. 2252A(g)(2); see also *United States v. Daniels*, 653 F.3d 399, 411 (6th Cir. 2011)("The statute thus requires that the government prove: (1) the defendant committed at least three separate predicate offenses; (2) more than one underage victim was involved; and (3) at least three other persons acted 'in concert' with the defendant to commit the predicate offenses").

[598] *United States v. Daniels*, 653 F.3d 399, 412 (6th Cir. 2011).

[599] *United States v. Wayerski*, 624 F.3d 1342, 1351 (11th Cir. 2010)("Because the defendants' conspiracy convictions did not require proof of facts different from the child exploitation enterprise offense's in concert requirement, we that the defendants' conspiracy convictions were lesser included offenses and violated the Double Jeopardy Clause"). The Court held, however, that subsection 2252A(g) was not unconstitutional vague as applied to the defendants, *id.* at 1349.

[600] United States Sentencing Commission, Results of Survey of United States District Court Judges, January 2010 through March 2010, Question 1 (June 2010), available at http://www.ussc.gov/Research/Research_Projects/Surveys/ 20100608_judge_Survey.pdf.

[601] *Commission Report II*, 365, available at http://www.ussc.gov.

[602] *Id.* at 369.

[603] 18 U.S.C. 1028A(a)(2), (a)(1).

[604] United States Sentencing Commission, *Results of Survey of United States District Judges, January 2010 through March 2010, Question 1* (June 2010), available at http://www.ussc.gov/Research/Research_Projects/Surveys/ 20100608_Judge_Survey.pdf.

[605] *Commission Report II*, 325-44.

[606] *Id.* at 366-67.

[607] *United States v. Barrington*, 648 F.3d 1178, 1192 (11th Cir. 2011)("To prove a violation of 18 U.S.C. §1028A, the evidence must establish that the defendant: (1) knowingly transferred, possessed, or used; (2) the means of identification of another person; (3) without lawful authority; (4) during and in relation to a felony enumerated in §1028A(c)"); *see also, United States v. Abdelshafi*, 592 F.3d 602, 607 (4th Cir. 2010).

[608] 1 U.S.C. 1.

[609] "(a) Whoever commits an offense against the United States or aids, abets, counsels, commands, induces or procures its commission, is punishable as a principal. (b) Whoever willfully causes an act to be done which if directly performed by him or another would be an offense against the United States, is punishable as a principal," 18 U.S.C. 2.

[610] *Id.*

[611] 18 U.S.C. 371. Examples of cases affirming the convictions of individuals charged with conspiracy to commit aggravated identity theft include, *United States v. Blechman*, 657 F.3d 1052, 1054 (10th Cir. 2011), and *United States v. Jenkins-Watts*, 574 F.3d 950, 955 (8th Cir. 2009).

[612] 18 U.S.C. 371 (emphasis added)("If two or more persons conspire either to commit any offense against the United States, or to defraud the United States, or any agency thereof in any manner or for any purpose, and one or more of such persons do any act to effect the object of the conspiracy, *each shall be fined under this title* or imprisoned not more than five years, or both ...").

[613] 18 U.S.C. 924(c)(1)(A).

[614] *Smith v. United States*, 508 U.S. 223, 239 (1993).

[615] *United States v. Mobley*, 618 F.3d 539, 548-50 (6th Cir. 2010).

[616] See e.g., *United States v. Rodriguez-Moreno*, 526 U.S. 275 (1999)("Section 924(c)(1) criminalized a defendant's use of a firearm 'during and in relation to' a crime of violence; in doing so, Congress proscribed both the use of the firearm and the commission of acts that constitute a violent crime. It does not matter that respondent used the .357 magnum revolver, as the Government concedes, only in Maryland because he did so 'during and in relation to' a kidnaping that was begun in Texas and continued in New York, New Jersey, and Maryland")

[617] *United States v. Curtis*, 635 F.3d 704, 718 n.49 (5th Cir. 2011), citing *Flores-Figueroa v. United States*, 556 U.S. 646 (2009); see also, *United Sates v. Magassouba*, 619 F.3d 202, 205 (2d Cir. 2010); *United States v. Jenkins-Watts*, 574 F.3d 950, 969 (8th Cir. 2009).

[618] *United States v. Jenkins-Watts*, 574 F.3d at 970.

[619] *United States v. Bonilla*, 579 F.3d 1233, 1242-243 (11th Cir. 2009)("[A]ny conduct that would constitute a crime under §1028A(a)(1) would also be a crime covered by the provisions of §1028(a)(7). This is a clear example of one act violating two distinct statutory provisions and therefore violating the protection against double jeopardy").

[620] Subsection 2332b(g)(5) defines "federal crimes of terrorism" as any of the crimes listed in clause 2332b(g)(5)(B), consists of a list of federal crimes, when committed under the circumstances described in clause 2332b(g)(5)(A), is, when "calculated to influence or affect the conduct of government by intimidation or coercion, or to retaliate against government conduct." Subsection 1028A(a)(2) refers only to the list of offenses in clause (B), and therefore appears to have been intended to dispense with the requirements of clause (A).

[621] As of this date, none of the reported aggravated identity theft cases involved the five-year mandatory minimum sentence that accompanies a terrorism predicate offense, although some courts have mentioned it in their construction of the two-year offenses, e.g., *United States v. Maciel-Alcala*, 612 F.3d 1092, 1098 (9th Cir. 2010); *United States v. Godin*, 534 F.3d 51, 59 (1st Cir. 2008).

[622] *Flores-Figueroa v. United States*, 556 U.S 646, 649 (2009)("As a matter of ordinary English grammar, it seems natural to read the statute's word 'knowingly' as applying to all the subsequently listed elements of the crime").

[623] *Id.* (emphasis in the original)("All the parties agree that the provision applies only where the offender knows that he is transferring, possessing, or using *something*").

[624] *Id.* (emphasis in the original)("And the Government reluctantly concedes that the offender likely must know that he is transferring, possessing, or using that *something* without lawful authority").

[625] *Id.* (emphasis in the original)("The question is whether the statute requires the Government to show that the defendant *knew* that the 'means of identification' he or she unlawfully transferred, possessed, or used, in fact, belonged to 'another person.' We conclude that it does");see also, *United States v. Dvorak*, 617 F.3d 1017, 1025 (8th Cir. 2010).

[626] *United States v. Otuya*, 720 F.3d 183, 189 (4th Cir. 2013); *United States v. Lumbard*, 706 F.3d 716, 722-25 (6th Cir. 2013); *United States v. Ozuna-Cabrera*, 663 F.3d 496, 499 (1st Cir. 2011); *United States v. Retana*, 641 F.3d 272, 274-75 (8th Cir. 2011).

[627] *United States v. Abdelshafi*, 592 F.3d 602, 608 (4th Cir. 2010)("Abdelshafi came into lawful possess, initially, of Medicaid patients' identifying information and had 'lawful authority' to use that information for proper billing purposes. He did not have 'lawful authority,' however, to use Medicaid patients' identifying information to submit fraudulent billing claims").

[628] *United States v. Barrington*, 648 F.3d 1178, 1193 (11th Cir. 2011). Subsection 18 U.S.C. 1028(d)(7) states that, "the term 'means of identification' means any name or number that may be used, alone or in conjunction with any other information, to identify a specific individual, including any - (A) name, social security number, date of birth, official State or government issued driver's license or identification number, alien registration number, government passport number, employer or taxpayer identification number; (B) unique biometric data, such as fingerprint, voice print, retina or iris image, or other unique physical representation; (C) unique electronic identification number, address, or routing code; or (D) telecommunication identifying information or access device (as defined in section 1029(e))."

[629] *Id.*, quoting *United States v. Mitchell*, 518 F.3d 230, 234 (4th Cir. 2008).

[630] *United States v. Mitchell*, 518 F.3d at 234 ("A name alone, for example, would likely not be sufficiently unique to identify a specific individual because many persons have the same name").

[631] *United States v. Silva*, 554 F.3d 13, 23 n.14 (1st Cir. 2009)("Silva argues a forged prescription containing a forged doctor's name is excluded as a 'means of identification.' ... Silva's contention runs afoul of the plain language of the statute"); see also, *United States v. Blixt*, 548 F.3d 882, 886-88 (9th Cir. 2008).

[632] *Flores-Figueroa v. United States*, 556 U.S. 646, 649 (2009); *United States v. Soto*, 720 F.3d 51, 55 (1st Cir. 2013); *United States v. Clark*, 668 F.3d 568, 573-74 (8th Cir. 2012); *United States v. Mobley*, 618 F.3d 539, 547 (6th Cir. 2010); *United States v. Gomez-Castro*, 605 F.3d 1245, 1248 (11th Cir. 2010).

[633] *United States v. Zuniga-Arteaga*, 681 F.3d 1220, 1223 (11th Cir. 2012); *United States v. LaFaive*, 618 F.3d 613, 617 (7th Cir. 2010); *United States v. Maciel-Alcala*, 612 F.3d 1092, 1096-102 (9th Cir. 2010); *United States v. Kowal*, 527 F.3d 741, 745-47 (8th Cir. 2008).

[634] 18 U.S.C. 1028A(a)(1), (a)(2).

[635] E.g., 18 U.S.C. 1341("Whoever, having devised ... any scheme ... to defraud ... places in any post office ... any matter ... shall be ... imprisoned not more than 20 years ..."); 18 U.S.C. 1001(a)(1)(" ... whoever, in any matter within the jurisdiction of the executive ... branch ... of the United States ... (1) falsifies, conceals, or covers up by any trick, scheme, or device any material fact ... shall be ... imprisoned not more than 5 years ...").

[636] E.g., 21 U.S.C. 841(a)(1)(A)("In the case of a violation of subsection (a) of this section [relating to drug trafficking] involving 1 kilogram or more of ... heroin ... such person shall be sentenced to a term of imprisonment which may not be less than 10 years or more than life ... "); 18 U.S.C. 924(c)(1)(A)(i)(" ... any person who, during and in relation to a crime of violence ... uses or carries a firearm ... shall, in addition to the punishment provided for such crime of violence ... (i) be sentence to a term of not less than 5 years").

[637] 18 U.S.C. 1028A(b) 18 U.S.C. 1028A(b)(3)("[I]n determining any term of imprisonment to be imposed for the felony during which the means of identification was transferred, possessed, or used, a court shall not in any way reduce the term to be imposed for such crime so as to compensate for, or otherwise take into account, any separate term of imprisonment imposed

or to be imposed for a violation of this section"). Nevertheless, "a district court, in sentencing a defendant on a 18 U.S.C. §1028A aggravated identity theft conviction, is not precluded from taking §1028A's mandatory sentence into account in sentencing defendant on *other counts of conviction* charged in the same indictment that are *not predicate felonies* underlying the §1028A conviction," *United States v. Vidal-Reyes*, 562 F.3d 43, 56 (1st Cir. 2009)(emphasis added); *United States v. Wahid*, 614 F.3d 1009, 1014 (9th Cir. 2010). Moreover, sentence imposed for the predicate offense may not be *enhanced* to account for presence of the aggravate identity theft penalty to be imposed, U.S.S.G. §2B1.6, app.n.2; *United States v. Lyons*, 556 F.3d 703, 708 (8th Cir. 2009); *United States v. Sharapka*, 526 F.3d 58, 62 (1st Cir. 2008).

638 18 U.S.C. 1028A(b)(2)("[E]xcept as provided in paragraph (4), no term of imprisonment imposed on a person under this section shall run concurrently with any other term of imprisonment imposed on the person under any other provision of law, including any term of imprisonment imposed for the felony during which the means of identification was transferred, possessed, or used").

639 18 U.S.C. 1028A(b)(4)("[A] term of imprisonment imposed on a person for a violation of this section may, in the discretion of the court, run concurrently, in whole or in part, only with another term of imprisonment that is imposed by the court at the same time on that person for an additional violation of this section, provided that such discretion shall be exercised in accordance with any applicable guidelines and policy statements issued by the Sentencing Commission pursuant to section 994 of title 28"); see also, *United States v. Vidal-Reyes*, 562 F.3d 43, 50 (1st Cir. 2009)(internal citations omitted)("We note that the only exception to this statutorily mandated rule requiring that all other sentences run consecutively to a sentence under §1028A grants a district court discretion to run additional §1028A sentences imposed at the same time concurrently with each other"); *United States v. Lee*, 545 F.3d 678, 680 (8th Cir. 2008).

640 U.S.S.G. §5G1.2, app.n. 2.(B)("In determining whether multiple counts of 18 U.S.C. § 1028A should run concurrently with, or consecutively to, each other, the court should consider the following non-exhaustive list of factors: (i) The nature and seriousness of the underlying offenses. For example, the court should consider the appropriateness of imposing consecutive, or partially consecutive, terms of imprisonment for multiple counts of 18 U.S.C. § 1028A in a case in which an underlying offense for one of the 18 U.S.C. § 1028A offenses is a crime of violence or an offense enumerated in 18 U.S.C. § 2332b(g)(5)(B). (ii) Whether the underlying offenses are groupable under §3D1.2 (Groups of Closely Related Counts). Generally, multiple counts of 18 U.S.C. § 1028A should run concurrently with one another in cases in which the underlying offenses are groupable under §3D1.2. (iii) Whether the purposes of sentencing set forth in 18 U.S.C. § 3553(a)(2) are better achieved by imposing a concurrent or a consecutive sentence for multiple counts of 18 U.S.C. § 1028A"); see also, U.S.S.G. §2B1.6, app.n. 1.(B).

641 *United States v. Collins*, 640 F.3d 265, 269-70 (7th Cir. 2011), citing in accord *United States v. Kreitinger*, 576 F.3d 500, 504 (8th Cir. 2009). Subsection 3553(a)(2) states: "(a) The court shall impose a sentence sufficient, but not greater than necessary, to comply with the purposes set forth in paragraph (2) of this subsection. The court, in determining the particular sentence to be imposed, shall consider ... (2) the need for the sentence imposed - (A) to reflect the seriousness of the offense, to promote respect for the law, and to provide just punishment for the offense; (B) to afford adequate deterrence to criminal conduct; (C) to protect the public from further crimes of the defendant; and (D) to provide the defendant with needed educational or vocational training, medical care, or other correctional treatment in the most effective manner."

642 E.g., *United States v. Barrington*, 648 F.3d 1178, 1183-184 (11th Cir. 2011); *United States v. Moore*, 581 F.3d 681, 683 (8th Cir. 2009).

643 18 U.S.C. 3553(e)("Upon motion of the Government, the court shall have the authority to impose a sentence below a level established by statute as a minimum sentence so as to

reflect a defendant's substantial assistance in the investigation or prosecution of another person who has committed an offense. Such sentence shall be imposed in accordance with the guidelines and policy statements issued by the Sentencing Commission pursuant to section 994 of title 28, United States Code"); the Sentencing Guidelines carry the provision forward along with factors for determining the extent of the appropriate reduction below the minimum, U.S.S.G. §5K1.1.

[644] *Id.* at 369.

[645] 18 U.S.C. 3559(c).

[646] United States Sentencing Commission, *Results of Survey of United States District Judges: January 2010 through March 2010, Question 1. Mandatory Minimums* (June 2010), available at http://www.ussc.gov/ Judge_Survey/2010/JudgeSurvey_201006.pdf.

[647] *Id.* A majority found the statutory mandatory minimums appropriate for trafficking in heroin, powder cocaine and methamphetamine; for firearms offenses; for aggravated identity theft; for production and distribution of child pornography; and for other child exploitation offenses. On the other hand, a majority found them too high for trafficking in crack cocaine (76%) or marijuana (54%); or receipt of child pornography (71%). *Id.*

[648] 18 U.S.C. 3559(c)(4).

[649] 21 U.S.C. 851(a)(1)("No person who stands convicted of an offense under this part shall be sentenced to increased punishment by reason of one or more prior convictions, unless before trial, or before entry of a plea of guilty, the United States attorney files an information with the court (and serves a copy of such information on the person or counsel for the person) stating in writing the previous convictions to be relied upon.... "). *E.g.*, *United States v. Sanchez*, 586 F.3d 918, 929-30 (11th Cir. 2009)("Prior to trial, the Government notified the district court and Camejo, pursuant to 18 U.S.C. §851, that if Camejo was found guilty of Counts 3, 4, or 5, it would ask the court to impose a life sentence, pursuant to 18 U.S.C. §3559(c), because he previously had been convicted in Florida circuit court of what §3559(c)(1)(A) deemed a 'serious violent felony' and two 'serious drug offenses'").

[650] *United States v. Hood*, 615 F.3d 1293, 1302 (10th Cir. 2010); *United States v. Baugham*, 613 F.3d 291, 294 (D.C. Cir. 2010); *United States v. Morales*, 560 F.3d 112, 113 (2d Cir. 2009).

[651] *United States v. Baugham*, 613 F.3d at 294-95; *United States v. Lane*, 591 F.3d 921, 927 (7th Cir. 2010).

[652] *United States v. Hood*, 615 F.3d at 1302 (noting the appropriateness of "harmless error analysis" rather than "hypertechnical approach"); *United States v. Baugham*, 613 F.3d at 295 ("Our caselaw also makes clear, however, that to comply with §851(a) the information need not be perfect with respect to every jot and tittle"); *United States v. Boudreau*, 564 F.3d 431, 437 (6th Cir. 2009)("Indeed, we have regularly held that actual notice satisfies the requirements of Section 851(a)").

[653] 21 U.S.C. 848.

[654] 21 U.S.C. 841(b)(1)(A).

[655] 21 U.S.C. 960(b)(1)(A).

[656] 18 U.S.C. 3559(c)(2)(H).

[657] *United States v. Sanchez*, 586 F.3d 918, 930 (11th Cir. 2009)(parenthetical citations in the original)("A state drug offense qualifies as a 'serious drug offense' under §3559(c) only if the offense, if prosecuted in federal court, would have been punishable under [21 U.S.C. §841(b)(1)(A)] or [21 U.S.C. §960(b)(1)(A)].... [For example,] to qualify as a 'serious drug offense' under §3559(c)(2)(H)(ii), the drug offenses must have been punishable under 21 U.S.C. §841(b)(1)(A). Section 841(b)(1)(A), however, is limited only to offenses involving '5 kilograms or more' of cocaine or '50 grams or more' of cocaine base").

[658] 18 U.S.C. 3559(c)(2)(E)("the term 'kidnapping' means an offense that has as its elements the abduction, restraining, confining, or carrying away of another person by force or threat of force").

[659] 18 U.S.C. 3559(c)(2)(C)("the term 'extortion' means an offense that has as its elements the extraction of anything of value from another person by threatening or placing that person in fear of injury to any person or kidnapping of any person").

[660] 18 U.S.C. 3559(c)(2)(B)("the term 'arson' means an offense that has as its elements maliciously damaging or destroying any building, inhabited structure, vehicle, vessel, or real property by means of fire or an explosive").

[661] 18 U.S.C. 3559(c)(2)(D)("the term 'firearms use' means an offense that has as its elements those described in section 924(c) or 929(a), if the firearm was brandished, discharged, or otherwise used as a weapon and the crime of violence or drug trafficking crime during and relation to which the firearm was used was subject to prosecution in a court of the United States or a court of a State, or both").

[662] 18 U.S.C. 3559(c)(2)(F)(i).

[663] 18 U.S.C. 3559(c)(2)(F)(ii).

[664] 18 U.S.C. 3559(c)(3)(B).

[665] 18 U.S.C. 3559(c)(3)(A).

[666] *Id.*

[667] E.g., *United States v. Abraham*, 386 F.3d 1033, 1038 (11th Cir. 2004)(escape constitutes a serious violent felony for purposes of section 3559(c)); *United States v. Dobbs*, 449 F.3d 904, 913-14 (8th Cir. 2006)(burglary is not a violent felony for purposes of section 3559(c)); *United States v. Evans*, 478 F.3d 1332, 1342 (11th Cir. 2007) (conviction for an anthrax threat against a federal building is not a serious violent felony for purposes of section 3559(c)).

[668] *United States v. Rose*, 587 F.3d 695, 703-704 (5th Cir. 2009)(noting that circuit precedent construing the term "violent felony" in ACCA may be instructive when construing the term "serious violent felony" in section 3559(c)). The ACCA defines the term "violent felony" to mean "any crime punishable by imprisonment for a term exceeding one year ... that – (i) has as an element the use, attempted use, or threatened use of physical force against the person of another; or (ii) is burglary, arson, or extortion, involves use of explosives, or otherwise involves conduct that presents a serious potential risk of physical injury to another," 18 U.S.C. 924(e)(2)(B).

[669] *United States v. Gonzalez*, 682 F.3d 201, 204 (2d Cir. 2012); *United States v. Snype*, 441 F.3d 119, 148 (2d Cir. 2006)("Thus, *Almendarez-Torres* continues to bind this court in its application of *Apprendi*.... With this understanding of the law, we identify no Sixth Amendment error in the district court's findings as to the fact of Snype's prior state robbery convictions. Four of our sister circuits have considered this question and reached the same conclusion"), citing *United States v. Cooper*, 375 F.3d 1041, 1053 n.3 (10th Cir. 2004); *United States v. Bradshaw*, 281 F.3d 278, 294 (1st Cir. 2002); *United States v. Weaver*, 267 F.3d 231, 251 (3d Cir. 2001); *United States v. Davis*, 260 F.3d 965, 969 (8th Cir. 2001).

[670] *United States v. Washington*, 109 F.3d 335, 338 (7th Cir. 1997); *United States v. Farmer*, 73 F.3d 836, 841 (8th Cir. 1996). Equally unsuccessful was a defendant who claimed an equal protection violation based on disparate sentencing patterns from one state to another, *United States v. Wicks*, 132 F.3d 383, 389 (7th Cir. 1997)("Certain felonies—those described in (F)(i)—it [(Congress)] considered serious enough to include no matter how Draconian or lenient their treatment may be under state law, while others—those described in (F)(ii)—are subject to a congressional leveler through the requirement of the ten-year term of imprisonment. There is no federalism or equal protection issue at all in (F)(i), and none that survives rational basis analysis in (F)(ii)").

[671] *United States v. Rose*, 587 F.3d at 704-705; *United States v. Gurule*, 461 F.3d 1238, 1247 (10th Cir. 2006); *United States v. Snype*, 441 F.3d 119, 152 (2d Cir. 2006); *United States v. Kaluna*, 192 F.3d 1188, 1199-200 (9th Cir. 1999); *United States v. DeLuca*, 137 F.3d 24, 40 n.19 (1st Cir. 1998); *United States v. Washington*, 109 F.3d 335, 337-38 (7th Cir. 1997); *United States v. Farmer*, 73 F.3d 836, 840 (8th Cir. 1996).

[672] *United States v. Gonzalez*, 682 F.3d at 203; *United States v. Gurule*, 461 F.3d at 1246("As for the Three Strikes statute in particular, the few reported decisions of which we are aware from other circuits are unanimous in rejecting this [separation of powers] argument.... We agree with these precedents"), citing *United States v. Kaluna*, 192 F.3d 1188, 1199 (9th Cir. 1999); *United States v. Rasco*, 123 F.3d 222, 226-27 (5th Cir. 1997); *United States v. Washington*, 109 F.3d 335, 338 (7th Cir. 1997).

[673] *United States v. Kaluna*, 192 F.3d at 1198-199, quoting *Witte v. United States*, 515 U.S. 389, 400 (1995) and *Gryger v. Burke*, 334 U.S. 728, 732 (1948); see also *United States v. Washington*, 109 F.3d at 338; *United States v. Farmer,* 73 F.3d 836, 840 (8th Cir. 1996).

[674] *United States v. Abraham*, 386 F.3d 1033, 1038 (11th Cir. 2004); *United States v. Kaluna*, 192 F.3d at 1199; *United States v. Rasco*, 123 F.3d 222, 227 (5th Cir. 1997); *United States v. Washington*, 109 F.3d at 338; *United States v. Farmer*, 73 F.3d at 840-41.

[675] The lists do not include offenses under the Uniform Code of Military Justice, the District of Columbia Code, or any of the criminal codes of the various territories, commonwealths, or possessions over which Congress has authority.

In: Federal Mandatory Minimum Sentencing ISBN: 978-1-62948-557-7
Editor: Christophe Salaut © 2013 Nova Science Publishers, Inc.

Chapter 2

FEDERAL MANDATORY MINIMUM SENTENCES: THE SAFETY VALVE AND SUBSTANTIAL ASSISTANCE EXCEPTIONS*

Charles Doyle

SUMMARY

Federal law requires a sentencing judge to impose a minimum sentence of imprisonment following conviction for any of a number of federal offenses. Congress has created two exceptions. One is available in all cases when the prosecutor asserts that the defendant has provided substantial assistance in the criminal investigation or prosecution of another, 18 U.S.C. 3553(e). The other, commonly referred to as the safety value, is available, without the government's approval, for a handful of the more commonly prosecuted drug trafficking and unlawful possession offenses that carry minimum sentences, 18 U.S.C. 3553(f).

Qualification for the substantial assistance exception is ordinarily only possible upon the motion of the government. In rare cases, the court may compel the government to file such a motion when the defendant can establish that the refusal to do so was based on constitutionally invalid considerations, or was in derogation of a plea bargain obligation or was the product of bad faith.

---

* This is an edited, reformatted and augmented version of a Congressional Research Service publication, R41326, dated July 14, 2010.

Qualification for the safety valve exception requires a defendant to satisfy five criteria. His past criminal record must be minimal; he must not have been a leader, organizer, or supervisor in the commission of the offense; he must not have used violence in the commission or the offense, and the offense must not have resulted in serious injury; and prior to sentencing, he must tell the government all that he knows of the offense and any related misconduct.

Congress has instructed the United States Sentencing Commission to report on the operation of federal mandatory minimum sentencing provisions. A majority of the Federal judges responding to a Commission survey agree that the two exceptions should be expanded. A number of Commission hearing witnesses have also urged that the provisions be amended.

INTRODUCTION

Depending on how the class is defined, there are hundreds of federal mandatory minimum offenses.[1] Yet only a handful are prosecuted with any regularity, including under 21 U.S.C. 841 (trafficking in controlled substances), 844 (possession of controlled substances), and 960 (smuggling controlled substances). Congress has provided two escape hatches under which a court may sentence a defendant below the statutory mandatory minimum. One, 18 U.S.C. 3553(e), is available only on the motion of the prosecutor based on the defendant's substantial assistance to the government and without regard to the offense charged. The second, 18 U.S.C. 3553(f), requires neither substantial assistance nor the prosecutor's endorsement, but is limited to the mandatory minimum sentences required in five sections of the federal drug law.

In October, 2009, Congress instructed the United States Sentencing Commission to prepare a report on the mandatory minimum sentencing provisions under federal law.[2] In early 2010, the Commission conducted a survey of federal district court judges regarding their views on mandatory minimum sentencing. A majority of those responding endorsed amendments to the safety valve and substantial assistance exceptions.[3] The Commission also held a public hearing at which several witnesses urged adjustments in the safety valve and substantial assistance provisions.[4]

SUBSTANTIAL ASSISTANCE

Background

The substantial assistance provisions, 18 U.S.C. 3553(e), passed with little fanfare in the twilight of the 99th Congress as part of the massive Anti-Drug Abuse Act of 1986, legislation which established or increased a number of mandatory minimum sentencing provisions.[5] The section continues in its original form virtually unchanged:

> (e) Limited Authority To Impose a Sentence Below a Statutory Minimum. - Upon motion of the Government, the court shall have the authority to impose a sentence below a level established by statute as a minimum sentence so as to reflect a defendant's substantial assistance in the investigation or prosecution of another person who has committed an offense. Such sentence shall be imposed in accordance with the guidelines and policy statements issued by the Sentencing Commission pursuant to section 994 of title 28, United States Code.[6]

The section passed between the date authorizing the Sentencing Guidelines and the date they became effective. Rather than replicate the language of section 3553(e), the Guidelines contain an overlapping section which authorizes a sentencing court to depart from the minimum sentence called for by the Guidelines, U.S.S.G. §5K1.1.[7]

"Upon the Motion of the Government"

As a general rule, a defendant is entitled to a sentence below an otherwise applicable statutory minimum under the provisions of section 3553(e) only if the government agrees.[8] The courts have acknowledged that due process or equal protection or other constitutional guarantees may provide a narrow exception. "Thus, a defendant would be entitled to relief if a prosecutor refused to file a substantial-assistance motion, say, because of the defendant's race or religion."[9] A defendant is entitled to relief if the Government's refusal constitutes a breach of its plea agreement.[10] A defendant is also "entitled to relief if the prosecutor's refusal to move was not rationally related to any legitimate Government end."[11] Some courts have suggested that a defendant is entitled to relief if the prosecution refuses to move under circumstances that "shock the conscience of the court," or that demonstrate bad faith, or for reasons unrelated to substantial assistance.[12] A majority of the judges who answered the Sentencing Commission's survey agreed that relief under section 3553(e) should be available even in the absence of motion from the prosecutor.[13]

A motion under section 3553(e) for a sentence beneath the mandatory minimum and a motion under U.S.S.G. §5K1.1 for a sentence beneath the applicable Sentencing Guideline range are not the same. Thus, a motion under section 5K1.1 will ordinarily not be construed as a motion under section 3553(e).[14]

To Reflect a Defendant's Substantial Assistance"

Any sentence imposed below the statutory minimum by virtue of section 3553(e) must be based on the extent of the defendant's assistance; it may not reflect considerations unrelated to such assistance.[15] It has been suggested that a court may use the section 5K1.1 factors for that determination, i.e., "(1) the court's evaluation of the significance and usefulness of the defendant's assistance, taking into consideration the government's evaluation of the assistance rendered; (2) the truthfulness, completeness, and reliability of any information or testimony provided by the defendant; (3) the nature and extent of the defendant's assistance; (4) any injury suffered, or any danger or risk of injury to the defendant or his family resulting from his assistance; [and] (5) the timeliness of the defendant's assistance," U.S.S.G. §5K1.1(a).[16]

The substantial assistance exception makes possible convictions that might otherwise be unattainable. Yet, it may also lead to "inverted sentencing," i.e., a situation in which "the more serious the defendant's crimes, the lower the sentence – because the greater his wrongs, the more information and assistance he had to offer to a prosecutor;" while in contrast the exception is of no avail to the peripheral offender who can provide no substantial assistance.[17] Perhaps for this reason, most of the judges who responded to the Sentencing Commission survey agreed that a sentencing court should not be limited to assistance-related factors and should be allowed use the generally permissible sentencing factors when calculating a sentence under section 3553(e).[18]

Booker

Defendants, seeking relief on the basis of substantial assistance have often and unsuccessfully sought to claim benefits under the *Booker* line of cases. In *United States v. Booker*, the Supreme Court affirmed that "[a]ny fact (other than a prior conviction) which is necessary to support a sentence exceeding the maximum authorized by the facts established by a plea of guilty or a jury verdict must be admitted by the defendant or proved to a jury beyond a reasonable doubt."[19] Since this constitutional command would doom *mandatory* sentencing guidelines, the Court found unconstitutional that portion of the Sentencing Reform Act which purported to make the Sentencing Guidelines mandatory.[20] The fact that the Guidelines are advisory hardly renders them irrelevant, as the Court's decision in *Gall* makes clear:

> [A] district court should begin all sentencing proceedings by correctly calculating the applicable Guidelines range. . . The Guidelines are not the only consideration, however, Accordingly, after giving both parties an opportunity to argue for whatever sentence they deem appropriate, the district judge should then consider all of the §3553(a) factors to determine whether they support the sentence requested by a party. . . . If he decides that an outside-Guidelines sentence is warranted, he must consider the extent of the deviation and ensure that the justification is sufficiently compelling to support he degree of the variance.[21]

Nevertheless, as the Fifth Circuit recently observed, "[D]istrict courts [may] impose a sentence of imprisonment below a statutory minimum only if: (1) the government so moves pursuant to 18 U.S.C. §3553(e), asserting the defendant's substantial assistance to the government; or (2) the defendant meets the 'safety valve' criteria, set forth in 18 U.S.C. 3553(f). Otherwise post-*Booker* sentencing courts lack discretion to depart below relevant statutory minimums."[22]

Safety Valve

Background

Congress enacted section 3553(f), after it became concerned that the mandatory minimum sentencing provisions could resulted in equally severe penalties for both the more and the less culpable offenders.[23] The section permits a sentencing court to impose a shorter term of imprisonment for the covered controlled substance offenses, if the defendant satisfies five criteria:

> Notwithstanding any other provision of law, in the case of an offense under section 401, 404, or 406 of the Controlled Substances Act (21 U.S.C. 841, 844, 846) or section 1010 or 1013 of the Controlled Substances Import and Export Act (21 U.S.C. 960, 963), the court shall impose a sentence pursuant to guidelines promulgated by the United States Sentencing Commission under section 994 of title 28 without regard to any statutory minimum sentence, if the court finds at sentencing, after the Government has been afforded the opportunity to make a recommendation, that –
>
> (1) the defendant does not have more than 1 criminal history point, as determined under the sentencing guidelines;
> (2) the defendant did not use violence or credible threats of violence or possess a firearm or other dangerous weapon (or induce another participant to do so) in connection with the offense;
> (3) the offense did not result in death or serious bodily injury to any person;
> (4) the defendant was not an organizer, leader, manager, or supervisor of others in the offense, as determined under the sentencing guidelines and was not engaged in a continuing criminal enterprise, as defined in section 408 of the Controlled Substances Act; and
> (5) not later than the time of the sentencing hearing, the defendant has truthfully provided to the Government all information and evidence the defendant has concerning the offense or offenses that were part of the same course of conduct or of a common scheme or plan, but the fact that the defendant has no relevant or useful other information to provide or that the Government is already aware of the information shall not preclude a determination by the court that the defendant has complied with this requirement. 18 U.S.C. 3553(f).

The defendant has the burden of convincing the trial court by a preponderance of the evidence that he satisfies each of the criteria.[24] The appellate courts will afford a sentencing court considerable deference before concluding that the lower court has come to a clearly erroneous conclusion of fact.[25]

Offenses Covered

Section 3553(f) covers the mandatory minimum sentences ordinarily imposed for five offenses:

> (1) trafficking in various controlled substances (21 U.S.C. 841);
> (2) possession of certain controlled substances (21 U.S.C. 844);
> (3) attempt or conspiracy to violate controlled substance provisions carrying mandatory minimum sentences (21 U.S.C. 846);
> (4) smuggling controlled substances in violation of 21 U.S.C. 952, 953, 955, 957, or 959); and
> (5) attempt or conspiracy to violate the controlled substance import/export provisions (21 U.S.C. 963).

The safety valve is not available to avoid the mandatory minimum sentences that attend other offenses, even those closely related to the listed offenses. For instance, section 860 (21 U.S.C. 860) outlaws violations of section 841 near schools, playgrounds or public housing facilities and sets the penalties for violation at twice what they would be under section 841. Those charged with a violation of section 860 are not eligible for relief under the safety valve provisions.[26] In addition, safety valve relief is not available to those convicted under the Maritime Drug Law Enforcement Act, even though the Act proscribes conduct closely related to the smuggling and trafficking activities punished under sections 960 and 963.[27]

More than two-thirds of the judges responding to the Sentencing Commission's survey agreed that the safety valve should be expanded to cover any offense with a mandatory minimum.[28] An even higher percentage agreed that it should extended to all drug trafficking offenses[29] and to receipt of child pornography.[30] A number of witnesses at the Commission's hearing also spoke in favor of expanding the number of mandatory minimum statutes covered.[31]

One Point

> [T]he defendant does not have more than 1 criminal history point, as determined under the sentencing guidelines, 18 U.S.C. 3553(f)(1).[32]

The first safety valve criterion demands that a defendant have no more than one criminal history point. The Sentencing Guidelines assign criminal history points based on a defendant's past criminal record. Two or more points are assigned for every prior sentence of imprisonment or juvenile confinement of sixty days or more or for offenses committed while the defendant was in prison, was an escaped prisoner, or was on probation, parole, or supervised release.[33] A single point is assigned for every other federal or state prior sentence of conviction, with certain exceptions.[34]

Foreign sentences of imprisonment are not counted;[35] nor sentences imposed by tribal courts;[36] nor summary court martial sentences;[37] nor sentences imposed for expunged, reversed, vacated, or invalidated convictions;[38] nor sentences for certain petty offenses or minor misdemeanors.[39]

The Sentencing Guidelines list two classes of these minor misdemeanor or petty offenses that are not counted for criminal history purposes and thus for safety valve purposes. One class consists of eight types of minor offenses that are not counted regardless of the sentence imposed, i.e.,

- Fish and game violations,
- Hitchhiking,
- Juvenile status offenses and truancy,
- Local ordinance violations (except those violations that are also violations under state criminal law),
- Loitering,
- Minor traffic infractions (e.g., speeding),
- Public intoxication, [and]
- Vagrancy.[40]

The other class consists of arguable more serious offenses that only counted if the offender was sentenced to imprisonment for thirty days or more and to probation for more than a year, i.e.

- Careless or reckless driving,
- Contempt of court,
- Disorderly conduct or disturbing the peace,
- Driving without a license or with a revoked or suspended license,
- False information to a police officer,
- Gambling,
- Hindering or failure to obey a police officer,
- Insufficient funds check,
- Leaving the scene of an accident,
- Non-support,

- Prostitution,
- Resisting arrest, and
- Trespassing.[41]

Both classes also include similar offenses to those listed "by whatever name they are known."[42]

> The Sentencing Guidelines suggest a number of factors to assist in the determination of whether an unlisted offense may be consider "similar" for purposes of section 4A1.2(c):
>
> (i) a comparison of punishments imposed for the listed and unlisted offenses;
>
> (ii) the perceived seriousness of the offense as indicated by the level of punishment;
>
> (iii) the elements of the offense;
>
> (iv) the level of culpability involved; and
>
> (v) the degree to which the commission of the offense indicates a likelihood of recurring criminal conduct.[43]

A sentencing court is bound by the Sentencing Guidelines in its determination of criminal history points for purposes of section 3553(f).[44]

Two-thirds of the judges who responded to the Commission's survey favored expanding the safety valve criminal history criterion to encompass those with 2 or 3 criminal history points,[45] although fewer than one quarter favored expansion of the criterion further.[46] Some of the Commission's hearing witnesses concurred.[47]

Not Violent or Deadly

> [T]he defendant did not use violence or credible threats of violence or possess a firearm or other dangerous weapon (or induce another participant to do so) in connection with the offense, 18 U.SC. 3553(f)(2).[48]
>
> [T]he offense did not result in death or serious bodily injury to any person, 18 U.S.C. 3553(f)(3).[49]

The disqualification in section 3553(f)(2) turns upon the defendant's conduct or the conduct of those he "aided or abetted, counseled, commanded, induced, procured, or willfully caused."[50] It is not triggered by the conduct of a co-conspirator, unless the defendant aided, abetted, counsel . . . the co-

conspirator's violence or possession.[51] Disqualifying firearm possession may be either actual or constructive.[52] Constructive possession is the dominion or control over a firearm or the place where one is located.[53] Disqualification requires the threat of violence or possession of a firearm "in connection with the offense." In many instances, possession of a firearm in a location where drugs are stored or transported, or where transactions occur, will be enough to support an inference of possession in connection with the drug offense of conviction.[54]

The Sentencing Guidelines define 'serious bodily injury" for purposes of section 3553(f)(3) as an "injury involving extreme physical pain or the protracted impairment of a function of a bodily member, organ, or mental faculty; or requiring medical intervention such as surgery, hospitalization, or physical rehabilitation."[55] On its face, the definition would include serious bodily injuries, such as hospitalization, suffered by the defendant as a result of the offense.[56] Unlike the gun and violence disqualification in section 3553(f)(2), the serious injury disqualification in section 3553(f)(3) may be triggered by the conduct of a co-conspirator.[57]

Single or Low Level Offender

> [T]he defendant was not an organizer, leader, manager, or supervisor of others in the offense, as determined under the sentencing guidelines *and was not engaged in a continuing criminal enterprise, as defined in section 408 of the Controlled Substances A*ct, 18 U.S.C. 3553(f)(4)(emphasis added).[58]

The Sentence Guidelines limit disqualification to those who receive a guideline level increase for their aggravated role in the offense.[59] Thus, by implication, it does not require a defendant to have received a guideline increase based on his minimal or minor participation in a group offense nor does it disqualify a defendant who acted alone.[60]

The appellate case law construing section 3553(f)(4) and its Sentencing Guideline counterpart is largely devote to (1) the impact of *Booker*,[61] and (2) the observation that a finding that an defendant merits a sentencing level increase for his aggravating role in the offense under U.S.S.G. §3B1.1 triggers a safety valve disqualification under section 3553(f)(4).[62]

Tell All

> [N]ot later than the time of the sentencing hearing, the defendant has truthfully provided to the Government all information and evidence the defendant has concerning the offense or offenses that were part of the same course of conduct or of a common scheme or plan, but the fact that the defendant has no relevant or useful other information to provide or that the Government is already aware of the information shall not preclude a determination by the court that the defendant has complied with this requirement, 18 U.S.C. 3553(f)(5).[63]

The fifth and most heavily litigated safety valve criterion requires full disclosure on the part of the defendant. The requirement extends not only to information concerning the crimes of conviction, but also to information concerning other crimes that "were part of the same course of conduct or of a common scheme or plan," including uncharged related conduct.[64]

Neither section 3553(f) nor the Sentencing Guidelines explain what form the defendants' full disclosure must take. At least one court has held that under rare circumstances disclosure through the defendant's testimony at trial may suffice.[65] Most often the defendant provides the information during an interview with prosecutors or by a proffer. The defendant must disclose the information to the prosecutor, however. Disclosure to the probation officer during preparation of the presentence report is not sufficient.[66] Moreover, a defendant does not necessarily qualify for relief merely because he has proffered a statement and invited the prosecution to identify any addition information it seeks; for "the government is under no obligation to solicit information from a defendant."[67] On the other hand, past lies do not render a defendant ineligible for relief under the truthful disclosure criterion of the safety value, although they may undermine his creditability.[68]

End Notes

[1] See generally, CRS Report RL32040, *Federal Mandatory Minimum Sentencing Statutes*, by Charles Doyle; United States Sentencing Commission, *Special Report to the Congress: Mandatory Minimum Penalties in the Federal Criminal Justice System* (1991), available on July 5, 2010 at http://www.ussg.gov/manmin/manmin51.htm; Greenblatt, *How Mandatory Are Mandatory Minimums? How Judges Can Avoid Imposing Mandatory Minimum Sentences*, 36 AMERICAN JOURNAL OF CRIMINAL LAW 1, 27-28 (2008)("[P]rosecutors have power to offer plea deals, reduce charges, limit introduction of evidence, and decide whether to appeal judges' trial management decisions and other

orders. Each of these powers gives prosecutors the opportunity to allow a defendant to avoid a mandatory minimum sentence").

[2] Section 4713 of the National Defense Authorization Act for Fiscal Year 2010, found in the Matthew Shepard and James Byrd, Jr., Hate Crimes Prevention Act, P.L. 111-84, 123 Stat. 2843 (2009).

[3] See United States Sentencing Commission, *Results of Survey of United States District Judges January 2010 through March 2010: Question 2. Safety Valve* (June 2010)(*Survey*) available on July 5, 2010 at http://www.ussc.gov/Judge_Survey/2010/JudgeSurvey_20106.pdf.

[4] United States Sentencing Commission, *Public Hearing Agenda Thursday, May 28, 2010* (*Hearing*) available on July 5, 2010 at http://www.ussc.gov/AGENDA/20100527/Agenda.htm.

[5] Section 1007(a) of P.L. 99-570, 100 Stat. 32-07-7 (1986).

[6] In the only amendment to section 3553(e), section 4002(a)(8) of P.L. 107-273 (2002) changed the phrase "as minimum sentence" to "as a minimum sentence."

[7] "5K1.1. Substantial Assistance to Authorities (Policy Statement). Upon motion of the government stating that the defendant has provided substantial assistance in the investigation or prosecution of another person who has committed an offense, the court may depart from the guidelines.

(a) The appropriate reduction shall be determined by the court for reasons stated that may include, but are not limited to, consideration of the following:

(1) the court's evaluation of the significance and usefulness of the defendant's assistance, taking into consideration the government's evaluation of the assistance rendered;

(2) the truthfulness, completeness, and reliability of any information or testimony provided by the defendant;

(3) the nature and extent of the defendant's assistance;

(4) any injury suffered, or any danger or risk of injury to the defendant or his family resulting from his assistance;

(5) the timeliness of the defendant's assistance."

[8] *Melendez v. United States*, 518 U.S. 120, 125-26 (1996)("We believe that §3553(e) requires a government motion requesting or authorizing the district court to impose a sentence below a level established by statute as a[a] minimum sentence before the court may impose such a sentence").

[9] *Wade v. United States*, 504 U.S. 181, 186 (1992).

[10] *United States v. Motley*, 587 F.3d 1153, 1159 (D.C. Cir. 2009); *United States v. Smith*, 574 F.3d 521, 525 (8th Cir. 2009); *United States v. Doe*, 445 F.3d 202, 207 (2d Cir. 2006).

[11] *Wade v. United States*, 504 at 186.

[12] *United States v. Freemont*, 513 F.3d 884, 889 (8th Cir. 2008)("The district court may review the government's refusal to make a motion in limited circumstances. First, the district court may review the government's decision for an unconstitutional motive. . . . Second, a district court can compel a §3553(e) motion if the government acknowledges the defendant provided substantial assistance, but refuses to make a motion expressly because the defendant engaged in unrelated misconduct – a reason unrelated to the quality of the defendant's assistance. . . . Third, the district court may be able to compel a motion if the government acted in bad faith by refusing to make a motion"); but see *United States v. Perez*, 526 F.3d 1135, 1138 (8th Cir. 2008)(citing cases evidencing a split within the circuit over whether bad faith provides a sufficient based to compel a government motion).

[13] *Survey, Question 15. Substantial Assistance*. Only 35% of the respondents disagreed with the statement that "Congress should amend 18 USC §3553(e) to authorize judges to sentence a

defendant below the applicable statutory mandatory minimum to reflect a defendant's substantial assistance, even if the government does not make a motion," *Id.*

[14] *Melendez v. United States*, 518 U.S. 120, 126 (1996).

[15] *United States v. Burns*, 577 F.3d 887, 894 (8th Cir. 2009)(en banc)("Where a court has authority to sentence below a statutory minimum only by virtue of a government motion under §3553(e), the reduction below the statutory minimum must be based exclusively on assistance-related considerations"); *United States v. Jackson,* 577 F.3d 1032, 1036 (9th Cir. 2009); *United States v. Hood*, 556 F.3d 226, 234 n.2 (4th Cir. 2009), citing *inter alia United States v. Richardson,* 521 F.3d 149, 159 (2d Cir. 2008) and *United States v. Desselle,* 450F.3d 179, 182 (5th Cir. 2006).

[16] *United States v. Gabbard*, 586 F.3d 1046, 1051 (6th Cir. 2009), citing *United States v. Richardson*, 521 F.3d at 159.

[17] *Hearing, Testimony of Jeffrey B. Steinback on behalf of the Practitioner's Advisory Group* at 8, quoting *United States v. Brigham*, 977 F.2d 317, 318 (7th Cir. 1992); see also *Hearing, Written Statement of Cynthia Hujar Orr, President of the National Ass'n of Criminal Defense Lawyers* at 3 (defendants "who have little or no information to provide the government, end up with far more severe sentences than leaders of conspiracies who run the operations and know the other participants").

[18] *Survey, Question 15. Substantial Assistance*. Only 24% of the respondents disagreed with the statement that "In determining the extent of a reduction below the statutory mandatory minimum under 18 USC §3553(e). . . the court's consideration should not be limited to the nature of the defendant's substantial assistance but also should include consideration of the factors at 18 USC §3553(a)," *Id.*

[19] *United States v. Booker*, 543 U.S. 220, 244 (2005), citing *Apprendi v. New Jersey*, 530 U.S. 466, 490 (2000).

[20] *United States v. Booker*, 543 U.S. at 245.

[21] *Gall v. United States*, 552 U.S. 38, 49-50 (2007).

[22] *United States v. Montes*, 602 F.3d 381, 390 (5th Cir. 2010); see also, *United States v. Christensen*, 582 F.3d 860, 862 (8th Cir. 2009)("Nothing in the reasoning of *United States v. Booker*. . . expands the authority of a district court to sentence below a statutory minimum"); *United States v. Johnson*, 580 F.3d 666, 673 (7th Cir. 2009).

[23] H.Rept. 103-460, at 4 (1994).

[24] *United States v. Gales*, 603 F.3d 49, 52-3 (D.C.Cir. 2010); *United States v. Pena*, 598 F.3d 289, 292 (6th Cir. 2010); *United States v. Larios*, 593 F.3d 82, 89 (1st Cir. 2010); *United States v. Jackson*, 552 F.3d 908, 909 (8th Cir. 2009); *United States v. Altamirano-Quintero*, 511 F.3d 1087, 1098 (10th Cir. 2007); *United States v. Olivas-Ramirez*, 487 F.3d 512, 516-17(7th Cir. 2007); *United States v. Mejia-Pimental*, 477 F.3d 1100, 1104 (9th Cir. 2007).

[25] *United States v. Padilla-Colon*, 578 F.3d 23, 29-30 (1st Cir. 2009)("We review de novo safety valve determinations to the extent they rest on conclusions of law. We review for clear error safety-valve determinations to the extent they depend on findings of fact. The clear error standard is extremely deferential. Under it, an appellate court ought not to disturb either findings of fact or conclusions drawn from the record unless the whole of the record compels a strong, unyielding belief that a mistake has been made"); *United States v. Crumley*, 528 F.3d 1053, 1068 (8th Cir. 2008)("We give great weight to a district court's credibility determinations"); see also *United States v. Gales*, 603 F.3d 49, 54 (D.C.Cir. 2010)("The district court did not clearly err in thinking it highly unlikely that Gales did not have any further information on the identity of his steady, supplier, whom he claimed to have known for ten years, beyond the vague description given to the government").

[26] *United States v. Phillips*, 382 F.3d 489, 499-500 (5th Cir. 2004); *United States v. Koons*, 300 F.3d 985, 993 (8th Cir. 2002); *United States v. Kakatin*, 214 F.3d 1049, 1050-51 (9th Cir. 2000); *United States v. Anderson*, 200 F.3d 1344, 1346-348 (11th Cir. 2000); *United States v. McQuilkin*, 78 F.3d 105, 108 (3d Cir. 1996). One Commission witness indicated that "in districts where substantial portions of towns and cities fall within protected zones, prosecutors can, and some do, charge violations of 21 U.S.C. §860 for the purpose of preventing safety valve relief for offenders who would otherwise qualify," *Hearings, Statement of Michael Nachmanoff, Federal Public Defender for E.D. Va.* at 31.

[27] *United States v. Gamboa-Cardenas*, 508 F.3d 491, 496-503 (9th Cir. 2007).

[28] *Survey, Section 2. Safety Valve*. Only 18% disagreed; another 12% were neutral, *Id.*

[29] *Id.* Only 12% disagreed; another 12% were neutral, *Id.*

[30] *Id.* Only 15% disagreed; another 13% were neutral, *Id.*

[31] *Hearings, Statement of Michael Nachmanoff, Federal Public Defender for E.D. Va.* at 31 ("We also urge the Commission to recommend to Congress that it expand the safety valve to apply to all mandatory minimums. . . . The problems caused by mandatory minimums are present for all offenses subject to them. Worse, prosecutors in some districts exercise their charging discretion to require mandatory minimum sentences for defendants who would otherwise qualify fort the safety valve"); *Comments of Cory L. Andrews, Washington Legal Foundation* at 5 ("Expanding such mechanisms to other non-violent offenses would allow Congress to maintain the current mandatory minimum sentencing structure while providing district judges with meaningful opportunities to avoid harsh and unintended sentencing results"); *Statement of Jay Rorty, American Civil Liberties Union* at 4.

[32] See also U.S.S.G. §5C1.2(a)(1).

[33] U.S.S.G. §§4A1.1(a), (b), (d); 4A1.2(d).

[34] U.S.C.G. §§4A1.1(c); 4A1.2.

[35] U.S.S.G. §4A1.2(h).

[36] U.S.S.G. §4A1.2(i).

[37] U.S.S.G. §4A1.2(g). Sentences imposed by general and special courts martial are counted, *id.*

[38] U.S.S.G. §§4A1.2(j); 4A1.2, cmt. n.6.

[39] U.S.S.G. §4A1.2(c).

[40] U.S.S.G. §4A1.2(c)(2).

[41] U.S.S.G. §4A1.2(c)(1).

[42] U.S.S.G. §4A1.2(c)(1), (c)(2).

[43] U.S.S.G. §4A1.2, cmt. n.12(A). See e.g., *United States v. DeJesus-Concepcion*, 607 F.3d 303, 305-306 (2d Cir. 2010) (third degree unauthorized use of a vehicle is not a similar offense to careless or reckless driving); *United States v. Calderon Espinosa*, 569 F.3d 1005, 1008 (9th Cir. 2009)(offense of loitering for drug activities is loitering "by whatever name it is known"); *United States v. Russell*, 564 F.3d 200, 206 (3d Cir. 2009)(misdemeanor marijuana possession is not similar to public intoxication); *United States v. Pando*, 545 F.3d 682, 684 (8th Cir. 2008)(driving while intoxicated is not similar to careless or reckless driving, citing U.S.S.G. §4A1.2, cmt. n.5); *United States v. McKenzie*, 539 F.3d 15, 17-18 (1st Cir. 2008)(shoplifting is not similar to "insufficient funds check"); *United States v. Garrett*, 528 F.3d 525, 527-29 (7th Cir. 2008)(bail jumping is similar to contempt of court); *United States v. Sanchez-Cortez*, 530 F.3d 357, 359-60 (5th Cir. 2008)(military AWOL offense was not similar to truancy); *United States v. Cole*, 418 F.3d 592, 599-600 (6th Cir. 2005)(underage (over 18 but under 21) possession of alcohol was similar to a juvenile status offense).

[44] *United States v. Leon-Alvarez*, 532 F.3d 815, 818-19 (8th Cir. 2008)("several of our sister circuits have determined that the calculation of criminal history points is not advisory"), citing *United States v. Hernandez*, 473 F.3d 1004, 1007 (9th Cir. 2007); *United States v. McKoy*, 452 F.3d 234, 239-40 (3d Cir. 2006); *United States v. Brehm*, 442 F.3d 1291, 1300 (11th Cir. 2006); *United States v. Barrero*, 425 F.3d 154, 1567-58 (2d Cir. 2005); *United States v. Carpenter*, 406 F.3d 915, 917 (7th Cir. 2005).

[45] *Survey, Question 2. Safety Valve*. Only 22% disagreed and another 12% were neutral, *Id.*

[46] *Id.* Asked whether the criterion should be expanded to include offenders with 4, 5 or 6 criminal history points, only 22% agreed; 60% disagreed; and 18% were neutral, *Id.*

[47] *Hearing, Statement of Michael Nachmanoff, Federal Public Defender for E.D. Va.* at 30-31 ("In fiscal year 2009, only 5,447 (35%) of defendants subject to a mandatory minimum qualified for the safety valve, while 10,085 (65%) did not. Yet, 83.2% of all drug trafficking offenses involved no weapon, 94.1% of drug trafficking defendants played no aggravated role or a mitigated role, 51.4% had zero to one criminal history points, and another 11.7% had two to three criminal history points. By requiring no more than one criminal history point, the safety valve excludes many offenders who were not involved in any violence and whose role in the offense was not serious. The safety valve does not distinguish between high- and low-level offenders based on role in the offense, but instead distinguishes among low-level offenders who differ little from each other, i.e., by one criminal history point"); *Statement of Jay Rorty, American Civil Liberties Union* at 4.

[48] See also U.S.S.G. §5C1.2(a)(2).

[49] See also U.S.S.G. §5C1.2(3).

[50] U.S.S.G. §5C1.2, cmt., n.4.

[51] *United States v. Denis*, 560 F.3d 872, 873 (8th Cir. 2009); *United States v. Figueroa-Encarnacion*, 343 F.3d 23, 34 (1st Cir. 2003); *United States v. Sarabia*, 297 F.3d 983, 989 (10th Cir. 2002).

[52] *United States v. Jackson*, 552 F.3d 908, 909-10 (8th Cir. 2009), citing in accord *United States v. Matias*, 465 F.3d 169, 173-74 (5th Cir. 2006); *United States v. Herrera,* 446 F.3d 283, 287 (2d Cir. 2006); *United States v. McLean*, 409 F.3d 492, 501 (1st Cir. 2005); *United States v. Gomez,* 431 F.3d 818, 820-22 (D.C.Cir. 2005); *United States v. Stewart,* 306 F.3d 295, 327 n.19 (6th Cir. 2002), but noting in apparent disagreement *United States v. Zavalza-Rodriguez*, 379 F.3d 1182, 1186-187 (10th Cir. 2004).

[53] *United States v. Stewart*, 306 F.3d 295, 326 (6th Cir. 2002).

[54] *United States v. Jackson*, 552 F.3d 908, 910 (8th Cir. 2009); *United States v. Stark,* 499 F.3d 72, 80 (1st Cir. 2007); *United States v. Stewart*, 306 F.3d 295, 327 (6th Cir. 2002).

[55] U.S.S.G. §5c1.2, cmt. n.2; §1B1.1, cmt. n.1(L).

[56] The Eleventh Circuit in a nonbinding opinion seems to have come to same conclusion, *United States v. Valencia-Vergara*, 264 Fed.Appx. 832, 836 (11th Cir. 2008)("The district court did not clearly err in denying Valencia-Vergara a reduction under the safety valve provisions. The evidence shows that both he and one of his codefendants sustained second and third degree burns on their bodies, for which they had to be treated at a hospital").

[57] Cf., *United States v. Grimmett*, 150 F.3d 958, 960-61(8th Cir. 1998).

[58] See also U.S.S.G. §5C1.2(a)(4), which notes that the refer to the criminal enterprise section is redundant because "[a]s a practical matter, it should not be necessary to apply this prong of subsection (a)(4) because (i) this [safety valve] section does not apply to a conviction under 21 U.S.C. §848, and (ii) any defendant who 'engaged in a continuing criminal enterprise' but is convicted of an offense to which this section applies will be an 'organizer, leader, manage, or supervisor of others in the offense,'" U.S.S.G. 5C1.2 cmt. n.6.

[59] U.S.S.G. §5C1.2, cmt. n.5 ("'Organizer . . . supervisor of others in the offense, as determined under the sentencing guidelines' as used in subsection (a)(4), means a defendant who receives an adjustment for an aggravating role under §3B1.1 (Aggravating Role)").

[60] See U.S.S.G. §3B1.2 (Mitigating Role).

[61] In *United States v. Booker*, 543 U.S. 220, 244-45 (2005), the Supreme Court held that the Sixth Amendment entitles a criminal defendant to a jury determination, beyond a reasonable doubt, of any fact (other than a prior conviction) which is necessary to increase the maximum penalty for the offense of conviction and that consequently the Sentencing Guidelines may not be afforded binding effect. The First and Second Circuits have distinguished *Booker* and refused to hold that a trial court commits error when it requires a defendant to establish by a preponderance of the evidence his eligibility for safety valve relief (including satisfying the want of leadership requirements of section 3553(f)(4)), *United States v. Zayas*, 568 F.3d 43, 45-46 (1st Cir. 2009); *United States v. Holguin*, 436 F.3d 111, 119(2d Cir. 2006).

[62] E.g., *United States v. Gonzalez-Mendoza*, 584 F.3d 726, 729 (7th Cir. 2009); *United States v. Bonilla-Filomeno,* 579 F.3d 852, 858 (8th Cir. 2009); *United States v. Nobari*, 574 F.3d 1065, 1083-84 (9th Cir. 2009); *United States v. Rendon*, 354 F.3d 1320, 1333 (11th Cir. 2003).

[63] See also U.S.S.G. §5C1.2(a)(5).

[64] *United States v. Ceballos*, 605 F.3d 468, 472 (8th Cir. 2010); *United States v. Altamirano-Quintero*, 511 F.3d 1087, 1096 (10th Cir. 2007), citing *United States v. Montes*, 381 F.3d 631, 635-36 (7th Cir. 2004); *United States v. Johnson*, 375 F.3d 1300, 1302-303 (11th Cir. 2004); *United States v. Salgado*, 250 F.3d 438, 459 (6th Cir. 2001); *United States v. Cruz*, 156 F.3d 366, 371 (2d Cir. 1998); *United States v. Miller*, 151 F.3d 957, 958 (9th Cir. 1998); *United States v. Sabir*, 117 F.3d 750, 753 (3d Cir. 1997).

[65] *United States v. DeLaTorre*, 599 F.3d 1198, 1206 (10th Cir. 2010).

[66] *United States v. Cervantes*, 519 F.3d 1254, 1257 (10h Cir. 2008)(" In making this determination, we join the First, Second, Fourth, Fifth, Seventh, and Ninth Circuits in ruling that a probation officer is not the government for the purposes of the safety valve,"), citing *United States v. Wood*, 378 F.3d 342, 351 (4th Cir. 2004); *Emezuo v. United States*, 357 F.3d 703, 706 n.2(7th Cir. 2004); *United States v. Contreras*, 136 F.3d 1245, 1246 (9th Cir. 1998); *United States v. Jimenez Martinez*, 83 F.3d 488, 495-66 (1st Cir. 1996); *United States v. Rodriguez*, 60 F.3d 193, 195-96 (5th Cir. 1995); and *United States v. Smith*, 174 F.3d 52, 56 (2d Cir. 1999).

[67] *United States v. Milkintas,* 470 F.3d. 1339, 1345 (11th Cir. 2006), citing *United States v. O'Dell*, 247 F.3d 655, 675 (6th Cir. 2001); *United States v. Ortiz*, 136 F.3d 882, 884 (2d Cir. 1997); *United States v. Flanagan,* 80 F.3d 143, 146-47 (5th Cir. 1996); and *United States v. Ivester*, 75 F.3d 182, 185-86 (4th Cir. 1996).

[68] *United States v. Padilla-Colon*, 578 F.3d 23, 31-2 (1st Cir. 2009)(Inconsistencies between statements made during the proffer and statements made to the authorities on other occasions are not necessarily disqualifying. But the court may legitimately consider such inconsistencies in deciding on the truthfulness of the proffer"); *United States v. Mejia-Pimental*, 477 F.3d 1100, 1108 (9th Cir. 2007)("The district court therefore erred, as a matter of law, in finding MejiaPimental ineligible for safety valve relief on the basis of the lies and delays that preceded his final proffer"); *United States v. Jeffers*, 329 F.3d 94, 99-100 (2d Cir. 2003)("[A] sentencing court may not disqualify a defendant at the threshold from eligibility for safety valve relief based solely on his commission of perjury at trial, where the defendant otherwise fulfills the statutory criteria under 18 U.S.C. §3553(f)(1)-(5).

To do so would contradict the plain language of the statute and contravene the statutory deadline for full compliance with its criteria at the time of the commencement of the sentencing hearing. A court may, of course, consider the relevance of the prior perjury or other obstructive behavior in making a factual finding as to whether the defendant has made a complete and truthful proffer in compliance with 18 U.S.C. §3553(f)(5)").

INDEX

C

G

H

I

J

K

L

M

N

O

P

Q

R

S

T

U

V

W

Y